The High-Yield Debt Market:
Investment Performance and Economic Impact

THE HIGH-YIELD DEBT MARKET: INVESTMENT PERFORMANCE AND ECONOMIC IMPACT

Edited by
Edward I. Altman
New York University

Salomon Brothers Center
for the Study of
Financial Institutions

Leonard N. Stern
School of Business
New York University

DOW JONES-IRWIN
Homewood, Illinois 60430

© Salomon Brothers Center for the Study of Financial Institutions, 1990

Dow Jones-Irwin is a trademark of Dow Jones & Company, Inc.

This publication is designed to provide accurate and authoritative information in regard to the subject matter covered. It is sold with the understanding that neither the author nor the publisher is engaged in rendering legal, accounting, or other professional service. If legal advice or other expert assistance is required, the services of a competent professional person should be sought.

From a Declaration of Principles jointly adopted by a Committee of the American Bar Association and a Committee of Publishers.

Library of Congress Cataloging-in-Publication Data

The High yield debt market.

    1. Junk bonds—United States. I. Altman, Edward I., 1941-

HG4963.H53 1990   332.63'234   89–25996

ISBN 1–55623–235–7

Printed in the United States of America

1 2 3 4 5 6 7 8 9 0 DO 6 5 4 3 2 1 0 9

CONTENTS

PREFACE

The high-yield, noninvestment-grade debt market is now a relatively large and important segment of the corporate bond market in the United States, comprising over 20 percent of total corporate, publicly held indebtedness. The relatively recent growth of this market in the 1980s has financed a variety of corporate programs such as investments in capital projects and a broad range of restructurings, including leveraged buyouts, takeovers, and financial structure changes. The increase in high-yield debt has coincided with a general increase in indebtedness for the economy as a whole and has prompted renewed concern about the vulnerability of the U.S. economy and the corporations that comprise the private sector. This market is of interest and concern to many direct and indirect participants including the issuing firms, investors, underwriters, traders, regulators, and the media. Perhaps more than any other financing vehicle, the high-yield or "junk" bond market has been associated with emotional assertions and calls for new regulations and even legislation. Yet another result of the emergence of high-yield debt is the increase in academic and related scholarly research.

The purpose of this volume is to capture the existing state of analytical research being carried out on the subject of high-yield debt and the associated topic of credit quality. In addition, a keynote panel will focus on the market from public policy and regulatory/legislative aspects. Academics and practitioners have been invited to present their findings and views with the expectation that the resulting papers and discussions will form the basis for thoughtful conclusions about the impact and prospects for the high-yield debt market.

Edward I. Altman
Max L. Heine Professor of Finance

CONTRIBUTORS

Edward I. Altman, Max L. Heine Professor of Finance, New York University, Stern School of Business.

Ramasastry Ambarish, Visiting Professor of Finance, New York University, Stern School of Business.

James R. Barth, Lowder Eminent Scholar in Finance, Auburn University, formerly Director, Office of Policy and Economic Research, Federal Home Loan Bank Board.

Ben S. Bernanke, Professor of Economics and Public Affairs, Princeton University.

Marshall E. Blume, Professor of Finance and Director of Rodney White Center, University of Pennsylvania.

Michael A. Burnett, Assistant Director, U.S. General Accounting Office, Financial Institutions and Markets Issues Group.

John W. Campbell, Director, Multinational and Regional Bank Analysis, Comptroller of the Currency, Administrator of National Banks.

Jerome S. Fons, Assistant Vice President and Economic Advisor at Chemical Banking Corporation, formerly Economist, Federal Reserve Bank of New York.

Martin S. Fridson, Managing Director, Merchant Banking Group, Merrill Lynch Capital Markets, formerly Head of High-Yield Research at Morgan Stanley & Co. Incorporated.

Congressman Carroll Hubbard, Jr., Chairman, Subcommittee on General Oversight and Investigations, House Committee on Banking and Urban Affairs.

Michael C. Jensen, Edsel Bryant Ford Professor of Business Administration, Harvard Business School.

Frederick H. Joseph, Chief Executive Officer and Vice Chairman, Drexel Burnham Lambert.

Steven Kaplan, Assistant Professor of Finance, University of Chicago.

Donald B. Keim, Associate Professor of Finance, University of Pennsylvania.

Seth A. Klarman, Managing Director, The Baupost Group, Inc.

Kenneth Lehn, Chief Economist, Securities and Exchange Commission.

Jan G. Loeys, Vice President, J.P. Morgan Co., Inc.

Robert Long, Managing Director, High Yield Research Group, The First Boston Corporation.

Louis Lowenstein, Professor of Law, Columbia University.

Christopher K. Ma, Associate Professor of Finance, Texas Tech University.

Congressman Edward J. Markey, Chairman, Subcommittee on Telecommunications and Finance, House Committee on Energy and Commerce.

Arie L. Melnick, Professor of Economics, Haifa University and Visiting Professor, New York University.

Richard L. Peterson, Professor of Finance, Texas Tech University.

Frank Philippi, Evaluator, Information Management and Technologies, General Accounting Office.

Steven E. Plaut, University of California, Berkeley.

Ramash P. Rao, Assistant Professor of Finance, Texas Tech University.

F. M. Scherer, The Ford Motor Company Professor of Business and Government, John F. Kennedy School of Government, Harvard University, and formerly with Swarthmore College.

Laura E. Stiglin, Analysis Group, Belmont, Massachusetts.

Marti G. Subrahmanyam, Professor of Finance and Economics, New York University, Stern School of Business.

Robert A. Taggart, Professor of Finance, Boston College.

Sheridan Titman, Professor of Finance, University of California-Los Angeles and U.S. Treasury Department.

Glenn Yago, Associate Professor of Management and Policy, W. Averell Harriman School for Management and Policy, Economic Research Bureau, State University of New York at Stony Brook.

The High-Yield Debt Market:
Investment Performance and Economic Impact

PART 1

INVESTMENT PERFORMANCE OF FIXED-INCOME SECURITIES

CHAPTER 1

RISK AND RETURN CHARACTERISTICS OF LOWER-GRADE BONDS, 1977–1987[*]

Marshall E. Blume[†]
Donald B. Keim[‡]

INTRODUCTION

Since the passage of ERISA, institutional investors have been increasingly willing to consider investments that traditionally have been considered highly speculative. Indeed, some institutional investors now routinely use options and futures, instruments they formerly viewed as highly speculative and thus inappropriate investments. The new rationale is that these instruments, although risky if viewed alone, can produce conservative portfolios when combined with other assets (witness the writing of covered calls).

This article examines the risk and return characteristics of lower-grade corporate bonds. Institutional investors have generally considered

[*]This is an updated and revised version of our earlier paper "Lower-Grade Bonds: Their Risks and Returns" that appeared in the *Financial Analysts Journal*, July/August 1987.
[†]Professor of Finance and Director of Rodney L. White Center, University of Pennsylvania.
[‡]Associate Professor of Finance, University of Pennsylvania.

such bonds inappropriate for a conservative portfolio. But if diversification eliminates much of the risk of individual bonds, lower-grade bonds might have a place in conservative portfolios. Whether they do or not depends upon their prospective risk and return characteristics.

THE MARKET

An active and broad market for lower-grade corporate bonds emerged only relatively recently. Prior to the late '70s, the market for lower-grade corporate bonds was dominated by railroad issues and other "fallen angels"—issues of formerly financially sound corporations that had been downgraded by Standard & Poor's and Moody's rating services. A more active and considerably broader market developed only in the late '70s. The complexion of the market also changed considerably. For the first time, investment banking firms—notably Drexel Burnham Lambert—allowed firms of less than investment grade access to the (public) capital markets. No longer were high-yield bonds only those of "fallen angels."

Since the late '70s, the market has experienced considerable growth. According to estimates by Drexel Burnham, new issuances of lower-grade straight public debt amounted to $0.56 billion in 1977; in 1986 and 1987 combined, such new issuances totaled nearly $63 billion.[1] Drexel Burnham estimates that at the end of 1987 the lower-grade market amounted to $159 billion—a sizable percentage of the total market for straight corporate debt.[2]

THE DATA

A common approach to describing the risk and return characteristics of asset classes is to analyze broad market indexes (e.g., Ibbotson and Sinquefield's *Stocks, Bonds and Inflation*). Unfortunately, there are no widely accepted indexes for lower-grade bonds as there are for the equities market or for investment-grade bonds. Although several such indexes do exist, some investors have criticized them because the indexes themselves have on occasion been constructed from estimated prices (so-called matrix prices) and not prices at which trades could necessarily be executed.[3]

Both Salomon Brothers and Drexel Burnham produce high-yield indexes using actual dealer quotes. Salomon uses dealer quotes for a minimum trade of 500 bonds. Until recently, however, the return on their index was derived from the average yield, average coupon and average maturity of the bonds in the index, not from the realized returns of the individual bonds; it thus represented the return on a hypothetical bond and only approximated the returns of a portfolio of lower-grade bonds. In 1986, Salomon introduced a new index based on the realized returns of individual bonds, which more closely approximates the returns of an actual portfolio.

A more serious problem with both the Drexel Burnham and Salomon indexes is that they drop a bond from their indexes if the bond defaults, if the quality of the bond increases to investment grade, or if there is no demand for the bond. As none of these events is known in advance, excluding the bond return for the month in which the event occurs may bias the index. In particular, if bond prices fall upon default, the return implied by these indexes may overstate the returns an actual investor might obtain. The indexes constructed in this article address this problem. Recently, Salomon has changed the construction of its index to adjust for this problem.

Both Drexel Burnham and Salomon provided us with copies of internal worksheets that contained quotes for month-end bid prices for the lower-grade bonds included in their indexes. The bonds in the indexes calculated in this article have the following characteristics—(1) greater than $25 million outstanding; (2) greater than (or equal to) 10 years to maturity; and (3) nonconvertible. We use only those bonds from Drexel Burnham and Salomon Brothers that satisfy these criteria. The data cover the period from December 1981 through December 1987.

Before actually constructing a new index of lower-grade bonds, we assessed the quality of the prices in these two data sources. For bonds that appeared in both data sources in common months, we computed two series of equally weighted monthly indexes—one for Salomon Brothers and one for Drexel. Any substantial differences between the monthly returns implied by these two indexes would call into question the accuracy of the data in one or both of the sources. Figure 1–A provides a scatter plot of the corresponding monthly portfolio returns computed using the same bonds and the same time periods; it suggests that the Drexel and Salomon data contain similar assessments of changes in value, as the points plot close to the 45-degree line, and the correlation between the returns for the two separate portfolios is 0.89.

To avoid any bias due to dropping a bond before it defaults, we augment the basic Drexel-Salomon data files with total returns derived from prices in the S&P *Bond Guide* for the two months *following* the deletion of a bond from either the Salomon or Drexel sample.[4] We then construct the

FIGURE 1–A
Salomon vs. Drexel—Common months and securities

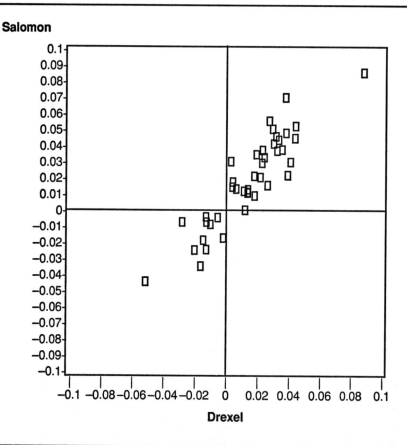

index as follows. For each month, we compute the total returns (coupon and capital appreciation) for all bonds in the Salomon and Drexel subsamples with more than 10 years to maturity.[5] For those bonds that appear in both subsamples, we compute the monthly return using the average of the prices from both subsamples. We then combine the individual bond returns with equal weights to arrive at a monthly total index return. The appendix gives the returns for this basic index.

The index (which we term the B-K index to differentiate it from Drexel and Salomon) represents a broadly diversified cross-section of the lower-grade market. For example, in December 1986, the index included

FIGURE 1–B
Industry breakdown of lower-grade index (December 1985)

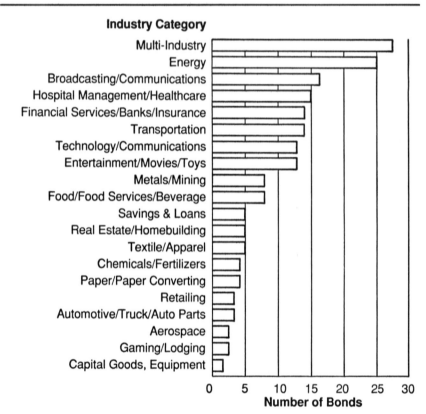

233 bonds issued by 146 companies. In 1985, the index included 197 bonds of 146 companies representing a broad range of industries (see Figure 1–B).

OVERALL RESULTS

Table 1–1 and Figure 1–C present data on the lower-grade bond index and investment alternatives over the period from January 1982 through December 1987. The lower-grade bonds had a geometric or compound rate of return per month of 1.26 percent—16.2 percent per year. By comparison, high-grade long-term corporate bonds (rated AAA-AA) returned 18.3 percent yearly and long-term governments 17.2 percent.[6] During this same period, the S&P 500 had an annual return of 17.3 percent.

Surprisingly, the lower-grade bonds experienced less volatility, or risk, than the high-grade corporates or equities, according to the standard deviations of monthly return. One possible explanation may be that lower-grade bonds, bearing higher coupons, have lower durations than high-grade bonds, hence are less sensitive to interest rate movements and have lower variability of price changes.

Another explanation may be that much of the risk of lower-grade bonds is firm-specific and can be eliminated through diversification. If so, the returns on a portfolio of lower-grade bonds may be considerably less volatile than the returns on the individual bonds. It is also possible that the prices quoted in this market do not adjust as rapidly to new information as prices in other markets.[7]

Of importance for diversification are the correlation coefficients of the returns in different markets. These coefficients suggest that lower-

TABLE 1–1
Monthly returns—January 1982 to December 1987

Portfolio	Geometric Mean (percent)	Arithmetic Mean (percent)	Standard Deviation (percent)	First-Order Auto-correlation
B-K Lower-Grade Bonds	1.26	1.29	2.32	0.31
High-Grade Bonds	1.41	1.46	3.23	0.13
Long-Term Government	1.33	1.39	3.64	0.04
Treasury Bills	0.65	0.65	—	—
S&P 500	1.34	1.47	5.20	0.06

Portfolio	Correlations between Index Returns		
	High-Grade	Long-Term Government	S&P 500
B-K Lower-Grade Bonds	0.71	0.61	0.53
High-Grade Bonds		0.92	0.29
Long-Term Government			0.31

FIGURE 1–C
Major market indexes—December 1981 through December 1987

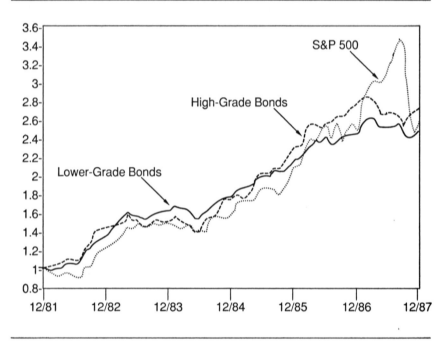

grade, high-grade, or government bonds would be effective diversification vehicles in combination with equities. Within the bond market, the relatively low correlation of lower-grade bonds with either high-grade or government bonds indicates that the inclusion of lower-grade bonds with high-grade or government bonds would result in the further diversification of a bond portfolio. Exactly how much, if any, of a bond portfolio should be invested in lower-grade bonds hinges not only upon the diversification effect, but also upon the expected returns of bonds of different qualities.

A commonly used measure of investment performance is the so-called "alpha coefficient." This can be interpreted as the return in excess of the return warranted by the beta risk of the investment. Beta is a measure of how the return on an investment tends to fluctuate with the return on some reference portfolio (frequently taken to be the S&P 500). A positive alpha for a particular investment vehicle means that an investor who currently holds the S&P 500 could obtain a higher rate of return with no increase in risk by reducing his investment in the index and shifting the proceeds to the investment under consideration.[8] (The alpha coefficient by itself does not indicate what proportion of the portfolio to shift.)

Table 1–2 shows that the beta coefficient is 0.24 for the lower-grade bonds and 0.18 for the high-grade bonds, indicating that their market volatility is about 15 to 25 percent of that of the stock market. The alpha coefficients for both classes of bonds are positive. Although the alpha for the high-grade bonds is greater than that for the lower-grade bonds, only the alpha for the lower-grade bonds is significantly different from zero. If these

TABLE 1–2
Characteristic line estimates—January 1982 to December 1987

$$R_{pt} - R_{Ft} = \alpha + \beta (R_{mt} - R_{Ft}) + e_{pt}$$

Portfolio	Alpha (percent)	(Standard Error)	Beta (percent)	(Standard Error)	R^2
B-K Lower-Grade Bonds	0.45	(0.23)	0.24	(0.04)	0.29
High-Grade Bonds	0.66	(0.37)	0.18	(0.07)	0.08

results are taken at face value, then an investor should find the inclusion of bonds in a portfolio to be beneficial; exactly what proportion of a total portfolio should be invested in bonds, and over what types of bonds, requires more analysis than contained in this article.

A LONGER TIME PERIOD

The period analyzed above is relatively short by usual standards. Since the market for lower-grade bonds in its current form began in the late '70s (some would pinpoint 1977 as its birth), it would be useful to have data back to that time. The S&P *Bond Guide* contains month-end prices for bonds prior to 1982, and these provide a source for earlier data. However, each price represents the closing price on the New York Bond Exchange (if listed and traded) or the average bid price from one or more market makers or a "matrix price." Thus a monthly return may reflect a price change using some combination of any of these three alternatives. The quality of these prices, from the perspective of constructing an index, can be evaluated directly against the data from Drexel and Salomon.

To assess the adequacy of the S&P prices for constructing indexes, we compared an index based upon S&P prices to an index based on Salomon and Drexel prices for common bonds and common time periods. As before, we computed two series of equally weighted monthly indexes, one for the S&P and one for our data, using only those bonds included in both sets of data and only common months.[9] A scatter plot of the corresponding monthly returns from these two indexes (Figure 1–D) suggests that the prices from S&P may be adequate for constructing indexes; the correlation between the

FIGURE 1–D
Blume-Keim vs. S&P Bonds—Common months and securities

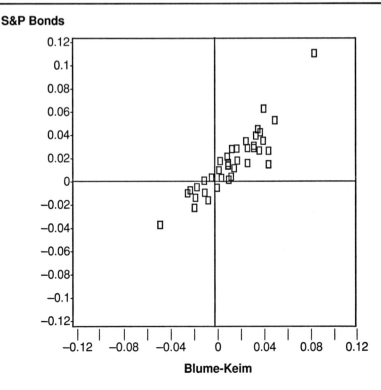

S&P Bonds

Blume-Keim

returns for the two indexes is 0.92. The portfolio returns based on the S&P prices behave similarly to the portfolio returns based on the Drexel-Salomon prices.

To extend our data back to 1977, we computed an S&P-based index return for each month (as described above) using *all* bonds listed in the S&P guide for that month that were rated below BBB, had an outstanding value in excess of $25 million, and had more than 10 years to maturity. As Tables 1–3 and 1–4 and Figure 1–E show, mean returns for lower-grade bonds over

TABLE 1–3
Monthly Returns—January 1977 to December 1987

Portfolio	Geometric Mean (percent)	Arithmetic Mean (percent)	Standard Deviation (percent)	First-Order Auto-correlation
B-K Lower-Grade Bonds	0.85	0.89	2.82	0.19
High-Grade Bonds	0.72	0.78	3.65	0.15
Long-Term Government	0.68	0.76	3.94	0.06
Treasury Bills	0.71	0.71	–	–
S&P 500	1.03	1.14	4.76	0.04

Portfolio	Correlations between Index Returns		
	High-Grade	Long-Term Government	S&P 500
B-K Lower-Grade Bonds	0.77	0.71	0.49
High-Grade Bonds		0.95	0.31
Long-Term Government			0.34

TABLE 1–4
Characteristic Line Estimates—January 1977 to December 1987

$$R_{pt} - R_{Ft} = \alpha + \beta (R_{mt} - R_{Ft}) + e_{pt}$$

Portfolio	Alpha (percent)	(Standard Error)	Beta (percent)	(Standard Error)	R^2
B-K Lower-Grade Bonds	0.06	(0.21)	0.29	(0.05)	0.24
High-Grade Bonds	−0.03	(0.30)	0.24	(0.06)	0.10

this extended 10-year period exceeded returns on the rest of the fixed income sector, but were lower than equity returns. Risk, as measured by the standard deviation of monthly returns, continued to be lower for the lower-grade bonds than for equities and high-grade corporate bonds, but not by nearly as large a magnitude as in the shorter time period of more volatile interest rates.

The correlations between the lower-grade returns and the returns on high-grade bonds and the S&P 500 still suggest that the inclusion of lower-grade bonds in a bond (or stock) portfolio can improve diversification. The beta coefficient for lower-grade bonds is roughly 0.30. Although considerably smaller than it was, the alpha coefficient for lower-grade bonds is still positive and now exceeds the alpha for higher-grade bonds, which is negative over the longer time period.

FIGURE 1–E
Major Market Indexes—December 1976 through December 1987

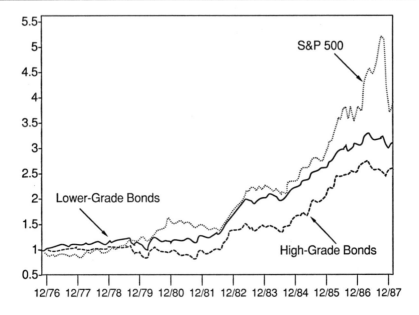

THE RETURNS ON COMMON STOCK

The lower-grade bonds in the B-K index are all nonconvertible. Nonetheless, the returns on these bonds may be closely related to the returns on the common stock of the issuers if both bond and equity returns are related to the credit risk of the company. To examine this possibility, we constructed a subsample of those bonds in the B-K index for which the issuing companies had stocks trading on the New York or American Stock Exchange.[10] For the same firms for which bond returns were available, we constructed an equally weighted index of the total returns on the common stocks. The returns for a particular firm were included in the stock index only for the months in which there were returns for its bonds.

Over the four-year period, the compound annual rate of return on the stocks for the lower-grade issuers was less than that for their bonds—11.9 percent versus 21.1 percent; the correlation between the returns was 0.43. The correlation between the stock returns and the S&P 500 was 0.836 from January 1982 through December 1985. The correlation with the small-stock (lower capitalization) index of Ibbotson-Sinquefield was 0.944, suggesting that these stocks were more closely related to smaller companies than to the larger companies in the S&P 500. Despite the high correlation of monthly returns, the realized equity return of those companies with lower-grade bonds was less than the 21.5 percent annual return realized by the Ibbotson-Sinquefield small-stock index. Perhaps there is some industry, or other, factor associated with companies that issue lower-grade bonds.

In sum, the returns on lower-grade bonds in the combined Drexel and Salomon universes are not perfect substitutes for the common stock of firms issuing the bonds. Depending upon their expected returns, a diversified portfolio might well contain both the bonds and equity of these companies.

CONCLUDING REMARKS

Over the eleven years from January 1977 through December 1987, the realized returns on a portfolio of lower-grade bonds exceeded those of high-grade bonds. One should be very cautious in predicting the same result for the future, however. The accuracy of measures of expected return depends upon the length of the period analyzed, and eleven years is a short period to estimate such statistics.

In the context of a well-diversified portfolio, we find the risk of lower-grade bonds to be no greater than the risk of high-grade bonds. Furthermore, lower-grade bonds provide good diversification when used with other risky assets. We are quite comfortable with this conclusion, as the accuracy of risk measures depends more on the number of independent observations than on the length of the time period under observation.

Notes

1. Drexel Burnham Lambert, *1988 Annual High Yield Market Report* (Los Angeles: Drexel Burnham Lambert), p. 25.
2. Ibid.
3. Kuhn Loeb and Merrill Lynch publish some bond indexes (based on matrix pricing) that would apply to the lower-grade bond market.
4. Through 1986, there were 226 bonds used in the construction of our indexes which Drexel or Salomon dropped from their databases, 98 of which were dropped in 1986. The S&P *Bond Guide* contains the needed price information for 177 of these bonds. A comparison of these added returns with the corresponding monthly returns for the Salomon database over 1982-85 shows that on average the added monthly returns are 1.2 percent less than the continuing returns in each of the two subsequent months. The returns of the 19 bonds not quoted in the S&P *Bond Guide* for 1982-85 are approximated in any month by the average monthly returns of the continuing bonds less 1.2 percent. For 1986, the average return for the dropped bonds for which price information was available was –8.2 percent for the month following the drop and zero for the subsequent month. For the 30 bonds in 1986 for which price information was not available in the *Bond Guide*, the returns for the first and second months following their elimination were assumed to be -8.2 percent and zero, respectively.
5. The return for each bond was calculated from the ratio of the monthly closing price of the bond plus accrued interest to the closing price of the bond in the previous month plus accrued interest.
6. The high-grade, long-term bond returns were provided by Salomon Brothers, and the long-term government bond returns were provided by R. G. Ibbotson Associates.
7. The reported autocorrelation coefficients are consistent with this explanation. The autocorrelation coefficient measure is the correlation between today's return and tomorrow's return. Whether profits can be made with a trading strategy designed to take advantage of such a slow adjustment hinges on the number of bonds that can be traded at these quoted prices without affecting the quoted price.

8. See M. E. Blume, "The Use of Alpha to Improve Performance," *Journal of Portfolio Management*, Fall 1984, for a further discussion of alpha and how it can be used in portfolio analysis.

9. Bond returns in month t are computed from S&P prices as

$$r_t = \frac{P_t + (c/12)}{P_{t-1}} - 1,$$

where c is the annual coupon. This approximation will slightly overstate the true return.

10. CUSIP numbers form the basis for determining a match. Stock return data are from the CRSP files of the University of Chicago; the most recent available file contained data through December 1985.

APPENDIX TO CHAPTER 1

Lower-Grade Bond Indexes

A. Returns (percent)

	1977	1978	1979	1980	1981	1982	1983	1984	1985	1986	1987
JAN	2.2	-1.3	5.1	-1.3	2.8	-1.6	5.5	3.6	3.5	0.6	4.1
FEB	1.9	0.3	-0.1	-6.0	-1.2	1.4	3.9	-1.2	1.4	3.3	2.2
MAR	-0.0	1.3	2.0	-5.7	2.0	1.0	4.3	-1.2	1.1	2.5	0.1
APR	0.9	0.0	0.5	13.0	-0.7	2.9	3.9	-1.1	1.2	2.4	-3.1
MAY	1.8	-1.1	0.5	6.6	0.5	2.0	-2.4	-4.5	4.2	-0.4	-0.5
JUN	3.3	1.0	1.8	3.3	3.8	-1.2	-0.6	1.1	1.2	2.6	0.4
JUL	-0.3	1.2	0.9	-1.9	-3.1	4.9	-1.5	3.0	0.2	-3.2	-0.4
AUG	0.3	2.9	0.8	-2.3	-2.2	8.7	0.9	2.2	1.5	1.6	1.8
SEP	-1.6	0.7	-2.1	-1.3	-2.9	3.6	2.5	3.9	0.4	1.0	-4.0
OCT	0.2	-5.8	-8.1	0.4	3.5	4.6	0.9	2.8	0.4	1.3	-2.7
NOV	2.3	0.8	3.2	-1.2	8.4	2.5	1.4	0.9	2.4	0.2	2.1
DEC	0.1	-1.2	-1.2	-1.0	-2.5	1.5	-0.3	0.0	3.2	0.4	1.6

B. Index Values (December 1976 = 1.00)

	1977	1978	1979	1980	1981	1982	1983	1984	1985	1986	1987
JAN	1.02	1.10	1.16	1.11	1.17	1.21	1.75	2.05	2.25	2.68	3.13
FEB	1.04	1.10	1.16	1.05	1.16	1.23	1.81	2.03	2.28	2.77	3.20
MAR	1.04	1.12	1.18	0.99	1.18	1.24	1.89	2.01	2.31	2.84	3.21
APR	1.05	1.12	1.18	1.12	1.17	1.28	1.97	1.98	2.33	2.91	3.11
MAY	1.07	1.11	1.19	1.19	1.18	1.30	1.92	1.90	2.43	2.90	3.09
JUN	1.10	1.12	1.21	1.23	1.23	1.29	1.91	1.92	2.46	2.97	3.11
JUL	1.10	1.13	1.22	1.21	1.19	1.35	1.88	1.97	2.46	2.88	3.09
AUG	1.10	1.16	1.23	1.18	1.16	1.47	1.90	2.02	2.50	2.93	3.15
SEP	1.09	1.17	1.21	1.16	1.13	1.52	1.94	2.09	2.51	2.96	3.02
OCT	1.09	1.10	1.11	1.17	1.17	1.59	1.96	2.15	2.52	2.99	2.94
NOV	1.11	1.11	1.14	1.15	1.26	1.63	1.99	2.17	2.58	3.00	3.00
DEC	1.12	1.10	1.13	1.14	1.23	1.65	1.98	2.17	2.66	3.01	3.05

Note: Due to revisions, the returns shown above may differ slightly from those shown in Blume and Keim, "Lower-Grade Bonds:Their Risks and Returns," *Financial Analysts Journal* (July/August 1987).

CHAPTER 2

DEFAULT RISKS AND DURATION ANALYSIS

Jerome S. Fons *

Today's fixed income manager can use several tools to quantify risk and other factors relevant to the performance of a portfolio. Among these tools, duration has assumed a central role. Macaulay (1938) introduced the concept of duration to help analyze the behavior of default-free fixed income securities. Since then, there has been rapid growth in the proportion of debt outstanding that is low-rated or default-prone. The analysis of these issues requires a modified concept of duration. This paper proposes a modification, notes its relation to Macaulay duration, and provides estimates of both measures using recent bond price and yield data.

MACAULAY DURATION AND DEFAULT RISK

Duration is simply the price elasticity of a coupon bond with respect to (infinitesimal) changes in its own yield to maturity. Algebraically, it is the

*The author is Assistant Vice President and Economic Advisor at Chemical Banking Corporation and formerly Economist of the Federal Reserve Bank of New York. He thanks Arturo Estrella and Gerald Bierwag for their comments and Nina Huffman for research assistance. The views expressed in this chapter are those of the author and do not necessarily reflect those of the Federal Reserve Bank of New York or the Federal Reserve System.

product of the derivative of the price V of a default-free coupon bond with respect to the yield to maturity i corresponding to that price and the term $-(1 + i) / V$:

$$D = - \frac{dV}{di} \frac{(1 + i)}{V}. \tag{1}$$

Duration can also be interpreted as a weighted time to maturity. Moreover, the duration of a portfolio of bonds is the weighted average of the individual bonds' durations (where the weights are the ratio of the market value of each bond to the market value of the entire portfolio). Equation (1) therefore suggests that a portfolio of bonds can be structured to minimize any adverse consequences of unanticipated interest rate changes.[1]

One of the most attractive features of Macaulay's duration formula is its ease of computation, especially in its closed form. Ignoring semiannual coupons, his formula for a coupon bond promising \$1 at maturity takes the form:

$$D = \frac{1}{V} \left\{ \sum_{t=1}^{M} \frac{tC_i}{(1 + i)^t} + \frac{M}{(1 + i)^M} \right\}, \tag{2}$$

where C_i is the coupon as a fraction of the face value (both being default-free), t is the date at which the cash flow is due, M is the number of years to maturity, and V is the price of the bond, found by computing the present value of all cash flows at the default-free yield to maturity i. To account for semiannual coupon payments, the coupon C_i and the discount rate i are divided by 2 while the maturity M is replaced by $2M$; duration in years is then $D / 2$. This representation assumes that cash flows are fixed and independent of interest rates.

Since duration is a weighted average of cash flows, the introduction of default risk should lower Macaulay duration. All else fixed, a coupon bond's duration decreases as either the coupon rate or the yield to maturity increases. Since default-prone instruments normally carry higher coupon rates than their default-free counterparts, more weight is shifted to earlier periods, thereby reducing duration. They also promise higher yields to maturity, which reduces duration by lowering the discount factor proportionately more for distant promised payments. The implied reduction in Macaulay duration suggests less price sensitivity to changing interest rates—a conclusion that may lead some to argue that so-called high-yield bonds partly compensate holders for their added credit risk.

The flaw in this reasoning stems from the misinterpretation of the yield to maturity on low-rated debt. Durand (1967) notes that "In periods of stress, formally computed yields to maturity for low grade bonds are largely fictitious because the market must expect defaults of principal, interest, or both." He argues that the "expected" and the "prospective" (i.e., promised) yields generally differ "because the market must anticipate some early defaults of interest among the lower grade bonds of any maturity— especially in periods of stress." Immunization strategies that attempt to lock in the higher promised yields can therefore misfire.

The interpretation of duration as a price elasticity and as a weighted time to maturity suggests two alternative routes for handling default risk. The weighted time route is explored by Bierwag and Kaufman (1988) who discuss duration in the context of the time pattern of omitted (defaulted) income flows. Their model allows the resumption of payments after a specified period, though the analyst must provide estimates of the timing and size of the omitted payments. Given the range of possibilities, there is considerable room for error. For this reason, I use the elasticity framework.

EFFECTIVE DURATION

By definition, the price (relative to par) of a default-prone bond, B, is a simple function of the instrument's risky coupon rate C_r, its maturity M, and its yield to maturity r :

$$B \equiv f(C_r, M, r) . \tag{3}$$

Conceptually, the default-prone instrument's yield to maturity is itself a complicated function of the default-free yield to maturity for bonds of the same maturity, i, its risky promised coupon rate, the corresponding coupon rate of the default-free bond C_i, the conditional probability P of receiving all risky promised payments in each period when due (given that the bond has not defaulted), and investors' degree of risk aversion, δ:[2]

$$r = g(i, C_r, M, C_i, P, \delta) . \tag{4}$$

In this notation, Macaulay duration for default-prone bonds is defined as:

$$D = - \frac{df}{dr} \frac{(1+r)}{B},$$

(5)

the price elasticity of a risky bond with respect to the risky bond's own yield to maturity. To calculate this measure, simply replace C_i with C_r, i with r, and V with B in equation (2).

However, if one has forecast a change in the level of (default-free) interest rates, (5) will not necessarily be the measure of interest. What is required instead is an estimate of the change in the price of the risky bond resulting from the forecast change in the general level of rates. To contrast this with Macaulay duration, first take the derivative of (3) with respect to i:

$$\frac{\partial B}{\partial i} = \frac{df}{dr} \frac{\partial r}{\partial i}.$$

(6)

Multiplying both sides of (6) by $-(1 + i) / B$ gives:

$$- \frac{(1+i)}{B} \frac{\partial B}{\partial i} = - \frac{df}{dr} \frac{\partial r}{\partial i} \frac{(1+i)}{B}.$$

(7)

Using (5) to eliminate df / dr yields:

$$- \frac{(1+i)}{B} \frac{\partial B}{\partial i} = D \frac{\partial r}{\partial i} \frac{1+i}{1+r}.$$

(8)

In the terminology of Leibowitz (1986), this measure represents the *effective duration* of the risky bond. It is simply the product of Macaulay duration and an elasticity representing the sensitivity of the risky rate to changes in the level of the risk-free interest rate.

PARTIAL EFFECTS

Unfortunately, it will be extremely difficult to derive a simple algorithm, such as equation (2), for the calculation of a default-prone bond's effective duration. This stems from the contradictory effects on prices from changes in the level of rates. Note that equation (4) implies the following relation:

$$\frac{\partial r}{\partial i} = \frac{\partial g}{\partial i} + \frac{\partial g}{\partial P}\frac{\partial P}{\partial i}, \qquad (9)$$

since C_r, M, C_i, and δ are assumed fixed with respect to i. Equation (9) indicates that the change in default-prone yields due to a change in the default-free yield to maturity has two components: a term representing a shift of the entire risk structure of rates, $\partial g / \partial i$, and a second-order term describing the impact of changes in the level of default-free rates on payment probabilities and on the promised risky yield. The $\partial g / \partial i$ term is assumed positive. The derivative $\partial g / \partial P$ is negative, since a higher likelihood of payment lowers risky promised yields, all else equal. The product $(\partial g / \partial P)(\partial P / \partial i)$, however, may be positive, negative, or zero, and may in fact change over time.

Higher interest rates, for instance, will increase a firm's cost of short-term financing, thereby reducing available cash flows and limiting the firm's ability to raise long-term capital. Rising rates should therefore increase expected defaults.

But high interest rates are usually associated with high inflation via the Fisher Effect. In an inflationary environment, industrial firms may find that the inflation-induced growth in revenues and in misstated accounting earnings raises cash flow.[3] Recent financial innovations may also help limit firms' exposure to fluctuating interest rates.

From a macroeconomic perspective, it may not be the increase in interest rates per se that leads to higher anticipated rates of default. Rather, it may be the expected decline in aggregate demand and economic activity following high interest rates that portends rising default rates. Falling interest rates are normally associated with declining economic activity. As a result, expectations of defaults generally rise as interest rates fall.

The latter point is clear from inspection of Figure 2–1, a time series depiction of the risk structure of interest rates, plotted at month-end, for the period covering December 31, 1979 through July 31, 1988. The bottom curve is the yield to maturity for the 10-year constant maturity Treasury security. Above that, respectively, lie the yields on corporate bonds rated Aaa, A, Baa (Moody's rating), BB, and B (S&P's rating). The investment grade yields (Aaa, A, and Baa) are constructed by Moody's Investors

FIGURE 2–1
Yields to Maturity

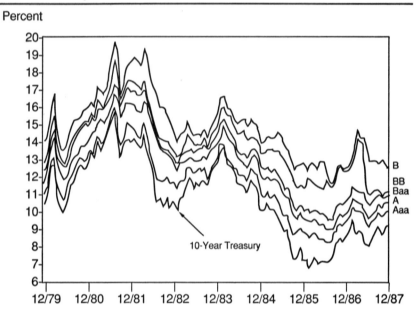

Percent

B
BB
Baa
A
Aaa

10-Year Treasury

12/79   12/80   12/81   12/82   12/83   12/84   12/85   12/86   12/87

Service while the speculative grade yields (BB and B) were obtained from Salomon Brothers' Corporate Bond Research Department.[4]

Note that promised yield spreads widen as rates fall and narrow as rates rise. This can also be seen in Figure 2–2 which depicts the spread between promised yields on corporate bonds rated B and the Treasury 10-year constant maturity rate. A proxy for expected default rates on bonds rated B, the mean of this series is 4.0 percent and its minimum and maximum values are, respectively, 2.58 percent and 5.86 percent. This measure tends to decline when interest rates are rising and increase when interest rates are falling. The scatterplot of Figure 2–3 illustrates this point by plotting this risk spread against the level of the Treasury rate. The correlation between these series for the entire sample period is –0.59. Interestingly, their correlation is only 0.005 during the 22 months marking the two recessions in this sample as against –0.85 in the 81 months of expansion. Altogether, the risk spread was at its highest when long-term interest rates reached their minimum for the past decade.

Finally, the condition of a bond issuer can be expected to change in ways unrelated to the level of interest rates. If this causes investors to alter the required yield on the firm's securities, r, the calculated Macaulay duration D will change, in turn, changing the effective duration of the firm's bonds.[5] The complex interaction of these partial effects prevents the derivation of a robust algorithm for calculating effective duration. As an alternative, I estimate effective duration from historic bond prices and yields.

ESTIMATION OF EFFECTIVE DURATION

Equation (8) suggests two alternatives for estimating a default-prone bond's effective duration. The first—equivalent to measuring the right hand side of (8)—involves calculating the Macaulay duration for a bond of a particular rating and scaling the result by an appropriate factor for that rating. The second method—corresponding to the left hand side of (8)— is simply to estimate the elasticity of the instrument's price with respect to the default-free level of interest rates. The first approach is discussed below; the second is addressed in the following section.

The compression of yields as interest rates rise and the widening as rates fall suggests that the factor $(\partial r / \partial i)[(1 + i)/(1 + r)]$ from the right hand side of (8) should be positive and less than one. For very highly rated fixed income instruments, it should be close to unity. That is, the percentage change in high-grade rates approximately equals the percentage change in default-free rates, causing the Macaulay duration of prime bonds to equal the bonds' effective duration.

Letting monthly first differences of the Treasury yield approximate the instantaneous change ∂i and first differences of the default-prone yield approximate ∂r, and using contemporaneous observations for the $(1 + i)$ and $(1 + r)$ terms (all yields are expressed as decimals), we can generate a time series for the term $(\Delta r / \Delta i)[(1 + i)/(1 + r)]$. The average value of this series can be multiplied by the risky security's own Macaulay duration, D, to obtain an estimate of the issue's effective duration. When the yield on bonds rated Aaa is used as the default-prone yield, r, the average value of this series is 0.7382. When using the yield on bonds rated A as the default-prone yield, we find an average value of 0.6247. The corresponding figure for bonds rated Baa is 0.4847.

FIGURE 2–2
Yield to maturity (B) minus 10-year Treasury

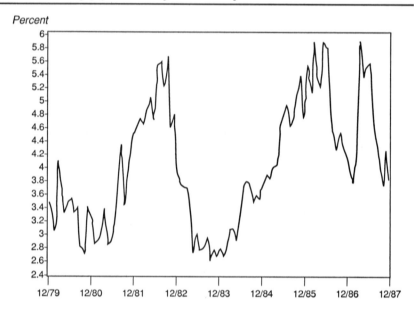

FIGURE 2–3
Scatterplot of (B-Treasury) spread against 10-year Treasury yield

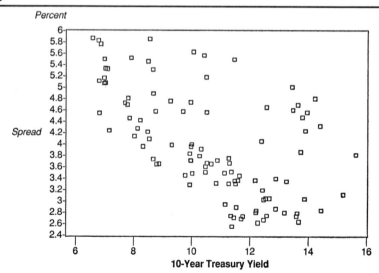

Several large (positive and negative) observations cause the average value of $(\Delta r / \Delta i)[(1 + i)/(1 + r)]$, calculated with the yield on bonds rated BB as the risky rate, to be –0.3841. The exclusion of observations outside the interval (–4, 4) raises this value to 0.5527. When the yield on bonds rated B is used as the risky yield, the average value of this series is 0.1256. This series also contains roughly a half dozen outliers over the sample period. Again, excluding observations outside the interval (–4, 4) raises the average for this series to 0.3931. Thus, consistent with our priors, this exercise indicates that the effective duration of a default-prone bond, as a fraction of its own Macaulay duration, declines as credit quality falls.

A rule of thumb consistent with these results is that the effective duration of bonds rated Aaa is roughly 74 percent of their Macaulay duration. For A-rated bonds, the fraction is 62 percent; and for issues rated Baa, 48 percent. For BB-rated bonds, the (adjusted) figure is 55 percent; for single B bonds, 39 percent.

Regression techniques can provide another estimate of this factor. Table 2–1 lists results of regressions of the natural log of (1 + the corporate yield) for each rating category on the natural log of (1 + 10-year Treasury yield) and a constant. A Cochrane-Orcutt adjustment for the first-order serial correlation was used in each case. The coefficient on the variable $ln(1 + \text{Treasury Yield})$ corresponds to the elasticity $(\partial r / \partial i)[(1 + i)/(1 + r)]$. The estimated coefficients are positive, less than one, and decline with the rating category for the top three ratings. Differences in data sources may contribute to a slight jump in coefficient values for the two speculative grades. The declining pattern, though less pronounced, is nevertheless maintained within the speculative grades.

Moreover, t-statistics for the hypothesis that these estimates are equal to unity range between –4.12 for the B rating and –11.41 for the Baa rating. Such results make this hypothesis untenable. This exercise reveals that the effective duration of a bond rated Aaa may be 81 percent of its calculated Macaulay duration. For bonds rated A, the figure falls to 60 percent of its Macaulay duration. For issues rated Baa, the corresponding figure is 59 percent. The estimate for bonds rated BB and B turns out to be the same: 76 percent of their Macaulay durations. As estimates of instantaneous percent changes in yields, these figures may be more accurate than the first-difference estimates. They also conform more closely to the results of the next section.

TABLE 2–1
Regressions of natural log of (1 + Yield) on natural log of
(1 + 10-Year Treasury Rate) and a constant, month-end
1979:12–1988:06

In(1+Yld)	In(1+Treas)	Constant	R^2	DW
Aaa	0.8104 (0.022)	0.0262 (0.002)	0.95	2.17
A	0.6014 (0.037)	0.0541 (0.006)	0.81	1.99
Baa	0.5854 (0.036)	0.0610 (0.006)	0.81	1.80
BB	0.7599 (0.054)	0.0514 (0.006)	0.79	1.88
B	0.7567 (0.059)	0.0604 (0.006)	0.77	2.09

Note: Standard errors in parentheses. All regressions run using a first-order serial correlation adjustment.

PRICE EFFECTS

The second method of estimating effective duration relates the historic price response of default-prone corporate bonds to changes in the level of interest rates.

Prices of straight default-free coupon bonds with fixed income streams respond to changes in their yields to maturity in a manner that can be characterized as convex. That is, the absolute value of the slope of the price-yield relationship increases as yields fall and decreases as yields rise.

Several factors, however, prevent corporate bonds from consistently exhibiting price convexity with respect to default-free yields. One of these is the embedded call option found in many corporate issues which gives the issuing firm the right to redeem the bond at a specified price, usually at a small premium over par. As interest rates decline, the value of this option (which the bond holder has implicitly sold) increases, causing the bond's price to rise by a smaller amount than it would in the absence of such an option. As a result, callable bonds exhibit concavity (or "negative convexity") at low interest rates. This may partly account for the previously mentioned widening of (promised) corporate yield spreads against Treasury yields when rates fall.[6] However, it would not account for widening spreads within the corporate sector. Because of the high coupon rates on low-rated bonds, the call provision is usually assumed to be less of a factor as credit quality declines. The increase in spreads can therefore be attributed to expected losses from defaults.

Conversely, in a high interest rate setting, the value of the call option falls. This reduces the extent of price erosion and results in a normal convex price/yield relationship at high interest rates. The compression of promised yield spreads within the corporate sector as interest rates rise further implies that default-prone prices fall proportionately less than their default-free counterparts. This too suggests greater convexity for default-prone bonds at high interest rates.

Figures 2–4 through 2–8 represent scatterplots of index prices of bonds for the rating categories used above against the promised yield to maturity for that rating group at each month-end from December 1979 through July 1988. Price index data for the investment grades (Aaa, A, and Baa) are from Shearson Lehman Hutton and conform very closely to the Moody's yield series. While yields were unchanged, however, the Aaa price series dropped sharply between November and December 1984 (perhaps resulting from replacement of the index's issues due to scarcity or even downgrades). To compensate, post-November 1984 Aaa prices were adjusted upwards by 16.26 points. The A and Baa ratings seem to be free of a similar anomaly.

Speculative grade price indices were constructed from weighted average current yield and coupon rate data for issues rated BB and B in Salomon Brothers High Yield Bond Index from the end of December 1979 through the end of December 1984 and updated from principal return data through July 1988.

Index prices per se are not of interest here because they are functions of the characteristics of issues within each index. Instead the focus is on the pattern of bond prices associated with the level of interest rates. Consequently, the data must be cautiously interpreted because of the changing composition of the portfolios that make up each price index. This is especially true for the small-sample low rated indices.

FIGURE 2–4
Scatterplot of price of Aaa bonds against Aaa yield

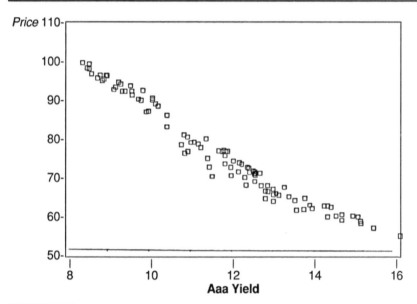

FIGURE 2–5
Scatterplot of price of A bonds against A yield

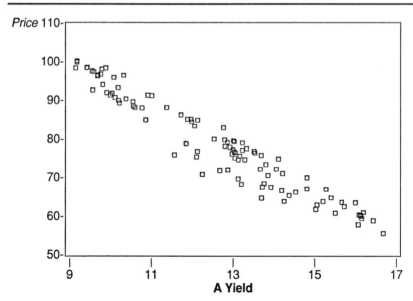

FIGURE 2–6
Scatterplot of price of Baa bonds against Baa yield

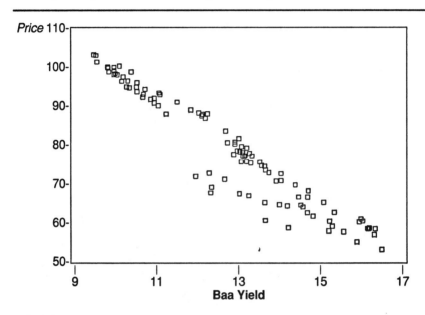

FIGURE 2–7
Scatterplot of price of BB bonds against BB yield

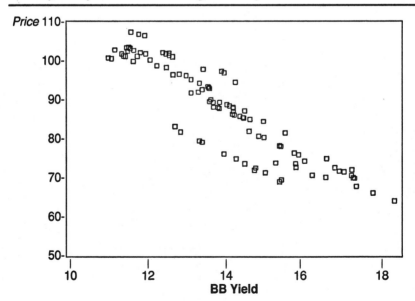

FIGURE 2–8
Scatterplot of price of B bonds against B yield

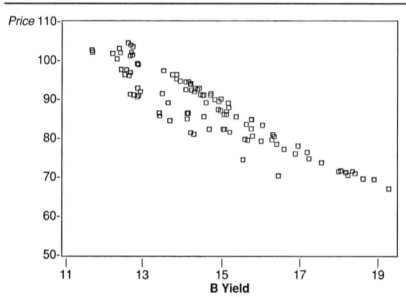

Evident in these diagrams is the changing nature of the components of each rating index. Generally, the differences between rating categories appear slight, though the smaller-sample low-grade indices exhibit greater issue turnover.

An estimate of Macaulay duration may be obtained from this data through regression techniques: When the natural log of bond prices is regressed on a constant and the natural log of $(1 + r)$ (where r is the risky security's own yield), the regression coefficient for $ln(1 + r)$ is simply the term $[(1 + r) / B]\, dB / dr$. (No adjustment for serial correlation is made because this would yield something other than the required slope between these variables.) Results of these regressions are found in Table 2–2. The Macaulay duration estimates for each of these rating groups are 9.35 for bonds rated Aaa, 8.30 for A-rated bonds, and 9.39 for Baa-rated bonds. For BB issues, the coefficient is 7.88, while for bonds rated B it is 6.41. All are highly significant at the 0.05 level. In general, these estimates of Macaulay duration decline as ratings fall. Actual calculations of Macaulay duration for this sample also decline with rating.

TABLE 2–2
Regressions of natural log of price on natural log of (1 + Own Yield) and a constant, month-end 1979:12–1988:06

In(Price)	In(1+Yld)	Constant	R^2	DW
Aaa	−9.3512 (0.155)	5.3454 (0.017)	0.97	0.20
A	−8.2950 (0.226)	5.3385 (0.027)	0.93	0.16
Baa	−9.3929 (0.284)	5.5063 (0.036)	0.91	0.09
BB	−7.8847 (0.370)	5.5054 (0.049)	0.82	0.11
B	−6.4102 (0.255)	5.3494 (0.036)	0.86	0.07

Note: Standard errors in parentheses.

Calculated Macaulay durations for the issues in the investment grade indices were provided at each month-end. Average values (across issues and time) are 8.71 for the corporate bonds rated Aaa, 8.02 for those rated A, and 7.62 for those rated Baa. Macaulay durations for the issues in the low-rated category are provided only for the entire low-rated index (which includes CCC-rated bonds) for the period covering the end of January 1985 through December 1987. These average 6.43. Starting in 1988, Salomon Brothers' yield and duration data are calculated only on a yield-to-worst basis. This duration measure averages 5.59 for the end of January 1987 through August 1988. Generally speaking, the estimates are quite close to the average values calculated directly.

Figures 2–9 through 2–13 illustrate the price/yield relationships once more, except that the own-class yield to maturity is replaced by the yield on the 10-year Treasury issue for each rating category. The period used to construct these diagrams was one in which interest rates initially rose and slowly declined. It also encompasses two peaks and two troughs of the most recent business cycles. According to the National Bureau of Economic

FIGURE 2–9
Scatterplot of price of Aaa bonds against 10-year Treasury yield

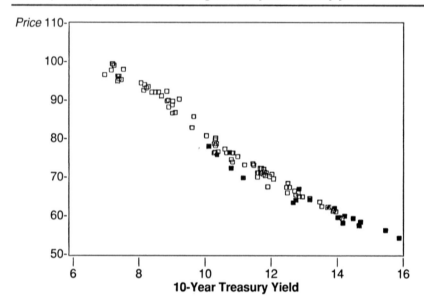

FIGURE 2–10
Scatterplot of price of A bonds against 10-year Treasury yield

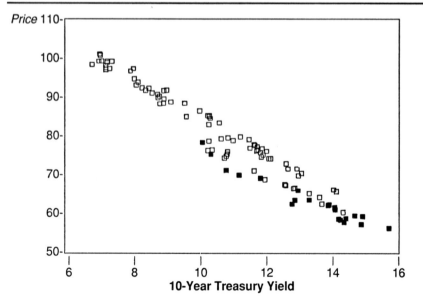

FIGURE 2–11
Scatterplot of price of Baa bonds against 10-year Treasury yield

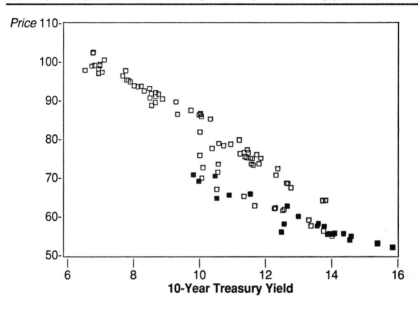

FIGURE 2–12
Scatterplot of price of BB bonds against 10-year Treasury yield

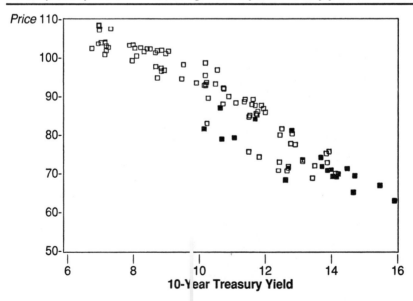

FIGURE 2–13
Scatterplot of price of B bonds against 10-year Treasury yield

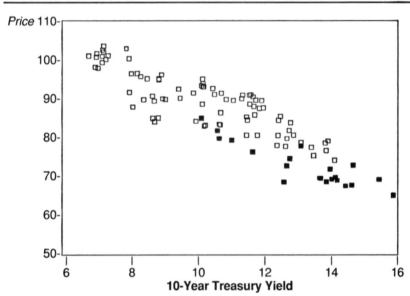

Research, peaks occurred at January 1980 and July 1981, while troughs occurred at July 1980 and November 1982. As noted earlier, macroeconomic factors other than interest rates may have a stronger influence on the performance of low-rated bonds than on their high-grade counterparts. Price/yield observations that occurred during the two most recent recessions appear shaded in these figures to distinguish the performance of low-rated bonds over periods of economic weakness.

These plots show clearly that low-rated bond prices are generally lower for a given Treasury yield during recessions. Further evidence is found in Table 2–3, a correlation matrix of the percent change in bond index prices and the level of monthly industrial production (a proxy for aggregate output) over the period January 1980 through June 1988. Note that, as the difference between rating categories widens, the correlation between each group's price return falls: More important, however, is the increase in the (negative) correlation between industrial production and the growth of prices as rating declines: Industrial production's correlation with the growth in B-rated bond prices is nearly 10 times its correlation with the

TABLE 2–3
Correlation matrix of percent change in prices and the level of industrial production

	Aaa	A	Baa	BB	B	IP
Aaa	1.00					
A	0.98	1.00				
Baa	0.95	0.97	1.00			
BB	0.85	0.86	0.88	1.00		
B	0.81	0.83	0.85	0.91	1.00	
IP	−0.01	−0.06	−0.07	−0.06	−0.10	1.00

growth in Aaa-rated bond prices. Though not presented here, the same pattern holds when the growth in bond prices is replaced with bond yields. These results may account for an apparent shift in the bond price/Treasury yield relationship, especially for low-rated bonds, in periods of economic stress.

Figures 2–9 through 2–13 also suggest that the price/riskless-yield relationship deteriorates as credit quality declines. The depiction of Aaa-rated bond prices in Figure 2–9 shows a generally tight and convex response to changing Treasury yields. The same plot for A-rated corporate bonds, shown in Figure 2–10, still suggests a convex pattern, but now, especially at lower interest rates, one can identify a second lower curve corresponding to the two recession periods.

The shift effect is even more pronounced for bonds rated Baa (Figure 2–11). It is also evident that the convex price/Treasury yield relation of the Aaa and A ratings has switched to concavity. Figure 2–12 depicts the relation between bonds rated BB and the Treasury yield. Here there is even more evidence of concavity. Though the "second curve" is largely absent, the pattern of prices against Treasury yields is much more dispersed. Even more dispersion is evident in the plot for B-rated bonds, illustrated in Figure 2–13. Another feature that emerges is the decline in the slope of the price/ Treasury yield relation as the rating falls. (Axis values are fixed in Figures 2–9 through 2–13 to allow this comparison.) The slope of the ln(price) / $ln(1 + i)$ relation, however, is of greater concern.

Estimates of the effective duration measure $-[(1 + i) / B] \partial B / \partial i$ can be obtained from this data through regression techniques. Table 2–4 shows the results of regressions of the natural log of bond index prices on a constant and the natural log of $(1 + i)$, where i is the Treasury yield. In absolute value, the coefficient on $ln(1 + i)$ is 8.01 for bonds rated Aaa, 7.72 for bonds rated A, 8.74 for bonds rated Baa, 6.36 for bonds rated BB, and 4.81 for bonds rated B.

The last two sets of regressions allow the construction of the ratio of effective duration to Macaulay duration for comparison with the previous section's results. The estimates indicate that the effective duration of bonds rated Aaa is 85.64 percent of their Macaulay duration. The effective duration for bonds rated A is 93.18 percent of their Macaulay duration. For bonds rated Baa, the corresponding figure is 93.09 percent, and for bonds rated BB, it is 80.60 percent. The effective duration of bonds rated B is 75.03 percent of their Macaulay duration. The estimates for bonds rated Aaa, BB, and B are quite close to those obtained in the previous section using regressions of logs of gross yields.

TABLE 2–4
Regressions of natural log of price on natural log of (1 + 10-Year Treasury Rate) and a constant, month-end 1979:12–1988:06

In(Price)	In(1+Treas)	Constant	R^2	DW
Aaa	−8.0079 (0.101)	5.1432 (0.011)	0.98	0.40
A	−7.7293 (0.178)	5.1517 (0.019)	0.95	0.11
Baa	−8.7442 (0.297)	5.2450 (0.031)	0.89	0.09
BB	−6.3553 (0.244)	5.1308 (0.026)	0.87	0.19
B	−4.8098 (0.262)	4.9558 (0.028)	0.77	0.20

Note: Standard errors in parentheses.

The regression results of Table 2–4 are also consistent with estimates of the correlation of returns for portfolios of low-rated bonds with those of long-term government bonds. Bookstaber and Jacob (1986) report a correlation (over an unspecified period) between returns on a portfolio of bonds rated Aaa to A and Treasuries of 0.86, as against a correlation between returns on a portfolio of bonds rated B to Caa and Treasuries of 0.51. Similarly, for the period covering January 1982 through December 1986, Blume and Keim (1987) find that monthly returns of high-grade corporate bonds had a correlation with Treasuries of 0.91, whereas the correlation between an index of returns on lower-grade corporate bonds and Treasuries was only 0.65. Blume and Keim also note that low-rated bond returns have been less volatile than their investment-grade counterparts. Both studies conclude that low-rated bonds offer diversification benefits.

CONCLUSION

This paper argues that the appropriate duration for default-prone bonds is their effective duration. However, because of the complicated way default-prone bonds respond to changing interest rates, a simple algorithm for this measure is not available. As an alternative, we estimate the effective durations of default-prone bonds, as well as their Macaulay durations, from historic corporate bond price and yield data. We find that the effective duration of risky bonds, perhaps because of firm-specific and macroeconomic partial effects, is lower than the commonly used Macaulay duration and find that the difference between these measures widens as credit quality falls. The lower price sensitivity of default-prone bonds to changing interest rates, however, does not mean these securities are in fact less risky than default-free bonds.

Notes

1. For an excellent exposition of the properties and uses of this measure, see Bierwag (1987).
2. Fisher (1927) was probably the first to suggest such a representation and Pye (1974) was among the first to express it mathematically.
3. For instance, Modigliani & Cohn (1979) argue that conventional accounting procedures cause a levered firm's profits, and subsequently its taxes, to be under-stated in a rising inflation environment.
4. For several reasons, the low-rated data used here are market capitalization-weighted yields for a portfolio of bonds rather than yields of individual issues. First, holders of risky bonds tend to (and should) diversify their holdings to minimize losses from default. Second, pricing information on individual issues is usually sketchy in the best of times. An index of yields compensates for the thin and illiquid nature of the high-yield bond market by smoothing anomalous observations.
5. Indeed, as the likelihood of default rises, the risky bond's price behavior may have more to do with firm-specific characteristics of the issuing firm than the general level of interest rates. Bookstaber and Jacob (1986) relate this to the options-like character of corporate debt: the firm's debt represents a claim to the minimum of a) the promised payment stream or b) the liquidation value of the firm (in the event of a default). As the financial position of the firm deteriorates to the point of imminent default, its bonds will represent claims on the assets of the firm. Prices of such a firm's bonds will correspond to idiosyncrasies of the firm rather than the level of interest rates. See Merton (1974) for an option pricing framework for corporate debt valuation. Theoretically, one can derive a bond's effective duration by differentiating its option representation. To date, there is no tractable option formula for the standard coupon bond.
6. See Dunetz and Mahoney (1988) for a discussion of the effects of call provisions on a default-free bond's duration and convexity.

References

Bierwag, G. O. (1987). *Duration analysis: Managing interest rate risk.* Cambridge, MA: Ballinger.

Bierwag, G. O., and Kaufman, George. (July-August 1988). Durations of nondefault-free securities. *Financial Analysts Journal*, pp. 39–45.

Blume, Marshall E., and Keim, Donald. (July/August 1987). Lower-grade bonds: Their risks and returns. *Financial Analysts Journal*, pp. 26–33.

Bookstaber, Richard, and Jacob, David P. (March/April 1986). The composite hedge: Controlling the credit risk of high-yield bonds. *Financial Analysts Journal*, pp. 25–36.

Dunetz, Mark L., and Mahoney, James. (May/June 1988). Using duration and convexity in the analysis of callable bonds. *Financial Analysts Journal*, pp. 53–72.

Durand, David. (1967). (Discussion of) The term structure of corporate bond yields as a function of risk of default, by Raymon E. Johnson. *Journal of Finance*, vol. 22, pp. 348–350.

Fisher, Irving. (1927). *Nature of capital and income*. New York: Macmillan.

Leibowitz, Martin L. (September/October 1986). Total portfolio duration: A new perspective on asset allocation. *Financial Analysts Journal*, pp. 18–29.

Macaulay, Frederick R. (1938). *The movement of interest rates, bonds, yields and stock prices in the United States since 1865*. New York: Columbia University Press.

Merton, Robert. (1974). On the pricing of corporate debt: The risk structure of interest rates. *Journal of Finance*, vol. 29, pp. 141–183.

Modigliani, Franco, and Cohn, Richard (March/April 1979). Inflation, rational valuation and the market. *Financial Analysts Journal*, pp. 24–44.

Pye, Gordon B. (January/February 1974). Gauging the default premium. *Financial Analysts Journal*, pp. 49–52.

CHAPTER 3

MEASURING CORPORATE BOND MORTALITY AND PERFORMANCE *

Edward I. Altman †

INTRODUCTION

The recent emergence of the high-yield corporate debt market in the United States has intensified interest into the relation between expected yield spreads of bonds of various credit quality and expected losses from defaults. In addition to default risk, investors also consider the effects of the two other major risk dimensions of investing in fixed-interest instruments, i.e., interest-rate risk and liquidity risk. The interaction among the three dimensions of risk has raised the analytic content of fixed-income assessment to an increasingly sophisticated level. The analysis of default risk, however, has probably been the area of most concern and empirical measurement over the years since the initial pioneering work by Hickman (1958).

The appropriate measure of default risk and the accuracy of its measurement is critical in the pricing of debt instruments, in the measurement of their performance, and in the assessment of market efficiency.

*A prior and longer version of this paper was published in the *Journal of Finance,* September 1989.
†Max L. Heine Professor of Finance, Stern School of Business, New York University.

Analysts have concentrated their efforts on measuring the default rate for finite periods of time—for example, one year—and then averaging the annual rates for longer periods. In almost all previous studies, the rate of default has been measured simply as the value of defaulting issues for some specific population of debt compared with the value of bonds outstanding that could have defaulted. Annual default rates are then usually compared with observed promised yield spreads in order to assess the attractiveness of particular bonds or classes of bonds. A corollary approach is to compare default rates with ex-post returns to assess whether investors are compensated for the risks they bear.

This study seeks to explore further the notion of default risk by developing an alternative way of measuring that risk and utilizes this measure to assess the performance of fixed-income investment strategies over the entire spectrum of credit-quality classes. Our approach seeks to measure the expected mortality of bonds in a manner similar to that used by actuaries in assessing human mortality. Our use of the term mortality refers specifically to a life expectancy or survival rate for various periods of time after issuance. Although it is informative to measure default rates and losses based on the average annual rate method, that traditional technique has at least two deficiencies. It fails to consider that there are other ways in which a bond dies, namely redemptions from calls, sinking funds, and maturation. Therefore, it fails to consider the surviving population of bonds. Nor does it answer the question of the probability of default for various time periods in the future on the basis of an issue's specific attributes at issuance, summarized into its bond rating. This study does explicitly consider the surviving population as the relevant basis or denominator in the default calculation and addresses the initial default assessment by the following:

Given an issue's initial bond rating:

(1) What is the estimated probability of default and loss from default over a specific time horizon of one year, 2 years, 3 years, or N years?

(2) What are the estimates of the cumulative annual mortality rates and losses for various time frames as well as the marginal rates for specific one-year periods?

(3) Given estimates of cumulative mortality losses suffered by investors and expected return spreads earned on the surviving population of bonds, what were the net return spreads earned or lost in comparison with returns on risk-free securities?

This paper is organized as follows. In Section I, we review prior studies in the default risk area. In Section II, we expand on traditional measures of default rates and losses. The new concept of mortality rates is then presented in Section III, indicating what we believe to be a more comprehensive and meaningful measure. Section IV presents empirical results including new issue volume by bond rating, adjusted mortality rates and losses, and, finally, net return spreads received by investors in different risk categories of bonds. The final section reviews the paper's implications.

I. PRIOR STUDIES

Previous works in the area of default were of three general kinds. The first example, which might be called Hickman-style (1958) reports, usually present statistics on annual default rates and actual returns to bond holders over various time frames.

A second kind of study emphasized the default risk potential of individual-company debt by examining the determinants of risk premiums over risk-free securities, e.g., Fisher (1959), or by constructing univariate (Beaver, 1966) or multivariate classification models, Altman (1968) and others, based on the combination of micro-finance measures and statistical classification techniques. Variants on those models were based on the gambler's ruin concept, Wilcox (1971), recursive partitioning techniques, Frydman, Altman, and Kao (1985) and market indicators of survival, Queen and Roll (1987). The latter study is particularly relevant because it emphasizes the distinction between favorable and unfavorable disappearance. Our measure of mortality of bonds has similar qualities in that we adjust the population for various kinds of redemptions.

Finally, a study by Fons (1987) attempts to combine observed pricing and the inherent default risk premium with estimates of corporate bond default experience. He incorporates default experience measured by Altman and Nammacher (1985 & 1987) and others with a risk-neutral investment strategy—that is, where the only factor that matters is the return distribution of debt with no relevance for volatility or liquidity factors. Fons did not believe, however, that default rates on particular bond-rating classes could be meaningfully addressed because the ratings are not permanent designations. Yet, it does appear to be relevant to measure losses to investors by original investment in specific bond-rating categories.

II. TRADITIONAL MEASURES OF DEFAULT RATES AND LOSSES

The corporate debt market has pretty much accepted the distinction between the so-called investment-grade and noninvestment-grade categories. At the same time, bonds receive more precise ratings with four classes of investment-grade debt and essentially three classes of lower-quality junk bonds. Despite the finer distinctions, all published analytical works concentrate on either the entire corporate-bond universe or just the high yield, noninvestment-grade sector. Default rates are calculated on an average annual basis, with individual rates for each year combined with rates for other years, over some longer time horizon to form the estimate for the average annual rate. Our own results (Table 3–1) show that the average annual default rate, measured in the traditional way, for the period 1978-1988 was 1.92% per year.[1]

A. Default Losses

The more relevant default statistic for investors is not the rate of default but the amount lost from defaults.[2] Altman and Nammacher (1987) measured the amount lost from defaults by tracking the price for the defaulting issue just after default and assuming the investor had purchased the issue at par value and sold the issue just after default. The investor also is assumed to lose one coupon payment. The average annual default loss over the sample period has been approximately 1.3% per year. That lower percentage of loss compared with default rates stems from the fact that defaulting debt, on average, sells for approximately 40% of par at the end of the defaulting month.

III. THE MORTALITY RATE CONCEPT

We retain the notion that default rates for individual periods—yearly, for example—are measured on the basis of defaults in the period in relation to some base population in that same period. The calculation, however, becomes more complex when we begin with a specific cohort group such as a bond-rating category and track that group's performance for multiple

TABLE 3–1
Historical default rate—low rated, straight debt only through December 1988 ($ millions)

Year	Par Value Outstanding	Par Value Default		Default Rate	
1988	$159,223	$3,944.20		2.477%	
1987	136,952	7,485.50	(1,841.7)[a]	5.466%	(1.34)%[a]
1986	92,985	3,155.76		3.394%	
1985	59,078	992.10		1.679%	
1984	41,700	34.16		0.825%	
1983	28,233	301.08		1.066%	
1982	18,536	577.34		3.115%	
1981	17,362	27.00		0.156%	
1980	15,126	224.11		1.482%	
1979	10,675	20.00		0.187%	
1978	9,401	118.90		1.265%	

Average Default Rate 1970 to 1988   2.404%
Average Default Rate 1978 to 1988   1.919%
Average Default Rate 1983 to 1988   2.485%

[a]$1,841.7 million without Texaco, Inc., Texaco Capital and Texaco Capital N.V. The default rate without these is 1.34%.

time periods. Because the original population can change over time as a result of a number of different events, we consider mortalities in relation to a survival population and then input the defaults to calculate mortality rates. Bonds can exit from the original population by means of at least four different events: defaults; calls; sinking funds; and maturities.

The individual mortality rate for each year (marginal mortality rate = MMR) is calculated by:

$$MMR_{(t)} = \frac{\text{Total Value of Defaulting Debt in the Year } (t)}{\begin{array}{c}\text{Total Value of the Population of Bonds at} \\ \text{the Start of the Year } (t)\end{array}}$$

We then measure the cumulative mortality rate (CMR) over a specific time period (1, 2,...., T years) by subtracting the product of the surviving populations of each of the previous years from one (1.0), that is:

$$CMR_{(T)} = 1 - \prod_{t=1}^{T} SR_t$$

where $CMR_{(T)}$ = cumulative mortality rate in (T)
   $SR_{(t)}$ = survival rate in (t); $1 - MMR_{(t)}$

The individual-year marginal mortality rates for each bond rating are based on a compilation of that year's mortality measured from issuance. For example, all the one-year mortalities are combined for the 17-year sample period to arrive at the one-year rate, all the second-year mortalities are combined to get the two-year rate, etc.

The mortality rate is a value-weighted rate for the particular year after issuance, rather than an unweighted average. If we were to simply average each of the year one rates, year two rates, etc., our results would be susceptible to significant specific year bias. If, for example, the amount of new issues is very small and the defaults emanating from that year are high in relation to the amount issued, the unweighted average could be improperly affected. Our weighted-average technique correctly biases the results toward the larger-issue years, especially the more recent years.

IV. EMPIRICAL RESULTS

Table 3–2 lists the dollar amount, by bond rating, issued for the period 1971–1988 according to statistics compiled from *Standard & Poor's Bond Guide*. Note that investment-grade categories dominated new listings over much of the sample period. During the 1971-1981 period, the below investment-grade sector showed small, relatively consistent BB-rated issues ranging from a low of $20 million in 1975 to a high of $579 million in 1977. Since 1982, however, BB new issues exceeded $1 billion each year. Single-B debt had small, sporadic new issues from 1971–1976. Since 1977, volume has picked up with more than $500 million issued in 1977; more than $1 billion issued in 1978; more than $6 billion in 1984–1985 and over $21 billion in 1986.[3] The number of issues in each year is also indicated for the junk bond sector (lower three categories of ratings) since 1977, showing its impressive growth.

Table 3–2
Corporate bond total new issue amounts by S&P bond rating, 1971–1988 ($ million)

Bond Rating	1971	1972	1973	1974	1975	1976	1977	1978	1979	1980	1981	1982	1983	1984	1985	1986	1987	1988
AAA	5125	3179	4046	7420	11348	9907	11046	7967	10400	10109	11835	6197	3920	2350	9016	14438	10540	18540
AA	5467	4332	3670	8797	9654	9560	7494	7374	5910	10497	11748	14597	14110	18291	23223	46978	30880	19280
A	6688	4745	4254	8388	12752	8103	5236	5330	6489	12195	12432	13315	5516	12252	23381	34173	23200	30190
BBB	2139	1198	937	1248	2367	2938	1558	1513	1225	2595	3900	5738	5827	5194	11068	21993	16240	19450
BB†	292	258	105	250	20	397	579	408	359	418	290	1378	2894	4698	2041	7098	5000	2570
						(10)	(15)	(10)	(8)	(9)	(6)	(16)	(24)	(23)	(23)	(37)	(31)	(13)
B†	112	1-1	140	19	27	59	526	1029	917	879	894	1122	3713	6485	5945	21260	17830	18170
						(3)	(17)	(39)	(33)	(28)	(15)	(24)	(46)	(68)	(77)	(133)	(109)	(102)
CCC†	0	0	0	0	14	75	78	34	91	25	0	145	285	1901	1668	4668	4620	5640
					(1)	(5)	(1)	(1)	(3)	(1)	(0)	(2)	(5)	(9)	(14)	(40)	(23)	(36)
Total Rated	19823	13813	13152	26121	36182	31026	26485	23606	25350	36681	41078	42452	36195	51080	76242	150438	108170	113725

†Number of issues of low-rated bonds in parentheses; from S&P Bond Guides.

A. Mortality Rates

The data in Table 3-3 show our mortality rate computations, adjusted for redemptions and defaults, for the entire period 1971-1988. The data include cumulative mortalities for up to 10 years after issuance. It is possible to list the data for beyond 10 years, but the number of observations obviously diminishes as the number of years after issuance increases.

The relative results across cohort groups are pretty much in line with expectations, with the mortality rates very low for the higher-rated bonds and increasing for lower-rated issues. For example, AAA-rated debt had a zero mortality rate for the first five years after issuance and then only 0.15% in year 6 and 0.21% for 10 years. AA-rated and A-rated debt mortalities reached just 2.42% and 1.13%, respectively, over a 10-year period. The mortality rates for BBB and lower bonds begin to increase almost immediately after issuance, with BBB (the lowest investment-grade debt level) showing a cumulative rate of 1.00% after five years and 2.13% after 10 years.

The single-B mortality rates were relatively high throughout the period and particularly in the later years. The marginal mortality rates are fairly constant after year three. The single-B-rated debt, however, had relatively small issue amounts throughout the 1970s, and when we calculate mortality rates for 7-10 years after issuance, the number of observations is quite small. For example, years 1971-1978 are the only years contributing to our 10-year results; 1971-1979 to nine-year results, and so on. Hence, we emphasize that the longer-term mortality results should be analyzed with considerable caution with respect to expectations about future mortality rates and return spreads.[4] Despite the high cumulative mortality rate, for single B's we will show that the net return to investors remains very attractive.

The results for five years after issuance do provide more observations, but they too lack results for new issues in the most recent, high-growth years (1983-1987). The five-year cumulative rate of 11.5% for B-rated debt might also be considered to be surprisingly high, but is it really? Consider that the average annual default rate calculated in the traditional way is 1.92% per year for the period 1978-1988. If we simply sum the one-year rates, the result is 9.60% for five years compared with our CMR of 11.5%. In addition, the traditional default rates are calculated on the basis of the population on June 30 while our mortality rates use survival population data

TABLE 3–3
Cumulative mortality rates by original S&P bond rating covering defaults and issues from 1971–1988

Original Rating	Years After Issuance									
	1	2	3	4	5	6	7	8	9	10
AAA	0.00%	0.00%	0.00%	0.00%	0.00%	0.15%	0.21%	0.21%	0.21%	0.21%
AA	0.00	0.00	1.39	1.72	1.92	1.92	2.18	2.18	2.29	2.42
A	0.00	0.39	0.71	0.71	0.71	0.82	0.93	1.00	1.13	1.13
BBB	0.03	0.23	0.35	0.61	1.00	1.00	1.14	1.14	1.34	2.13
BB	0.00	0.50	1.07	1.34	1.86	4.59	7.48	7.48	7.48	10.70
B	1.40	2.04	4.72	8.24	11.54	14.95	20.31	22.95	28.22	30.88
CCC	1.97	3.81	8.01	23.05	24.64	24.64	n/a	n/a	n/a	n/a

from the start of each year. Therefore, the "old" way probably understates default rates somewhat. As for the six- to ten-year results, only time will tell if the relatively large marginal one-year rates, especially for the ninth year, continue in the future.[5] There are other biases, positive and negative, in the calculation of traditional default rates and we will return to these points when we discuss several studies which which were published after our original working paper, Altman (1988).

Since we adjust the population for all redemptions as well as defaults, the mortality rates listed in Table 3–3 will be higher than if the population data was unadjusted. For example, the B-rated cumulative mortality rates, unadjusted for redemptions was 27.4% for 10 years. I believe that both the adjusted and unadjusted methods of calculating the results are meaningful. The mortality figures over time should adjust for changing population size while the unadjusted data could be helpful in examining the probability of default of a particular rating category from a given year's issuance. Strictly speaking, however, the unadjusted figures are not "rates." For a more in-depth discussion of this and a presentation of the entire unadjusted default amounts, see Altman (1989).

B. Losses

As in the previous discussion on traditional measurements of default, the loss to investors from defaults is of paramount importance. In our ensuing analysis of net return spreads for each category of bond rating, we use the actual recovery amount that investors were able to sell the defaulting issue for and also assume that one coupon payment was lost. The average recovery rate was slightly below 40% of par.

We did look at the relation between individual bond ratings at issuance and the subsequent average price that could be realized upon default and found essentially that no relationship existed. Table 3–4 lists those results for 222 defaulting issues and shows that the average retention rate was actually 43.2% (including Texaco and 38.8% without Texaco). Note that there is virtually no correlation between initial bond rating and average price after default.

There also does not appear to be a correlation between the price after default and the number of years that a bond is in existence before default (Table 3–5). Therefore, while the marginal default rate is relatively low in

TABLE 3–4
Average price after default by original bond rating

Original Rating	Average Price After Default (per $100)	Number of Observations
AAA	65.48	7
AA	63.88	21
A	54.11	27
BBB	45.08	23
BB	36.03	20
B	40.09	81
CCC	42.80	16
C	10.00	2
Nonrated	31.18	25
Average	**43.18**	**222**

the first three years after issuance (Table 3–3), the recovery rate is unaffected by the age of the issue.

C. Net Return Performance

An important dimension to our analysis is the ability to track performance of bonds from issuance, across bond ratings, and over relevant time horizons. This analysis enables us to compare the performance of various risky bond categories with default risk-free U.S. Treasury securities. By factoring into the analysis actual losses from defaults and yield spreads over Treasuries, a more complete analysis results. We calculate actual return-spread performance, but the algorithm used is sufficiently robust to handle any set of assumptions on the variables analyzed.

Table 3–6 and Figure 3–1 present the return spread results across bond ratings over the sample period 1971-1988. The spreads, expressed in terms of basis points compounded over a 10-year investment horizon are based on actual yield spreads for the 19-year period. The average yield spreads were 0.47% (AAA), 0.81% (AA), 1.09% (A), 1.76% (BBB), 2.99% (BB), 4.08% (B), and 7.08% (CCC).[6]

TABLE 3–5
Average price after default by number of years after issuance

Number of Years After Issuance	Average Price After Degault (per $100)	Number of Observations
<1	45.41	10
1–2	44.74	19
2–3	57.06	36
3–4	40.08	23
4–5	42.75	24
5–6	45.50	19
6–7	41.01	21
7–8	37.17	6
8–9	41.42	8
9–10	42.30	11
>10	43.94	42

The body of Table 3–6 represents returns realized above what would have been earned on risk-free treasuries, measured in basis points. Table 3–6 uses actual long-term treasury coupon rates, yield spreads at birth for the different rating categories, the sale of defaulted debt, the loss of one coupon payment, and the reinvestment of cash flows at the then prevailing interest rates for that bond rating group. Cash flows are reinvested from coupon payments on the surviving population as well as the reinvestment of sinking funds, calls, and the recovery from defaulted debt. The results assume no capital gains or losses over the measurement period and the investor follows a buy-and-hold strategy for the various horizons.

Results show that AAA-rated bonds can be expected to earn 45 basis points (0.45%) *more than* Treasuries over one year (two semi-annual coupon payments) and 1201 bp. after 10 years. BB-rated bonds earn 313 bp. more than treasuries after one year and an impressive 6233 after 10 years. Another way to put this is an investment of $100 would return $66.23 more than treasuries over 10 years.

Of interest is that for the first three years after issuance, the lower the bond rating the higher the net return spread, with triple CCC-rated bonds doing best. In the fourth year, the CCC-rated bonds do best but the B's drop off. After the fifth year, however, the BB-rated category begins to dominate while the B-rated bonds continue to lose ground. That relationship is

TABLE 3–6
Return spreads earned by corporate bonds over Treasury bonds
(measured in Basis Points compounded over time)

Years After Issuance	Bond Rating at Issuance						
	AAA	AA	A	BBB	BB	B	CCC
1	45	76	105	171	313	370	572
2	100	169	222	367	666	849	1421
3	165	254	369	614	1097	1225	2312
4	246	373	558	901	1653	1583	1899
5	343	529	786	1229	2289	2077	3083
6	447	725	1051	1671	2714	2589	n/a
7	578	924	1370	2190	3164	2838	n/a
8	747	1215	1775	2856	4316	3515	n/a
9	954	1554	2259	3641	5639	3421	n/a
10	1201	1949	2853	4493	6233	4215	n/a

illustrated in Figure 3–1. For all holding periods, all bond types do well and have positive spreads over treasuries.

As indicated, the historical average 4.08% yield spread for B-rated debt provides an ample cushion to compensate for losses, but the performance relative to the BB-rated category is inferior in the later years. This changes, however, if we adjust our initial yield spread assumptions to reflect different market conditions, assuming the same default experience. For example, in the period October 1987 to early 1988 and again in Fall 1989, yield spreads on single-B-rated bonds jumped to over 5.5%. Under this assumption, the resulting net return spreads over Treasuries are higher for the lower-rated bonds, with B-rated debt dominating all others for the entire 10-year time frame (See Altman, 1988).

V. IMPLICATIONS

The results indicate the expected adjusted mortality rates and losses, cumulated for a number of years after issuance, for all bond-rating categories. Despite some relatively high cumulative mortality rates over long holding periods, return spreads on all corporate bonds are positive, with

FIGURE 3–1
**Realized return spread on net investment in corporate bonds
over risk-free governments**

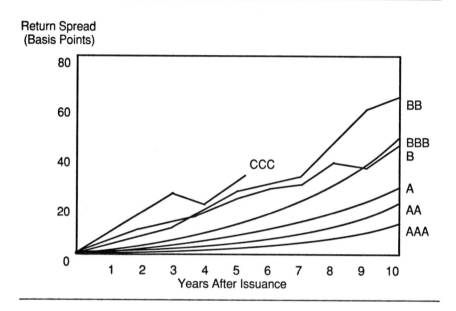

Return Spread
(Basis Points)

impressive results for the high-yield, low-grade categories. If the analyst wishes to use higher (or lower) than historic mortality rates to reflect a number of macro and microeconomic uncertainties, or different yield spread assumptions, that is certainly feasible.

Why do we observe such relatively consistent positive return spreads for all rating categories? The results show that investors have been more than satisfactorily compensated for investing in high-risk securities. Indeed, if expected default losses are fully discounted in the prices (and yields) of securities, our return spread results should be insignificantly different from zero. The fact that the spreads are so positive has a number of possible explanations—none of them easily corroborated.

One possible explanation is that the fixed-income market has been mispricing corporate debt issues and the discrepancy has persisted, perhaps because of the lack of appropriate information. That implies market inefficiency; if default losses are consistently lower than yield spreads and this comparison is the only relevant determinant of future yield spreads, inefficiency is a reasonable conclusion.

If all other things are not equal, however, for determining yield spreads on corporate bonds, then the market inefficiency conclusion is difficult to reach. For example, liquidity risk is often mentioned as important to price determination. If liquidity risk increases with lower bond ratings, then the excess returns noted earlier may in part be the returns necessary to bear this risk. Indeed, during the post-October 19, 1987 period, poor liquidity was cited as one cause of the precipitous drop in common-stock prices and the rise in yields of certain high-yield debt issues.

The other risk element that is not isolated in our study is interest-rate or reinvestment risk. Actual returns on bonds are obviously affected by interest-rate changes. Our results include actual reinvestment rates over time and we have not factored in any capital gains or losses, assuming a buy and hold strategy for investors. Blume and Keim (1987) and Altman and Nammacher (1985) have shown, however, that if anything lower-grade bonds have lower volatility from interest rate changes than risk-free, lower-coupon treasuries.

Another explanation of the persistent positive return spreads attributed to lower-rated bonds is the variability of retention values after default. Our observation of a recovery rate of an average 40% of par value just after default is an expected value. Investors might require positive spreads based on the possibility that retention values will be below the 40% average. In addition, the 40% retention is relevant only for a portfolio of defaulting bonds. An investor may not be well diversified and may be vulnerable to higher-than-average mortality losses on specific issues. Therefore, if the market prices low-quality issues as individual investments and not as portfolios, required spreads are likely to be higher than is perhaps necessary. On the other hand, if defaults are correlated with market returns, risks may not be as diversifiable as we assume to be the case for equities.

Investors might also be restricted in relation to the risk class of possible investments, thereby creating an artificial barrier to supply-demand equilibrium. For instance, certain institutions are prohibited from investing in low-grade bonds or are limited in the amount that they can invest in such securities. That reduces demand and inflates yield and possibly return spreads.

Notes

1. The default rate through the first nine methods of 1989 was 2.6% with $5.3 billion of defaults.

2. An additional item of importance is the amount lost not just from defaults but also from other crisis situations, such as distressed exchange issues. Fridson, Wahl, and Jones [1988] did look at the loss on distressed exchange issues as well as losses from defaults and found that the overall average annual loss for the period 1978-1987 was 1.88%. Their base and reference population was only original issue high-yield debt.

3. Nonrated debt is not included in our formal analysis because the risk nature of those issues appears to have shifted over the years with the most recent data probably dominated by low-rated equivalent securities. The earlier nonrated debt data appear to have included all risk types.

4. In addition, the later year results could be biased since a portion of the original population of bonds will be redeemed by then. If more credit worthy firms tend to be called earlier than more risky ones, then the later year mortality rates would be biased upward. In addition, we did not include in our return calculation any call premiums or warrant value which might have been attached to the bond issue. Our results, however, did not show a great deal of difference when we did not exclude redemptions (results without redemptions are available from the author).

5. If we begin our analysis in 1976, rather than in 1971, the five-year B-rated cumulative rate is slightly higher at 11.7%; the eight-year rate is 23.7%; and the 10-year rate is 36.4%. The latter is due to the relatively high nine- and ten-year defaults of 1977 new issues ($85.5 million and $26.7 million, respectively, from the $526 million issued).

6. In an earlier version of this paper, Altman (1988), we assumed yield spreads of 0.50, 1.0, 1.5, 2.0, 3.0, 4.0, and 5.0 percent for AAA, AA, A, etc., respectively. Except for the CCC rate, the actual average yield spreads are quite similar to these assumptions.

References

Altman, E. I. (September 1968). Financial ratios, discriminant analysis and the prediction of corporate bankruptcy. *Journal of Finance*, 589–609.

Altman, E. I. (September 1989). Measuring corporate bond mortality and performance. *Journal of Finance*, 44-4, 909–922. Also (February 1988) New York University working paper.

Altman, E. I. (Fall 1989). *Default risk, mortality rates and the performance of corporate bonds: 1970–1988.* Charlottesville, VA: Foundation for Research of the Institute for Chartered Financial Analysts.

Altman, E. I., and Nammacher, S. A. (July/August 1985). Default rate experience on high yield corporate debt. *Financial Analysts Journal.* Also (March 1985) Morgan Stanley & Co., Inc.

Altman, E. I., and Nammacher, S. A. (1987). *Investing in junk bonds: Inside the high-yield debt market.* New York: John Wiley.

Asquith, P., Mullins, D., and Wolff, E. (September 1989). Original issue high yield bonds: Aging analysis of defaults, exchanges and calls. *Journal of Finance,* *44–4*, 923–953.

Atkinson, T. R. (1967). *Trends in corporate bond quality.* New York: National Bureau of Economic Research.

Beaver, W. (January 1967). Financial ratios as predictors of failure. *Empirical research in accounting.* Selected studies supplement to *Journal of Accounting Research,* 71–111.

Blume, M. E., and Keim, D. B. (July/August 1987). Risk and return characteristics of lower-grade bonds. *Financial Analysts Journal,* 26–33.

Blume, M. E., and Keim, D. B. (August 1989). Realized returns and defaults on lower-grade bonds: The cohort of 1977 and 1978. University of Pennsylvania, The Wharton School, Rodney L. White Center working paper.

Fisher, L. (June 1959). Determinants of risk premiums on corporate bonds. *Journal of Political Economy,* 67, 217–237.

Fons, J. S. (March 1987). The default premium and corporate bond experience. *Journal of Finance,* 81–97.

Fridson, M. S., Wahl, F., and Jones, S. B. (January 1988). New techniques for analyzing default risk. *High Performance,* 4–11.

Frydman, H., Altman, E. I., and Kao, D-L. (1985). Introducing recursive partitioning analysis to financial analysis: The case of financial distress classification. *Journal of Finance,* 269–291.

Goodman, L. (April 1989). High-yield default rates: Is there cause for concern. *Goldman, Sachs Fixed Income Research.*

Hickman, W. B. (1958). *Corporate bond quality and investor experience.* Princeton University Press and the National Bureau of Economic Research.

Lucas, D., and Douglas, S. (July 1989). Historical default rates of corporate bond issuers 1970–1988. Moody's *Structured finance.*

Queen, M., and Roll, R. (May/June 1987). Firm mortality: Using market indicators to predict survival. *Financial Analysts Journal,* 9–26.

Wilcox, J. W. (September 1971). A gambler's ruin prediction of business failure using accounting data. *Sloan Management Review,* 12, 1–10.

Wyss, D., Probyn, C., and de Angelis, R. (July 1989). *The impact of recession on high-yield bonds.* Washington, DC: DRI/McGraw-Hill.

CHAPTER 4

RESILIENCY OF THE HIGH-YIELD BOND MARKET[*]

Christopher K. Ma
Ramesh P. Rao
Richard L. Peterson[†]

In recent years, high-yield debt has become a significant segment of the corporate bond market. The main source of the growth has come from new issues of high-yield corporate bonds, rather than an increase in "fallen angels."[1] The driving force behind this new breed of high-yield debt growth has been its use as a means to tap the capital markets to finance increasingly common leveraged buyouts, hostile takeovers, and major corporate restructurings. The market acceptance of high-yield bonds was further enhanced by empirical evidence that net returns on a diversified portfolio of low-grade bonds exceeded those on high-grade bonds while the volatility of their monthly returns was no greater.[2]

The frenzied pace of growth in the high-yield debt market, however, has been accompanied by increasing concerns from various quarters.[3] Critics have characterized the high-yield bond market as a house of cards

[*]This study is partially financed by Delaware Investment Advisors, Inc. A shorter version of this chapter was published in *Journal of Finance*, September 1989.
[†]Richard L. Peterson is Professor of Finance at Texas Tech University; Christopher Ma and Ramash Rao are Associate Professors of Finance, also at Texas Tech University.

ready to collapse with the slightest whiff of an economic downturn. Detractors appear to suggest that the market for high-yield bonds is "built on sand," with a price structure that does not reflect the risk inherent in these securities. Others suggest that a crisis, such as a major bankruptcy or an economic downturn, could cascade into a wave of defaults engulfing the entire high-yield debt market. The projection of a contagion effect no doubt stems from the thin equity cushion and high debt service requirements that are typical of most high-yield debt issuers. The situation could be exacerbated if a major default caused lenders to demand higher interest rates on credit extended to high-yield debt issuers, thereby causing the already suspect financial condition of such issuers to worsen. Thus, the resiliency of the high-yield debt market subsequent to adverse economic events has been seriously questioned.

The concern with market resiliency of high-yield debt was brought into sharp focus since 1986 when the high-yield debt market had witnessed several significant adverse events. First, the entire capital market had suffered the largest corporate failure until that time — the bankruptcy of the LTV Corporation.[4] The filing of bankruptcy by the LTV corporation and its various subsidiaries had its historical significance since $1.766 billion of debt was thrown into default, representing 56% of total debt defaulting in 1986. Another first of the LTV bankruptcy is that it was the first major default on new high-yield debt that was issued as a result of takeover contests and reorganizations. Immediately following the LTV shock, the high-yield bond market was hurt by the notorious "insider trading scandal" which began with the indictment of Ivan Boesky on November 24, 1986. On October 19, 1987, the U.S. stock market experienced the most significant crash in its history; and more recently in September 1988, the "Junk Bond King," Michael Milken, and the most active firm in trading junk bonds, Drexel Burnham Lambert, Inc. were indicted for violations of security laws. Within a period of less than two years, all these events share a common significance in that they represent either the largest bankruptcy in magnitude until that time, or a highly significant collapse of investors' confidence in financial markets. Considering that high-yield bond pricing is most sensitive to default risk, these events demonstrate real challenges to the market. Therefore, examining the change in investors' default risk perceptions around these events provides an excellent test of the resiliency of the high-yield debt market.

Previous studies have explored the impact of prominent cases of default on bonds that were originally investment-grade.[5] While some studies find that major defaults on investment-grade securities could affect the pricing of similar issues shortly after default, the extant evidence fails to indicate a permanent impact on the interest cost structure. These results, however, are not totally surprising inasmuch as all of these studies dealt with bonds that were originally investment-grade. For such bonds, the default component in their original pricing is not substantial, and any default of any unrelated issuer is likely to be viewed as an isolated case of mismanagement or fiscal irresponsibility. Consequently, a widespread and permanent impact may not be evident. However, this is not necessarily true in the high-yield debt market, where the pricing structure is strongly affected by the perceived default probability of the issuer.

The major findings of this study are that the high-yield bond pricing demonstrates suprisingly strong resiliency with respect to major adverse events in both the primary and secondary markets. The evidence indicates that, in general, there was a sharp upward revision in the market's assessment of future default probabilities on high-yield debt immediately following each of the adverse events under investigation. The effect, however, was transitory. Contrary to popular belief, the high-yield bond market exhibits a strong ability to recover swiftly from severe adversities.

The remainder of this study is organized as follows: The following section describes the empirical design which includes a description of the sample and of the methodology used to test the hypothesis. The second, third, and fourth sections present the empirical results. Finally, the last section summarizes the paper and presents conclusions.

EMPIRICAL DESIGN

Methodology

The methodology is designed to test the hypothesis that major adverse economic events caused a revision in the probability of default perceived by investors in the high-yield bond market. The hypothesis is tested by examining whether announcements of the events caused a change in the implied default risk premium or yield spread inherent in the pricing of both new issues and secondary market trading of high-yield bonds. In section two (page 64), this is done by comparing the probabilities of default implied in the actual yields of high-yield bonds issued after the adverse event and those implied from estimated instrumental yields assuming that the LTV event and other adversities had not occurred.

Essentially, for each new issue of high-yield bonds beginning in July 1986 (e.g., the LTV bankruptcy), we first compute the instrumental yields using a pricing model estimated in the pre-LTV environment. The estimated yield gives us the projected interest cost of a bond assuming the LTV bankruptcy did not occur. Furthermore, based on the actual yield and the instrumental yield for each issue, we estimate the default probability implied from each yield. The comparison of default probabilities from actual yields relative to those estimated from instrumental yields enables us to test the hypothesis that the LTV crisis (or other events) affected the subjective default probabilities in the low-grade, high-yield bond markets. In section three (page 70), we estimate the cross-section time-series model developed below to explain the yield spread for new-issue high-yield bonds directly, with dummy variables used to identify changes in yield spreads that occurred after each event. In section four (page 72), similar tests are conducted in the secondary markets. For comparative purposes, we examine the changes in yield spreads between bonds of various ratings and 10-year Treasury bond yields in the secondary market (a proxy for changes in default risk premia) around the four events.

A Model to Estimate Yields

Previous studies have identified a fairly consistent set of macroeconomic variables and issuer/issue characteristics to explain the yield on risky bonds.[6] Generally, it is acknowledged that the yield spread between a risky bond and a riskless bond is determined by the likelihood of default of the issuing firm, stage of the economic cycle, market uncertainty at the time of the issue, the maturity and marketability of the issue, and other issue characteristics such as conservative sinking fund provisions, etc. For high-yield bond pricing, we also include an additional variable, the purpose of the issue; takeover high-yield bonds have higher yields than otherwise similar nontakeover high-yield bonds (see Rao and Ma, 1988). Identifying the purpose of the issue allows us to measure the impact of bond purpose and uncertainty of the use of the funds on yield spreads. Thus, the model used in this study is:

$$YS = f(PUR, RATG, DUR, SIZE, CV, BC) \qquad (1)$$

where:

YS = Yield spread measured as the difference between the yield to maturity on a bond relative to the yield for constant maturity Treasury bonds with a duration approximately equal to the duration of the bond at the time of issue. Because of high and risky coupon payments, a high-yield bond's pricing is likely to be more closely related to its duration than its maturity.[7]

PUR = Dummy variable to capture the purpose of the issue. Two dummy variables were used (P1, P2), where P1 = 1 if the bond was used to finance a specific impending acquisition or to refinance a previously undertaken loan that was used to consummate a merger or acquisition and P2 = 1 if the issue was to finance future takeovers where no specific target was identified.

RATG = A series of dummy variables is used to capture default risk based on Moody's ratings. A total of five dummy variables were used (BA2, BA3, B1, B2, and B3) with the excluded set being bonds with a BA1 rating. The expected sign is positive with the magnitude of the coefficient increasing monotonically from BA2 to B3.

DUR = Duration of the bond calculated on the assumption the bond will be called at the end of the call deferment period. The expected sign is positive. Duration to first call is used rather than maturity because high-yield bond issues are generally considered the first candidates to be called, ceteris paribus.

SIZE = Issue size in millions of dollars. Previous studies generally have documented that larger-size issues have lower yield premiums. This is attributed to economies of scale arising from the selling effort and fixed costs associated with the flotation process.

CV = Dummy variable equal to 1 if bond is convertible, zero otherwise. The expected sign is negative.

BC = A variable measuring the stage of business cycle. This is computed by the difference in the average yield on Moody's AAA corporate bond index and Moody's 30-year Treasury bond index in the month of issuance. Previous studies by Jaffee (1975) and others have documented that yield differentials fluctuate with credit risk over the business cycle. The expected sign is positive.

A Model to Estimate Default Probabilities from Bond Yields

To estimate the default probability implied in yields, we rely on the theoretical work of Bierman and Hass (1975), Yawitz (1977), and Yawitz, Maloney, and Ederington (1983). Given a recovery rate on promised payments, the following relationship holds in a perfect market:

$$\sum_{t=1}^{n-1} \frac{P^t C + P^{t-1}(1-P)\, g\,(C+1)}{(1+i)^t} + \frac{P^n(C+1) + P^{n-1}(1-P)\, g\,(C+1)}{(1+i)^n}$$

$$= \sum_{t=1}^{n} \frac{C}{(1+r)^t} + \frac{1}{(1+r)^n} \tag{2}$$

where

n = number of periods to maturity;

C = coupon rate on the risky bond per period;

P = probability of the firm surviving from one period to the next;

r = yield on the risky bond;

i = yield on an otherwise identical riskless bond; this is proxied by the yield on the Moody's Treasury bond index in the month of issuance for bonds with a duration approximate equal to the duration of the bond.

g = proportion of the sum of the period's coupon and face value of the bond that would be paid as settlement if default were to occur. In this we are guided by the findings of Altman and Nammacher (1987) on default losses in the high-yield bond market. They estimate the recovery rate to have averaged 41 percent for the period 1975-1985.

The left hand side in the above equation is the present value of the certainty equivalent stream of cash flows from the risky bond discounted at the risk-free rate; the right hand side is the risky stream of cash flows from the bond discounted at the risk-adjusted discount rate. From the above equation, given the known parameters, $r, i, n, c,$ and g, one can compute the probability of survival from one period to the next (P) or its complement, the default probability ($1-P$).[8]

The probability of default is calculated using both observed yields and instrumental yields estimated from (1). The comparison of the default probability implied by the actual yields, 1–Pa, and that implied by the instrumental yields, 1–Pe, enables us to test the null hypothesis, i.e., 1–Pa = 1–Pe.[9] The difference in theoretical default probabilities is tested using both parametric (T test) and nonparametric (Wilcoxon) tests.

EMPIRICAL RESULTS: IMPLIED DEFAULT PROBABILITIES IN NEW-ISSUE MARKETS

The sample used in the tests consists of all high-yield bonds with Moody's ratings of BA1, BA2, BA3, B1, B2, and B3 that have all the requisite data and were issued between January 1980 and November 1988 as reported in *Moody's Bond Survey*. Descriptive statistics for the entire sample are presented at the bottom of Table 4–1.

Table 4–2 presents the least squares estimate of the relationship in (1) using the 506 high-yield bonds issued from January 1980 through June 1986 (pre-LTV period). The regression model explains 79 percent of the cross-sectional variation in yield spreads and its coefficients are generally significant and have the expected signs. The only exceptions were P2, SIZE, and BA2. P2 (which denoted issues used to finance unspecified takeovers) was not significant even though the coefficient for P1 (which denotes bonds used to finance or refinance specific acquisitions) is significantly greater than the omitted (non-takeover) category. The coefficient for size is not significant, suggesting that economies of scale are not as significant for issuing and marketing high-yield bonds as investment-grade bonds. The coefficients for the rating dummies increase monotonically and all but BA2, which is closest in quality to the omitted category, are significant.[10]

Table 4–2 presents mean default probabilities based on the actual and instrumental yields for various months beginning in the month LTV declared bankruptcy (July 1986), through Boesky's indictment (November 1986), the stock market crash (October 1987), and Drexel's indictment (September-October 1988), and ending in November 1988. Also summarized for each month are the number of issues, the number of cases where default probabilities estimated from actual yields exceed those estimated from the instrumental yields, and the significance of the difference using both the t-test and the Wilcoxon test statistic.[11]

TABLE 4–1
Sample statistics, January 1980–November 1988

Variable

Number of issues 876

Takeover Issues (P1 and P2) 400
Non-takeover Issues 476
Convertible Issues (CV = 1) 370
Non-convertible Issues...506

Average Issue Size ....$72.0 million
Range ....$10.0–975.0 million

    < 25 million 114
    25–50 million 262
    50–75 million 112
    75–100 million 121
    >100 million 267

Average Yield to Maturity 12.45%

Average Coupon Rate 11.99%

Average Years to Maturity ....14.3 years

    < 10 years...337
    10–15 years...218
    15–20 years...150
    >20 years...171

Average Duration[a]...3.78 years

    ≤ 2 years 81
    2–6 years 692
    >6 years 103

Average Years to Call ....4.2 years

Agency ratings

BA1	37	B1	172
BA2	60	B2	281
BA3	103	B3	223

[a]The duration is computed using the call deferment period in lieu of the actual maturity.

Source: *Moody's Bond Survey*, all issues, January 1980 through November 1988

TABLE 4–2
Estimates of the regression equation for yield sSpreads on high-yield debt

---

Regression Estimate

$$YS = 1.2269 + 0.3391 \ P1 + 0.0184 \ P2 + 0.4203 \ BA2 + 0.7347 \ BA3$$
$$\quad (3.588)^* \quad (2.110)^{**} \quad 0.124) \quad (0.1353) \quad (2.3131)^{**}$$

$$0.8477B1 + 1.2452B2 + 1.7011B3 + 0.0886DUR + 0.0011SIZE - 5.0603CV + 1.2647BC$$
$$(2.659)^* \quad (4.384)^* \quad (5.570)^* \quad (2.378)^{**} \quad (1.369) \quad (-33.539)^* \quad (8.293)^*$$

R-Square 0.7940
F-Ratio 173.05
Prob > F 0.0001
Degrees of freedom 494

YS = Yield spread on new issue versus T-bond with the same duration
P1 = Dummy variable for bond issues to finance or refinance specific mergers or acquisitions
P2 = Dummy variable for bonds issued to finance unspecified mergers or acquisitions
BA2,
... B3 = Dummy variables to reflect Moody's bond rating categories, = 1 if in category; the omitted category is BA1
DUR = Duration to first call for the new issue
SIZE = Size of the new issue in millions of dollars
CV = Dummy variable that equals 1 for convertible bonds
BC = Business conditions as measured by the yield spread between Moody's 30-year AAA bond and 30-year Treasury bond series

* = Significant at 1% level
** = Significant at 5% level

Sources: *Moody's Bond Survey*, all issues from January 1980 through May 1987 and U.S. Treasury constant maturity Treasury bond yield series.

For the month of July 1986, the statistics are split between the two halves of the month to reflect better the timing of the LTV bankruptcy, which occurred on July 17, 1986. The same procedure of splitting the month for observations is also done for the exact timing of other events. Interestingly, the figures show that there was no significant increase in implied default probabilities in the first half of July 1986; however, there was a significant increase in the second half of the month. This suggests that the declaration of bankruptcy by LTV caused a systematic upward revision in estimated default probabilities for low-grade bonds issued immediately after the LTV bankruptcy. This upward revision persisted through December 1986. Note that the difference between the default probabilities implied in the actual yield and in the instrumental yield began to narrow in September. However, it sharply increased in November and December, after Ivan Boesky was indicted and the high-yield bond market was placed under a regulatory cloud. However, even after these two most damaging impacts on the high-yield bond market, beginning early in 1987, no significant difference in default probabilities estimated, using actual and instrumental yields is evident.

A similar pattern can be observed for the October 19th stock market crash. While there was a significant increase in default perception before the end of 1987, the duration for the increase only persisted six to eight months till June 1988. The fourth and a more recent test on the high-yield bond market is the indictment of Drexel Burnham Lambert, Inc. and its star player of junk bonds, Michael Milken on September 19, 1988. The high-yield market again experienced an increase in risk premium, as evidenced by the significant jump in default risk probability in October and November of the year. While only time can tell the ultimate reaction of the market, there was some sign of recovery from this negative event on the high-yield bond market, as indicated by the narrowing difference in default probability in November.

In Figure 4–1, the percentage increase in subjective default risk perception and the timing of the major events are presented from May 1986 to November 1988. In sum, the evidence in Table 4–2 and in Figure 4–1 indicate that the LTV crisis and other events caused only a short-lived increase in the high-yield bonds' estimated default probabilities, as the effect lasted six to eight months at most, then dissipated.

FIGURE 4–1
Increase in perception of default probability around major events

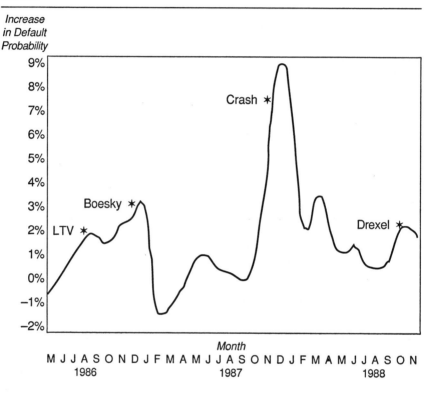

Source: Moody's Bond Survey

EMPIRICAL RESULTS: YIELD SPREADS IN NEW-ISSUE MARKETS

The default probability model generates results that depend monotonically, but not linearly upon yield spreads. For that reason, many previous researchers have used yield spreads as a proxy for default probabilities. Thus, to investigate the robustness of these findings to the measure of default risk perceptions, we conducted an alternative test based only upon

TABLE 4–3
Estimates of post-LTV default probabilities based on actual and instrumental yields of new issue high-yield bonds

Time Period	Actual Yield Avg.Def. Prob. (1)	Instrumental Yield Avg.Def. Prob. (2)	No. of Issues (3)	No. where Actual > Instrumental (4)	T Test (5)	Wilcoxon Chi-square (6)
May 86	9.10	9.70	33	9	−1.16	−1.23
June 86	8.78	8.76	19	7	0.03	0.42
July 1-15/86	8.63	8.46	23	13	0.40	0.35
LTV	**9.44**	**7.51**	**18**	**15**	**3.46***	**9.85***
Aug. 86	9.94	8.28	34	28	2.75*	13.36*
Sep. 86	8.85	7.11	22	19	3.21*	5.73**
Oct. 86	8.82	7.28	20	18	3.19*	8.01*
Nov. 1-15/86	10.59	7.63	10	8	2.94**	1.70
Boesky	**8.90**	**7.16**	**7**	**5**	**2.51****	**2.57*****
Dec. 86	9.40	6.73	16	15	8.83*	22.40*
Jan.-Feb. 87	7.80	6.47	13	7	1.39	0.13
Mar.-Apr. 87	6.02	6.56	18	4	−1.30	2.88
May 87	6.54	6.08	11	7	1.34	1.11
June 87	7.52	6.49	26	24	2.41**	2.30*
July 87	6.99	6.59	19	10	0.87	0.90
Aug. 87	6.77	6.43	12	7	0.52	1.07
Sep. 87	6.81	6.79	15	9	0.03	0.91
Oct. 1-15/87	6.90	7.45	6	4	−0.51	0.08
Crash	**11.96**	**6.55**	**2**	**2**	**9.47***	**1.16**
Dec. 87	13.97	6.37	3	3	2.44***	1.77***
Jan. 88	12.75	5.80	2	2	0.88	0.38
Feb. 88	7.90	5.66	5	3	1.91***	1.26
Mar. 88	9.60	6.12	5	5	1.72	2.52**
Apr. 88	8.50	5.87	3	3	2.90**	1.75***
May 88	7.02	5.93	6	5	1.62	1.54
June 88	7.13	5.64	15	13	2.03**	2.26**
July 88	6.91	6.10	11	8	1.00	0.51
Aug. 88	6.37	5.73	7	5	1.56	1.67
Sep. 88	6.71	5.86	8	6	1.06	1.20
Drexel	**7.73**	**5.56**	**11**	**9**	**3.09***	**2.86***
Nov.88	8.68	6.78	13	10	2.09**	2.49*

* Significant at the 1% level
** Significant at the 5% level
*** Significant at the 10% level

Source:

(1) Actual implied default probabilities were calculated using equation (2) from actual new issue rates and terms, taken in comparison with prevailing Treasury bond rates.

(2) Instrumental yields were calculated using the regression presented in Table 4–2 to estimate the implied yield spread and default probability that would be expected to apply based only on the objective terms surrounding the new issue.

(3) The number where the actual implied default probabilities exceed calculated default probabilities obtained from the instrumental yield equation was then calculated.

(5) T-tests and (6) Wilcoxon Chi-square tests were then calculated to determine if the difference in implied and actual default probabilities each month was statistically significant.

TABLE 4–4

Yield spreads before and after the LTV default: Pooled cross-section times series estimates

---

$$YS = 1.306 + 0.350\ P2 + 0.047\ P1 + 0.410\ BA2 + 0.708\ BA3 + 0.832\ B1 + 1.208\ B2$$
$$(3.172)^* (1.880)^{***}\ (0.271)\quad (1.09)\quad\ (1.856)^{***}\quad (2.192)^{**}\quad (3.528)$$

$$+ 1.674\ B3 + 0.082\ DUR + 0.00056\ SIZE - 5.089\ CV + 1.282\ BC + 0.048\ JY\ 186$$
$$(4.589)^*\quad (1.820)^{***}\qquad (0.688)\qquad (-28.494)\quad (6.877)^*\quad (0.123)$$

$$+ 1.014\ JY286 + 1.038\ AUG\ 86 + 0.830\ SEP\ 86 + 0.748\ OCT\ 86 + 1.136\ NOV\ 86$$
$$(2.350)^{**}\qquad (3.227)^*\qquad (2.208)^{**}\qquad (1.898)^{***}\qquad (2.677)^*$$

$$+ 1.546\ DEC\ 86 + 1.846\ JAN\ 87 - 0.251\ FEB\ 87 - 0.262\ MAR\ 87 - 0.262\ APR\ 87$$
$$(3.520)^*\qquad (2.665)^*\qquad (-0.376)\qquad (-0.372)\qquad (-0.522)$$

$$+ 0.422\ MAY\ 87$$
$$(0.815)$$

$$R^2 = 0.7019,\ F = 69,\ prob > F = 0.001,\ df = 674$$

YS	=	Yield spread on new issue versus T-bond with the same duration
P1	=	Dummy variable for bond issues to finance or refinance specific mergers or acquisitions
P2	=	Dummy variable for bonds issued to finance unspecified mergers or acquisitions
BA2, ... B3	=	Dummy variables to reflect Moody's bond rating categories, = 1 if in category; the omitted category is BA1
DUR	=	Duration to first call for the new issue
SIZE	=	Size of the new issue in millions of dollars
CV	=	Dummy variable that equals 1 for convertible bonds
BC	=	Business conditions as measured by the yield spread between Moody's 30-year AAA bond and 30-year Treasury bond series
AUG 88, SEP 86, ... , MAY 87	=	dummy variables that take the value for all bonds issued in that month
JY186 and JY286	=	dummy variables that take the value of 1 in the first and last halves of July 1986, respectively, since the LTV default occurred in mid-month

    * = Significant at 1% level
    ** = Significant at 5% level
    *** = Significant at 10% level

Sources: *Moody's Bond Survey* and U.S. Treasury constant maturity Treasury bond yield series.

FIGURE 4–2
Yield spreads of junk bond, industrial BBB, AA, AAA off 10-year
Treasury bond

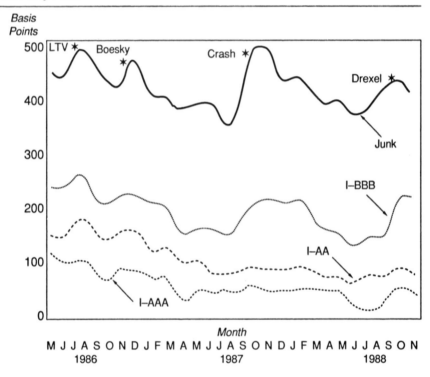

Source: Moody's Bond Survey

yield spreads. The test employs a dummy-variable regression model to estimate yield spreads on new issues of high-yield debt. Specifically, it estimates the yield-spread relationship described in equation (1) over the entire sample period from January 1980 through November 1988, using dummy variables for various months after each event. Note that the dummy variables, "LTV," "Boesky," "Crash," and "Drexel" represent the month that each event occurred. The advantage of this approach is that it makes full use of the information after each event to estimate the parameters of the yield-spread model. The results of the pooled cross-section, time-series estimation of equation (1) is presented in Table 4–4.[12] These results indicate that after controlling for other factors, yield spreads on new issues of high-yield bonds increased significantly in the post-LTV crisis period for

FIGURE 4–3
Yield spreads of junk bond, public utility BBB, A, AA off 10-year Treasury bond

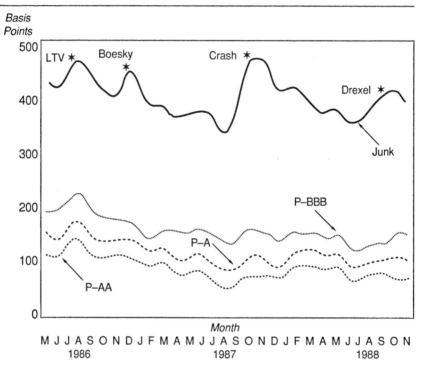

Source: Moody's Bond Survey

approximately six months. Beginning in early 1987, however, the effect appears to have dissipated. Even confounded by the indictment of Ivan Boesky on November 1986, the yield spread reflected no additional risk premium starting Feburary 1987. Similarily, the stock market crash did widen the yield spread by 3.56 percent for the high-yield bond market, but this additional premium turned insignificant no later than June 1988. As for the impact of Drexel's indictment, the yield spread increased by 1.24 percent.

These results are consistent with the findings from the default premium tests. They also imply that the temporary changes in the yield spread that occurred immediately after each event did not result from a permanent shift in the structure of the yield spread model.

EMPIRICAL RESULTS: YIELD SPREADS IN
SECONDARY MARKETS

In this section, we examine the impact of various negative events on the trading of bonds in secondary markets. For comparative purposes, yield spreads between bonds with different ratings and 10-year Treasury bonds, a common proxy for the default risk premium, are presented in Figures 4–2 and 4–3.

In Figures 4–2 and 4–3, the yield spreads are computed based on the weekly yield-to-maturity of Moody's Industrial BondIndex with ratings of AAA, AA, BBB, Moody's Public Utility Bond Index with ratings of AA, A, BBB, and Morgan Stanley High-Yield Composite, less the yield to maturity of 10-year Treasury bonds. Also plotted are the timing of each adverse economic event. It is clear that for the LTV bankruptcy, the Boesky affair, the stock market crash, and Drexel's indictment, there was a significant increase in yield spreads for all classes of bonds. While it appears that the high-yield bond market has been most sensitive to these events, the reaction reversed itself within a short period. Similar to the findings in the primary market, the evidence suggests that even for the controversial high-yield bond market, there is strong resiliency in secondary trading.

CONCLUSIONS

In contrast to popular conjectures, the high-yield bond market demonstrates surprisingly strong resiliency. This study compares implied default probabilities around four major adverse events between May 1986 and November 1988. A comparison of these default probabilities and the corresponding yield spreads in both new-issue and secondary markets reveals that the market's perception of default probabilities applicable to the high risk segment of the bond market increased significantly after each event. However, the effect was transitory, lasting for only six to eight months, as demonstrated by the swift recovery of the prices of high-yield bonds from economic misfortunes. The evidence indicates that the high-yield bond market is resilient with respect to major adverse economic events.

Notes

1. High-yield bonds are also known by such other versatile names as"junk" bonds, "low-rated" bonds, and "speculative-grade" bonds.
2. In a detailed examination of default rates on low-grade bonds, Altman and Nammacher (1985, 1987) and Altman (1987) estimated the default rate to be 1.53 percent for the period 1974 to 1985. This compares with an average of 0.173 percent for all corporate bonds over the same period. Further, they conclude that even after adjusting for the default loss rate, high-yield bonds yielded a respectable return of 16.1 percent over the period of study. Blume and Keim (1987) on the other hand show that the risk of high-yield bonds as measured by monthly return volatility over the period 1982-1986 was lower than corresponding risk estimates for long term U.S. government and investment-grade corporate bonds and equities.
3. See, for example, *The Wall Street Journal*, July 31, 1986; July 21, 1986; September 20, 1985; May 14, 1985; and April 29, 1985.
4. The LTV Corporation filed for protection under Chapter 11 of the federal bankruptcy code on July 17, 1986 (see *The Wall Street Journal,* July 18, 1986, p. 3 for further details).
5. See Forbes and Peterson (1975), Gramlich (1976), Hoffland (1977), and Kidwell and Trzcincka (1982 and 1983) with regard to the New York City crisis; Jaffee (1975) and Kidwell and Trzcincka (1979) with regard to the effect of the Penn-Central Crisis; and Peavy and Hempel (1987) with regard to the WPSS default.
6. See for instance, Benson, Kidwell, Koch, and Rogowski (1981), Fisher (1959), Jaffee (1975), Yawitz (1978), and Kessel (1971).
7. The Treasury bond yield series used were average "constant-maturity" rates. Thus we calculated the duration of each constant-maturity yield by assuming that a new Treasury bond of that maturity was issued at par carrying the current day's appropriate constant maturity rate. Since the duration did not match exactly when calculating the yield spread, we used the constant maturity yield of the Treasury bond with a duration closest in length to the duration of the new high-yield issue. Because the Treasury yield curve usually is relatively flat at longer maturities, and duration and maturity differ little for short maturities, the empirical results obtained in the paper were very similar regardless of whether the yield spread was obtained by using yields for constant-maturity T-bonds with a *maturity* or a *duration* equal to the duration of the high-yield bond.
8. Evidence developed by Kim (1988) indicates that the implied default probability measure developed by Fons (1987) provides a better estimate of near-term high-yield bond default probabilities than either the traditional risk premium (the actual bond rate minus the riskless bond yield) or the relative risk premium (the bond yield divided by the actual bond yield).

9. Fons (1987) used the formulation in (2) to relate calculated default probabilities to actual default probabilities and various macroeconomic factors.

10. To ensure that the yield-spread model is well specified (equation 1), we split the sample into an estimation sample and a test sample and examined the residuals in the test sample for possible biases. The estimation sample comprised 80 percent of the total sample selected randomly, while the remaining 20 percent of the observations served as the test sample. The estimation sample was used to generate the coefficients for equation (1) which were then used to estimate the yield spreads for the test sample observations. The estimated yield spreads for the test sample were then compared to the actual yield spreads. A check of the residuals in the test sample showed no bias. Specifically, a t-test of the null hypothesis of mean zero residuals could not be rejected at the one percent level of significance. The residual test was also conducted by various rating classes and, as before, the null hypothesis of mean zero residuals could not be rejected at conventional levels of significance. These results indicate that the model is well specified and that the error structure is not biased.

11. The estimated default probabilities are not substantially higher than those estimated by Fons for higher yielding bonds. While default probabilities using this methodology are relatively high (at up to ten percent), when we consider that estimated losses upon default are barely more than half the principal amount, the estimated default rates for high yield bonds do not seem excessive.

12. A *Journal of Finance* referee appropriately noted that the equation estimated in Table 4–4 may overstate the effect of yield changes in the post-LTV period if the model is inappropriately specified. Because of the pooled cross-section, time-series methodology, any month-specific error in the model would be represented n_i times in the residuals of the model, where n_i is the number of high-yield security issues floated in month i. In order to eliminate the multiplication of error that is possible in a cross-section, time-series framework, we reran the model two ways, both of which confirmed the results presented in the text. The first approach used the average yield spread for all high-yield bonds issued in month i as the dependent variable and also averaged all independent variables for all high-yield bonds issued that month. This converted our model to a strict time-series model, but it reduced our degrees of freedom substantially. In addition, the rating variables no longer made sense. Furthermore, even though all other (nonrating) variables retained the expected signs, the average duration variable was no longer significant. However, a dummy variable for the second half of July through year end 1986 was strongly and significantly positive, as would be expected if, as we posit, a positive "LTV effect" existed. The results were:

$$YS = 1.282 + 1.325 \text{ P1} + 0.269 \text{ P2} - 0.231 \text{ BA2} - 0.252 \text{ BA3}$$
$$\quad (1.278) \quad (2.050)** \quad (0.552) \quad (-0.239) \quad (-0.205)$$

$$-0.421 \text{ B1} + 0.715 \text{ B2} + 1.021 \text{ B3} + 0.075 \text{ DUR}$$
$$(-0.381) \quad (0.815) \quad (0.975) \quad (0.692)$$

$$+ 0.049 \text{ SIZE} - 4.881 \text{ CV} + 1.038 \text{ BC} + 1.318 \text{ DUM LTV}$$
$$(1.903)*** \quad (-11.770)* \quad (2.583)** \quad (2.7880)*$$

$$R^2 = 0.8404, \quad F = 25.45, \quad \text{prob } F < 0.0001, \quad \text{D.F.} = 58,$$

where all variables are monthly averages of values applicable to each bond issue (see Table 4–2 for basic variable definitions) and DUM LTV is a dummy variable that equals 1 for all bonds issued from the last half of July through December 1986.

The second equation estimated used a pooled cross-section time series approach through the first half of July 1986, then treated each month or half month subsequent to the LTV event as if a single bond were issued at that time with the characteristics of the average high-yield bond issued that month. In that way, any bias in the model in the post-LTV period would enter the model only once each month, rather than n_i times. The extended results were very similar to those reported in the text, even the coefficients were very close in magnitude. The only difference of note was that the coefficient for JAN 87 was no longer significant.

References and Additional Reading

Altman, E. I. (July/August 1987a). The anatomy of the high-yield bond market. *Financial Analysts Journal, 43,* 12–25.

Altman, E. I. and Nammacher, S. A. (1987b). *Investing in junk bonds: Inside the high-yield debt market.* New York: John Wiley & Sons.

Altman, E. I. and Nammacher, S. A. (July/August 1985). The default rate experience on high-yield debt. *Financial Analysts Journal, 41,* 25–42.

Benson, E. D., Kidwell, D. S., Koch, T. W., and Rogowski, R. J. (December 1981). Systematic variation in yield spreads for tax-exempt general obligation bonds. *Journal of Financial and Quantitative Analysis, 15,* 685–702.

Bierman, H., Jr., and Hass, J. E. (1975). An analytical model of bond risk differentials. *Journal of Financial and Quantitative Analysis, 9,* 757–773.

Blume, M. E., and Keim, D. B. (July/August 1987). Risk and return characteristics of lower-grade bonds. *Financial Analysts Journal, 43,* 26–33.

Fisher, L. (June 1959). Determinants of risk premiums on corporate bonds. *Journal of Political Economy, 67*, 217–237.

Fons, J. S. (March 1987). The default premium and corporate bond experience. *Journal of Finance, 42*, 81–98.

Forbes, J. R., and Peterson, J. E. (1975). *Costs of credit erosion in the municipal bond market.* Chicago: Municipal Finance Officers Association.

Gramlich, E. M. (May 1976). New York ripple or tidal wave. *American Economic Review, 66*, 415–429.

Hoffland, D. L. (March/April 1977). The New York City effect in the municipal bond market. *Financial Analysts Journal, 33*, 36–39.

Jaffee, D. (July 1975). Cyclical variation in the risk structure of interest rates. *Journal of Monetary Economics, 1*, 309–325.

Kessel, R. (July/August 1971). A study of the effects of competition in the tax-exempt bond market. *Journal of Political Economy*, 706–738.

Kidwell, D. S., and Trzcinka, C. A. (December 1982). Municipal bond pricing and the New York City fiscal crisis. *Journal of Finance, 37*, 1239–1246.

Kidwell, D. S., and Trzcinka, C. A. (December 1983). The impact of the New York City fiscal crisis on the interest cost of new issue municipal bonds. *Journal of Financial and Quantitative Analysis, 37*, 1239–1246.

Kidwell, D. S., and Trzcinka, C. A. (June 1979). The risk structure of interest rates and the Penn-Central crisis. *Journal of Finance, 34*, 751–760.

Kim, S.-M. (1988). The prediction of default probabilities in the lower-rated corporate bond market: A comparison of three models of the default risk premium. Texas Tech University.

Peavy, J. W., III, and Hempel, G. H. (Fall 1987). The effect of the WPSS crisis on the tax-exempt bond market. *Journal of Financial Research, 10*, 239–247.

Rao, R. P., and Ma, C. K. (August 1988). The pricing of high-yield bonds. Texas Tech University working paper.

Standard & Poor's. (June 1987). Junk bond market's resiliency. *Credit Review*, 125–137.

Wall Street Journal, The. (April 29, 1985). Junk bonds don't merit a black-hat image. p. 18.

Wall Street Journal, The. (May 14, 1985). Fools and their takeover bonds. p. 34.

Wall Street Journal, The. (September 20, 1985). Bank board mulls curbs on thrifts buying junk bonds. p. 6.

Wall Street Journal, The. (July 18, 1986). The LTV Corp. files for protection from creditors under Chapter 11. p. 3.

Wall Street Journal, The. (July 21, 1986). LTV bankruptcy filing is likely to add to controversy surrounding two risky methods of corporate financing: Junk bonds and standby letters of credit. p. 2.

Wall Street Journal, The. (July 31, 1986). The $100 billion junk bond market is shaken by LTV recent bankruptcy-law filing. p. 53.

Yawitz, J. B. (September 1977). An analytical model of interest rate differentials and different default recoveries. *Journal of Financial and Quantitative Analysis, 12,* 481–490.

Yawitz, J. B. (September 1978). Risk premia on municipal bonds. *Journal of Financial and Quantitative Analysis, 13,* 475–486.

Yawitz, J. B., Maloney, K. J., and Ederington, L. H. (October 1983). Taxes, default risk, and yield spreads. NBER working paper No. 1215.

CHAPTER 5

DEFAULT RISK AND THE VALUATION OF HIGH-YIELD BONDS: A METHODOLOGICAL CRITIQUE

*Ramasastry Ambarish**
Marti G. Subrahmanyam[†]

INTRODUCTION

High-yield or "junk" bonds have been the subject of intensive research and analysis over the last decade, in large part due to the spectacular growth in that market during the period. Several of these research studies assess the performance of lower-grade corporate bonds in relation to higher-grade corporate/Treasury bonds.[1] Typically, these studies compare the mean returns and the standard deviations of return computed from a time-series of monthly realized returns on well-diversified portfolios of high-yield bonds, higher-grade corporate bonds, and Treasury bonds. The general conclusion is that an investment in a well-diversified portfolio of high-yield bonds, after adjusting for risk, tended to out-perform an investment in higher-grade corporate and Treasury bonds.

*Ramasastry Ambarish is a Visiting Professor of Finance, New York University, Stern School of Business.
†Marti G. Subrahmanyam is Professor of Finance and Economics, New York University, Stern School of Business.

The purpose of this paper is to examine critically the methodology used in previous research in the area of high-yield bonds. In particular, the use of the mean return and the standard deviation of return as measures of the reward and risk from investing in these financial instruments is questioned. The reason is that a risky corporate bond has an embedded put option due to the limited liability feature of corporate equity. This option feature of corporate debt assumes greater significance as the credit quality of bonds decline. Therefore, high-yield bonds share some of the properties of simple call and put options on common stock.

The option feature of risky corporate debt has two implications for the analysis of such securities. First, the mean return and the standard deviation of return traditionally applied to equity returns are not meaningful statistics for the reward and risk from high-yield instruments since the latter distributions of return are highly skewed as a result of the option feature. Second, the ex ante expected return and standard deviation of return are nonstationary. While the problem of non-stationarity of data is common in financial economics, ignoring it while analyzing returns on high-yield bonds may lead to misleading inferences. In this paper, results from option pricing theory are used to develop and elaborate on the empirical implications of the option feature of risky corporate debt.

This chapter is organized as follows: The second section, below, characterizes the put option embedded in risky corporate debt. The third section (page 82) develops expressions for the expected return and the standard deviation of return on risky bonds and discusses their relationship to the embedded put option. The fourth section (page 85) deals with the interest rate sensitivity of risky bonds and its relationship to credit quality. The fifth section (page 87) deals with the implication of this embedded put option for the comparative analysis of time-series sample statistics, and the sixth section concludes the chapter.

DEFAULT RISK AND THE EMBEDDED PUT OPTION IN CORPORATE DEBT

The "limited liability" feature of the corporate form of enterprise gives the equityholders of a corporation issuing debt the option to default on the payments they promise to the debtholders. This limited liability feature can be characterized and valued as an appropriate put option, since it confers on the equityholders the right to walk away from the firm if the value of the firm (i.e., its assets) falls below the promised payments to the debtholders.[2]

Due to this limited liability provision, a long position in any corporate bond can be viewed as a portfolio consisting of a long position in an "equivalent" default risk-free bond and a short position in a put option written on the market value of the firm issuing the debt.[3] For example, consider a firm with an outstanding issue of zero coupon debt of total face value F, maturing at time T.[4] A long position in this bond is equivalent to a long position in a default risk-free bond of face value F, and a maturity of T years, and a short position in an European put option on the market value of the firm with an exercise price F and an expiration date T years from now.

Risky bond $\equiv$ "Equivalent" Default Risk-free Bond

$\qquad$ – European Put on the Market Value of the Firm $\quad$ (1)

It should be emphasized that the European put option in equation (1) is *not a traded option*. It is an "embedded" put option, i.e., it is an option implicit in the risky bond and cannot be detached from the bond. However, it is possible to value this put option using the standard "no-arbitrage" arguments of option pricing theory. It is assumed that, corresponding to any corporate bond, an equivalent default risk-free bond (or a portfolio of such bonds) with an identical stream of promised cashflows can be identified. Then, in arbitrage free markets, the following relationship should hold between the market value of the risky bond and that of the equivalent default risk-free bond:

$$V_{rb}(F, T) = V_{tb}(F, T) - P(V; F, T) \qquad (2)$$

where

$\quad V_{rb}(F, T)$ = the market value of the risky bond,

$\quad V_{tb}(F, T)$ = the market value of the equivalent default risk-free bond,

$\quad P(V; F, T)$ = the market value of the European put option on the market value of the firm.

In equation (2), the value of the put option, P, measures the default risk premium on the risky bond. Other things being equal, the lower the quality of the bond, the higher will be the value of P. For the highest grade bonds, say AAA-rated bonds, P constitutes an insignificantly small part of the portfolio. However, for "junk" bonds, P constitutes a significant and material part of the portfolio. While the market value of default risk-free bonds such as U.S. Treasury bonds is determined *exclusively* by the term structure of risk-free interest rates, P depends on the following factors:

1. V, market value of the firm,
2. σ_v, the volatility of V,
3. σ_{vr}, the covariance between V and r, the risk-free rate, and
4. the term structure of risk-free interest rates.

The option feature of risky corporate debt has important implications for the measurement of the expected return and the standard deviation of return on corporate bonds, the duration and the convexity of such bonds, and the interpretation of comparative time-series sample statistics of realized returns on corporate bonds and Treasury bonds. These implications are especially relevant in any analysis of returns from "junk" bonds since P, the value of the embedded put option, is a significant part of the value of the "portfolio" of the long position in the default risk-free bond and the short position in the put option that is equivalent to the junk bond.

EXPECTED RETURN AND STANDARD DEVIATION OF RETURN ON RISKY BONDS

Given the characterization of a risky bond in equation (2), the expression for expected return on a corporate bond can be written as:

$$E\,[R_{rb}] = \omega_{tb}\,E\,[R_{tb}] - \omega_p\,E\,[R_p] \qquad (3)$$

where,

$E\,[R_{rb}]$ = the expected return on the risky bond,

$E\,[R_{tb}]$ = the expected return on the equivalent default risk-free bond,

$E\,[R_p]$ = the expected return on the embedded put option,

$\omega_{tb} = \dfrac{V_{tb}}{V_{tb} - P}$, is the portfolio weight of the equivalent default risk-free bond, and

$\omega_p = \dfrac{P}{V_{tb} - P}$, is the portfolio weight of the embedded put option.

Since the portfolio weights add up to 1, equation (3) can be simplified to the following expression.[5]

$$E\ [R_{rb}] = E\ [R_{tb}] + \omega_p\{E\ [R_{tb}] - E\ [R_p]\} \tag{4}$$

Two observations are in order here. First, in equation (4) ω_p is always positive. Also, in general, the difference between $E[R_{tb}]$ and $E[R_p]$ is positive.[6] Further, higher values of the embedded put option imply larger ω_p and larger differences between $E[R_{tb}]$ and $E[R_p]$. Therefore, the spread between the expected return on a corporate bond and an equivalent Treasury bond is always positive and this spread gets wider for lower quality bonds. Second, ω_p and $E[R_p]$ change every time *any* of the following variables change: $V, r, \sigma_v, \sigma_{vr}$ and the term structure of risk-free interest rates. As a result, even if the firm value and the interest rate follow a time-stationary process, the embedded put option, and, in turn, the expected return of the corporate bond will change every time there is a change in the firm value and/or the risk-free interest rate. Consequently, the expected return on a corporate bond will be highly *non-stationary*. This will be true even if the returns from the default risk-free bonds do not display nonstationarity, since changes in the firm value cause the depth-in-the-money of the embedded put option to vary.

Now, from standard portfolio theory, the expression for the standard deviation of return on a corporate bond can be written as follows:

$$\sigma_{rb}^2 = \omega_{tb}^2\ \sigma_{tb}^2 + \omega_p^2\ \sigma_p^2 - 2\ \omega_{tb}\ \omega_p\ \sigma_{tb,\,p} \tag{5}$$

where,

σ_{rb} = the standard deviation of return on the corporate bond,
σ_{tb} = the standard deviation of return on the "equivalent" default risk-free bond,
σ_p = the standard deviation of return on the embedded put option,
$\sigma_{tb,\,p}$ = the covariance between the return on the "equivalent" default risk-free bond and the embedded put option.

Again, using the relationship between portfolio weights from equation (3), equation (5) can be rewritten as follows:

$$\sigma_{rb}^2 = \sigma_{tb}^2 + \omega_p^2\ (\sigma_{tb}^2 - \sigma_{tb,\,p}) + \omega_p^2(\sigma_p^2 - \sigma_{tb,\,p}) + 2\omega_p\ (\sigma_{tb}^2 - \sigma_{tb,\,p}) \tag{6}$$

Ignoring terms containing ω_p^2, since ω_p is a small fraction, we obtain the following approximation for standard deviation of return on a corporate bond.

$$\sigma_{rb}^2 \cong \sigma_{tb}^2 + 2\omega_p \, (\sigma_{tb}^2 - \sigma_{tb, \, p}) \tag{7}$$

From equation (7), it is clear that the magnitude of σ_{rb} relative to σ_{tb} depends on $\sigma_{tb, \, p}$, the covariance between the return on the "equivalent" default risk-free bond and the return on the embedded put option. An increase in the risk-free interest rate, holding other things constant, leads to a decrease in the value of both the embedded put option and the equivalent default risk-free bond and *vice versa*. Therefore, a change in the risk-free interest rate induces a positive covariation between return on the embedded put option and that of the "equivalent" default risk-free bond. However, when interest rates and firm values are correlated, any change in the risk-free interest rate may also lead to a change in the depth-in-the-money of the embedded put option which, in turn, will lead to a change in P. The sign of this effect depends on the coefficient of correlation between the risk-free interest rate and the market value of the firm. If this coefficient of correlation is *negative,* an increase in interest rates will be accompanied by a decrease in the market value of the firm and the value of the embedded put option will increase. Therefore, in this case, the effect of the change in the depth-in-the-money of the embedded put option acts to mitigate the positive covariation between the return on "equivalent" default risk-free bond and that of embedded put option. If the coefficient of correlation between interest rates and firm values is *positive,* which is empirically more likely to be the case, an increase in interest rates will be accompanied by an increase in the market value of the firm, which, in turn, will lead to a decrease in value of the embedded put option. Thus, in this case, the depth-in-the-money effect acts to exacerbate the positive covariance between the return on "equivalent" default risk-free bond and that of embedded put option. Therefore, in this scenario, it is very likely that $(\sigma_{tb}^2 - \sigma_{tb, p})$ will be negative and, in turn, the standard deviation of the return on junk bonds will be smaller than that of default risk-free bonds.

The earlier comments about non-stationarity of the expected return on junk bonds are valid for the standard deviation of their return too. The standard deviation of return on all corporate bonds is highly *non-stationary* due to the changes in the depth-in-the-money of the embedded put option.

And the non-stationarity feature will be more important the higher the default risk or the lower the quality rating. Since both the expected return and the standard deviation of return of corporate bonds are nonstationary, any statistical methodology used to estimate them will have to explicitly recognize and adjust for this nonstationarity. *This is most important in the case of junk bonds, since the nonstationarity problem is most severe in their case, due to the relatively greater value of their embedded put option.*[7]

DURATION OF RISKY BONDS

The Macaulay duration of a bond is related to the sensitivity of its market price to changes in the risk-free interest rate.[8] We will demonstrate that the relationship between the duration of corporate bonds and credit quality depends on the behavior of the embedded put option.

Differentiating equation (2) with respect to r, we obtain the following expression for the sensitivity of corporate bonds to the risk-free interest rate.[9]

$$\frac{dV_{rb}}{dr} = \frac{dV_{tb}}{dr} - \frac{dP}{dr} \tag{8}$$

The first term on the right-hand side is negative from the definition of the value of a default risk-free bond. The second term is given by the following:

$$\frac{dP}{dr} = \frac{\delta P}{\delta V}\frac{dV}{dr} + \frac{\delta P}{\delta r} \tag{9}$$

The value of the embedded put option is a decreasing function of both V, the value of the firm, and r, the risk-free interest rate.

$$\frac{\delta P}{\delta V} < 0 \tag{10}$$

$$\frac{\delta P}{\delta r} < 0 \tag{11}$$

Further, the larger the depth-in-the-money of the embedded put, the larger are these partial derivatives (in absolute value).[10] The sign and magnitude of dV/dr depends on the coefficient of correlation between firm values and the risk-free interest rate. If this coefficient of correlation is non-negative, then dV/dr is non-negative. In this case, the value of the embedded put option always decreases when the risk-free interest rate increases and *vice versa*. Even if the coefficient of correlation between firm values and the risk-free interest rate is negative, for low (absolute) values of correlation the value of the embedded put option decreases when the risk-free interest rate increases. Only when the coefficient of correlation between firm values and the risk-free interest rate is sufficiently negative does the value of the embedded put option increase when the risk-free interest rate increases.[11]

In general, firm values and the risk-free interest rate are likely to be positively correlated. In this case, it can be seen that both V_{tb}, the value of the "equivalent" default risk-free bond, and P, the value of the embedded put option, move in the same direction when there is a change in the risk-free interest rate. Recall that a long position in a corporate bond is identical to a portfolio of a long position in the "equivalent" default risk-free bond and a short position in the embedded put option. Therefore, in this scenario, the embedded put option in corporate bonds provides a partial hedge against changes in the risk-free interest rate. Other things being equal, a corporate bond is less sensitive to changes in the risk-free interest rate than a Treasury bond.

The embedded put option is more sensitive to changes in the risk-free interest rate if it is more in-the-money. Therefore, the embedded put option provides a better partial hedge against changes in the risk-free interest rate as we move from high-grade to low-grade bonds. *A direct implication is that, other things being equal, a lower-grade bond is less sensitive to changes in the risk-free interest rate than a high-grade bond, when firm values and the risk-free interest rate are positively correlated.*[12]

The Macaulay duration measure, which was developed for a default risk-free bond, does not consider the effect of the embedded put option. As argued earlier, the embedded put option mitigates the interest rate sensitivity of corporate bonds. *Therefore, the "effective duration" of a corporate bond will be less than its Macaulay duration.*[13] *And, other things being equal, the "effective duration" of a risky bond decreases as we move from high quality to junk bonds.*

The methodology used by Jerome Fons (1989) to derive a measure of "effective duration" for risky bonds is conceptually related to our arguments above, although he does not explicitly consider the embedded put option. Further, his empirical estimates are largely consistent with our observations above. In particular, he finds that the "effective duration" of corporate bonds is always less than their Macaulay duration and the gap between the two widens as one moves from AAA- to B-rated bonds. However, he finds that the behavior of this gap is not monotonic in the bond rating. This may be due to the underlying non-monotonicity in the coefficient of correlation between the risk-free interest rate and the portfolios of market values of the firms issuing the bonds.

TIME-SERIES SAMPLE STATISTICS

In the third section (page 82), we argued that the expected return and the standard deviation of return on corporate bonds are inherently non-stationary due to the embedded put option. Consequently, any sample of time-series returns on a corporate bond portfolio is a heterogeneous sample, i.e., each data point is drawn from a distribution with a *different* mean and standard deviation. Therefore, time-series sample means and standard deviations would generally be poor estimators of the *ex ante* expected returns and the standard deviations of return. Moreover, since these sample statistics are based on the implicit assumption that the sample is drawn from a stationary distribution, when the underlying distribution is, in fact, non-stationary, it is extremely difficult to interpret these statistics.

Recently, several researchers have done a comparative analysis of realized returns on bond portfolios of different credit ratings.[14] These studies typically find that a portfolio of junk bonds yields a high mean return and has a lower standard deviation of return than a portfolio of Treasury bonds. For example, during the period from January 1, 1977 through December 31, 1987, the average monthly return on a portfolio of long-term government bonds and a portfolio of lower-grade corporate bonds were, respectively, 0.76% and 0.89%. Their respective standard deviations of return were 3.94% and 2.82%.[15] During the period from January 1, 1985 through December 31, 1988, the annual compound return and annualized standard deviation of return on the Salomon Brothers Long-Term High-Yield Index were 14.68% and 6.38%. The corresponding numbers of the

Salomon Brothers Index of Long-Term Investment-Grade Corporate Bonds ("Corporate Big") were 13.06% and 6.62%.[16] We will demonstrate that relative means and standard deviations of return on junk bonds and Treasury bonds depends on the sample path of the risk-free interest rate, the market value of the firm, and the sample coefficient of correlation between these two variables. We will do this with the aid of a numerical example that uses the binomial option pricing model.[17]

Assume that the market value of the firm and the one period risk-free rate follow, respectively, the binomial processes given in Figures 5–1 and 5–2.[18] For simplicity, we only consider a four-period model. (The conclusions hold even for a more general scenario.) The capital structure of the firm consists of equity and a zero coupon bond. The bond has a face value of 120 and matures at the end of period 4 (t=4). It is evident that this bond has default risk since there are many states at time t=4 where the value of the firm falls below 120. We also assume that there is an "equivalent" default risk-free, zero coupon, bond with a face value of 120 and a maturity

FIGURE 5–1
Binomial tree for the value of the firm

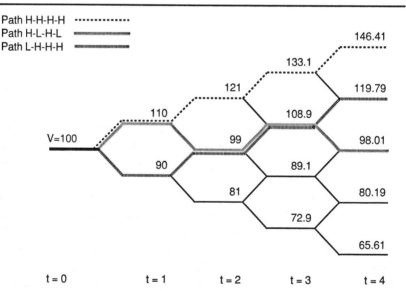

Note: Figure 5–1 is based on a firm value of 100 at time t=0 and proportionate up (u) and down (d) movements of 1.1 and 0.9, respectively.

of four periods. Figure 5–3 presents the binomial tree and the computed values of V_{rb}, V_{tb} and P at every node of the tree.[19] At each node in the binomial tree in Figure 5–3, the top number represents the value of the "equivalent" default risk-free bond, the middle number represents the value of the embedded put option and the bottom number represents the value of the risky corporate bond. Figure 5–3a is the case of perfect positive correlation between the value of the firm and the risk-free interest rate. Figure 5–3b corresponds to the case of perfect negative correlation between the value of the firm and the risk-free interest rate.[20]

Since we have a four-period binomial tree, the *ex post* realizations of the market value of the firm may correspond to any one of the 16 possible sample paths. For each possible sample path, using the values given in Figure 5–3, we can compute one-period return on the risky bond as well as the equivalent default-free bond for each of the four periods. Using this sample of four one-period returns, corresponding to each possible sample path, we can compute the sample mean returns and the sample standard

FIGURE 5–2
Binomial tree for the risk-free rate

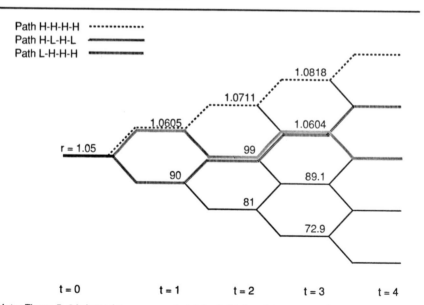

Note: Figure 5–2 is based on a one-period default risk-free interest rate of 5% at time t=0 and proportional up (u) and down (d) movements of 1.01 and 0.99, respectively.

FIGURE 5–3a
Binomial tree for the values of the "equivalent" default risk-free bond, the "embedded" put option, and the risky bond when the firm value and the risk-free interest rate are perfectly POSITIVELY correlated.

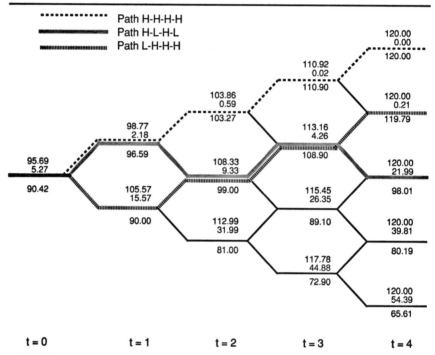

| | t = 0 | t = 1 | t = 2 | t = 3 | t = 4 |

NOTE: Figure 5–3a is based on the data in Figures 5–1 and 5–2 for the value of the firm and the risk-free interest rate, respectively. At each node in this tree, the top number is the value of the "equivalent" default risk-free bond, the middle number is the value of the "embedded" put option, and the bottom number is the value of the risky bond.

TABLE 5–1a

Sample Path	Bonds	Mean Return	Standard Deviation
H-H-H-H	Risky	7.34%	0.55%
	Default-free	5.84%	1.86%
H-L-H-L	Risky	2.33%	7.60%
	Default-free	5.85%	2.43%
L-H-H-H	Risky	7.26%	4.75%
	Default-free	5.86%	2.85%

FIGURE 5–3b
Binomial tree for the values of the "equivalent" default risk-free bond, the "embedded" put option, and the risky bond when the firm value and the risk-free interest rate are perfectly NEGATIVELY correlated.

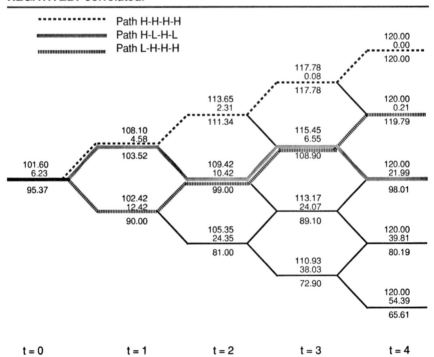

NOTE: Figure 5–3b is based on the data in Figures 5–1 and 5–2 for the value of the firm and the risk-free interest rate, respectively. At each node in this tree, the top number is the value of the "equivalent" default risk-free bond, the middle number is the value of the "embedded" put option, and the bottom number is the value of the risky bond.

TABLE 5–1b

Sample Path	Bonds	Mean Return	Standard Deviation
H-H-H-H	Risky	5.94%	2.52%
	Default-free	4.26%	1.69%
H-L-H-L	Risky	1.05%	8.48%
	Default-free	4.27%	1.97%
L-H-H-H	Risky	6.09%	6.77%
	Default-free	4.17%	2.13%

deviations of return on both the risky bond and the equivalent default risk-free bond. These sample statistics, computed for three specific sample paths, are tabulated in Table 5–1. Again, Tables 5–1a and 5–1b, respectively, correspond to the cases of perfect positive and negative correlation between the market value of the firm and the risk-free interest rate.

Three observations are in order here. First, in the case of perfect negative correlation between the market value of the firm and the risk-free interest rate (Table 5–1b), the standard deviation of return on the risky bond is higher than that of the default-free bond for all three sample paths. In Table 5–1a, i.e., the case of perfect positive correlation between the market value of the firm and the risk-free interest rate, the relative magnitude of these standard deviations depends on the sample path. For instance, in Table 5–1a, standard deviation of return on the risky bond is smaller than that of the default-free bond for sample path H-H-H-H. However, for sample paths H-L-H-L and L-H-H-H, it is larger than that on the default-free bond.[21] Second, the relative magnitude of mean return on the risky bond compared to that on the default-free bond is dependent on the sample path. For four out of the six sample paths, the risky bond has a higher mean return than the default-free bond. Third, the relative magnitudes of sample means and standard deviations depend on the trend in the market value of the firm along the sample path. For example, compare sample paths H-H-H-H and H-L-H-L in Table 5–1a. While the risky bond has a higher mean return and a lower standard deviation of return for path H-H-H-H, just the opposite is true for sample path H-L-H-L.[22] A more detailed, n-period (n large) binomial model is necessary in order to further elaborate on these points.

CONCLUSION

In this chapter, we have used insights from option pricing theory to analyze the expected return and risk characteristics of corporate bonds, especially junk bonds. Due to the limited liability provision on equity, risky corporate bonds have a put option embedded in them. This embedded put feature implies that the risk-return characteristics of junk bonds are different from those of default risk-free bonds such as U.S. Treasury bonds in a *fundamental* way. Consequently, it is inappropriate to draw inferences on relative risk-return characteristics of junk bonds and Treasury bonds based on a comparative analysis of time-series sample mean returns and standard deviations of return. Any exercise in the valuation of junk bonds, or the analysis of junk bond returns, should appropriately modify traditional tools of bond analysis with techniques from option pricing theory. We leave the detailed exposition of such a methodology to a future paper.

Notes

1. For example. see Altman (1987) and Blume and Keim (1987 and 1989).
2. This was originally pointed out by Black and Scholes (1973).
3. Here we are assuming that there are no other senior claims on the corporation. For a simple exposition of this idea, see Brealey and Myers (1988), chapter 20.
4. For simplicity, the analysis that follows assumes zero coupon debt. A similar, although more complex, characterization holds for coupon debt. In the case of coupon debt, the equityholders may be viewed as buyers of "compound" put options. Similarly, the holders of the risky bonds may be characterized as writers of "compound" put options.
5. Here $\omega_{tb} > 1$, $\omega_p > 0$ and $\omega_{tb} - \omega_p = 1$.
6. The expected return on the embedded put option depends on the market value of the firm, the value of the put option, the expected return on the firm, the hedge ratio or "delta" of the put and the risk-free rate. Further, it is never greater than the risk-free rate. It may even be negative. See Cox and Rubinstein (1985), pp. 211–212, for details.
7. By far the largest volume of junk bonds issued in the past few years is *not* among the higher noninvestment grades (say BB) but among B-rated issues. In 1988, for example, about two-thirds (by number and value) of the junk bonds issued were rated B, with another one-quarter of the issues rated CCC.
8. More formally, under continuous compounding, the change in the price of a bond for a small change in its yield to maturity is equal to the negative of the product of the duration of the bond and its price. In general, the Macaulay duration is replaced by the modified duration, which includes an adjustment for the effect of discrete compounding.
9. If we assume that the term structure of yields on default risk-free bonds is flat, dV_{tb} / dr will be equal to the dollar duration of the equivalent default risk-free bond. Similarly, if we assume that the term structure of yields on risky bonds is also flat, dV_{rb} / dr will be equal to the dollar duration of the risky bond. However, due to the embedded put option in risky bonds, the term structure of yields on risky bonds is unlikely to be flat even if it is so for default risk-free bonds.

10. Although this property cannot be demonstrated based on general arbitrage relationships, it is true in the context of most standard pricing models. For a demonstration in the context of the Black-Scholes model for European puts and a general discussion of the issue, see Cox and Rubinstein (1985), pp. 217–229.

11. This happens if dV/dr is such that $[dP/dr] = (\delta P/\delta V)(dV/dr) + [\delta P/\delta r]$ is positive.

12. This is true for a small (absolute) negative correlation as well. For larger (absolute) negative correlation, the results are ambiguous.

13. Just as it affects the duration of a corporate bond, the embedded put option changes the convexity of the bond. One can derive expressions for the "effective duration" and the "effective convexity" of a risky bond.

14. For example, refer to Blume and Keim (1989) and the references cited therein.

15. These figures are from Table 1 of Blume and Keim (1987).

16. These numbers have been computed using monthly return data. They are reported in Ross, Chacko, Palermo, and Warlick (1989).

17. See Cox and Rubinstein (1985), chapter 5, for an exposition of the binomial model.

18. We have set u = 1.1 and d = 0.9 for the market value of the firm in Figure 5–1. For the risk-free rate, u = 1.01 and d = 0.99; numbers reported in Figure 5–2 have been rounded to the fourth decimal.

19. We have implicitly assumed that the term structure of default risk-free interest rates is driven by a single factor, viz., the one-period risk-free interest rate.

20. We have considered only the polar cases of the coefficient of correlation between the market value of the firm and the risk-free interest rate, i.e., $\rho_{v,r} =$ +1 and –1. However, one can construct similar examples for arbitrary values of $\rho_{v,r}$. All our conclusions remain unchanged regardless of the value of $\rho_{v,r}$.

21. Note that the probability of exercising the put is one at some intermediate node along both these sample paths. We conjecture that, in the case of perfect positive correlation between the market value of the firm and the risk-free interest rate, as long as it is true that the probability of exercising the put is not one, the standard deviation of return on the risky bond will be smaller than that on the default-free bond.

22. Results reported in Table 1 of Blume and Keim (1987) are somewhat consistent with our observations. Note that their data is consistent with the coefficient of correlation between the market value of the firm and the risk-free interest rate being positive. They find that lower-grade bonds had a higher mean return than long-term government bonds during the periods from January 1977–December 1987 and January 1982–December 1984. The opposite is the case during the periods January 1982–December 1987 and January 1985–December 1987. The latter two periods happen to be the ones with higher standard deviations of return on the Standard & Poor's 500: 5.20% and 6.09% compared with 4.76% and 4.20% for the former two periods.

References

Altman, E. I. (July/August 1987). The anatomy of the high-yield bond market. *Financial Analysts Journal.*

Black, F., and Scholes, M. J. (1978). The pricing of options and corporate liabilities. *Journal of Political Economy, 81*, 637–654.

Blume, M. E., and Keim, D. B. (July/August 1987). Lower-grade bonds: Their risks and returns. *Financial Analysts Journal.*

Blume, M. E., and Keim, D. B. (1989). Volatility patterns of fixed-income securities. Chapter 1, this volume.

Brealey, R. A., and Myers, S. C. (1988). *Principles of corporate finance.* (3rd edition). New York: McGraw-Hill.

Cox, J., and Rubinstein, M. E. (1985). *Options markets.* Englewood Cliff, NJ: Prentice-Hall.

Fons, J. S. (1989). Default risk and duration analysis. Chapter 2, this volume.

Ross, P. H., Chacko, V. P., Palermo, V. J., and Warlick, P. M. (February 1989). High-yield corporate bonds: An asset class for the allocation decision. *Corporate bonds research.* New York: Salomon Brothers Inc.

CHAPTER 6

A LONG-TERM PERSPECTIVE
ON HIGH YIELD

Robert Long, CFA[*]

In the volatile securities markets of the last ten years, some of the conventional benchmarks of stocks and bonds have been changing. In particular, yields on all bonds have risen dramatically, while yields on stocks have fallen. In this upside down environment, high-yield bonds have become the fastest growing part of U.S. capital structure and have offered the highest returns of any security class. As long as interest rates remain at high levels by historic standards, these trends are likely to continue.

To some observers, high-yields bonds present an image of decaying credit quality, which increases risk of defaults and potential for widespread economic upheaval. This view assumes that there is no potential return that justifies risk of default. Yet the record of returns for high-yield securities, including the impact of credit defaults, shows a compelling case that higher-yielding securities tend to produce attractive returns. This has been true for stocks as well as bonds. Investors in more junior securities in the capital structure of a given company will expect higher returns to compensate for junior raking in the capital structure. Equity investors have traditionally expected better returns than more senior fixed income securities.

High-yield securities have existed in the U.S. for some time. What

---

[*]Robert Long is Managing Director, High-Yield Research Group, The First Boston Corporation.

High-yield securities have existed in the U.S. for some time. What may surprise some is that until quite recently stocks had higher yields than bonds (see Figure 6–1). Because equity is junior to debt in the capital structure, and because dividends can be omitted without fear of involuntary liquidation, risk is substantially greater. Thus, the concept that equity yields should be higher than debt is reasonable. Only since the 1960s have equity yields fallen below bond yields. This can be explained by the bull market of the 1950s and 1960s during which price appreciation provided approximately 75 percent of the returns on stocks, compared to only 25 percent from dividends. After these growth decades, it should not be surprising that equity returns underperformed in the 1970s and 1980s as price appreciation of stocks slowed.

While stock yields were falling in the 1960s and 1970s, bond yields were rising dramatically, a trend which made bond investments underperform. There are two important explanations for the sharp rise in bond yields.

FIGURE 6–1
Stock Yield vs. Bond Yield: A Long-Term Perspective

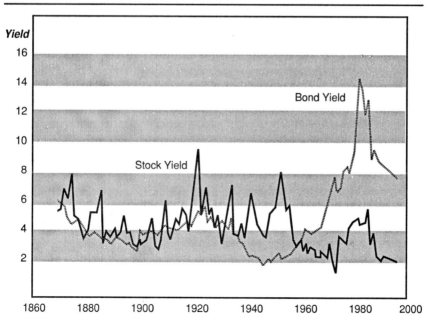

Source: First Boston High Yield Research

rates to rise through the conventional ceiling which had curtailed credit during previous periods of expansion. This policy led to a sharp recession and a cooling of the dangerous inflationary trends of the late 1970s. Partly as a result of this policy decision, price volatility of bonds rose sharply (see Figures 6–2a and 6–2b), thereby increasing the risk to investors and diminishing the appeal of bonds considerably. By the early 1980s, the yield levels on bonds and stocks reached a record gap.

During the recent period of historically high interest rates, the market saw the rapid growth of high-yield or "junk" bonds, with yields of 400–600 b.p. higher than treasury bonds. These securities have been used as a substitute for equity in the lower half of the capital structure of U.S. corporations. They have often appeared in reorganizations of corporations with low returns on equity which were restructured to improve utilization of capital. In fact, many high-yield investors have considered their investments much like equity. Thus, high-yield bonds may be compared to high-yielding equities of the earlier half of the twentieth century.

RISK VS. RETURN OF HIGH YIELD

The two primary risks of fixed income securities are default and price volatility. Studies of high-yield default rates by Altman and First Boston show that defaults of high-yield debt in recent years have been more than offset by the wide yield spreads over the "risk-free" treasury rate. Figure 6–3 compares the default rate of high-yield securities to the spread between treasuries and the high-yield market. In each of the last twelve years, the yield spread was greater than default losses, which leaves the residual "excess premium." This chart explains in part why high-yield bonds have outperformed treasuries. Investors in the high-yield sector currently have a substantial cushion should default rates rise. Furthermore, this comparison of default rates fails to consider upgrades and premium calls of high-yield bonds, which enhances returns.

A better comparison of relative performance is provided in Table 1, where returns of different security classes are compared. This also shows the effect of the other major risk: volatility. In Table 6–1, the returns and volatility of the First Boston High-Yield Index™ are compared to other fixed income and equity security types. Not only did the index post better returns than other security types, but with a surprisingly low volatility for

FIGURE 6–2a
Volatility of stocks and bonds

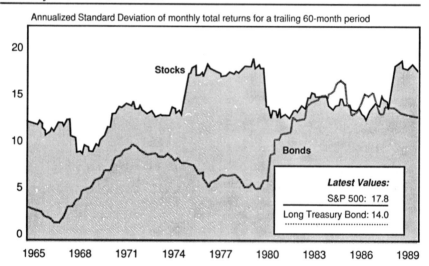

Annualized Standard Deviation of monthly total returns for a trailing 60-month period

Latest Values:
S&P 500: 17.8
Long Treasury Bond: 14.0

FIGURE 6–2b
Ratio between interest rates on long-term government bonds and S&P 500 earnings yield

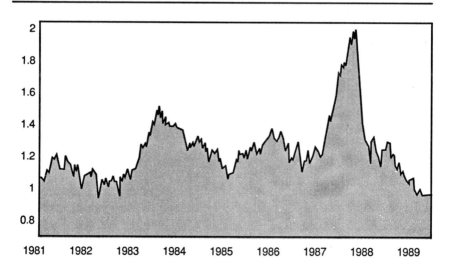

FIGURE 6–3
Excess Premiums vs. Default Losses, 1977–1988

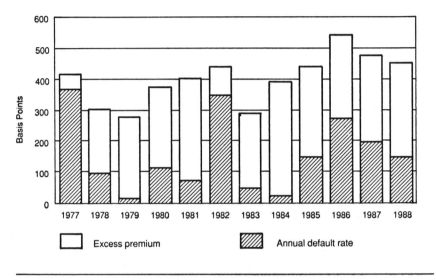

TABLE 6–1
Comparison of returns and volatility of return (1981–1988)

Index	Annualized Compound Total Return	Annualized Total Return Volatility
First Boston High Yield Index™	16.01%	9.21%
SLH Bond Index	14.30	11.51
SLH Government/Agency Index	12.74	7.72
Standard & Poor's 500	14.13	11.00
OTC Composite	8.25	13.77

Source: First Boston High-Yield Research Group

such a seemingly "risky" asset class. This can be explained in part by the shorter duration of high-yield securities, relative to lower-yield bonds of similar maturity. While the volatility of a particular high-yield bond may be quite high, the specific security risk is greatly reduced in a portfolio of securities. While future recessions may lead to higher default rates and possibly higher volatility, the 1987 experience during the crash is interesting to note. The price volatility and the returns of high-yield bonds held up well in comparison to stocks. Predictably, high-yield bonds outperformed stocks during the crash, as well as during the full year 1987.

Because high-yield bonds have recently been used as junior debt to replace equity in LBOs, recapitalizations, and leveraged acquisitions, many investors consider them as a form of equity. Therefore, it should not be surprising that returns of high-yield securities show closer correlation with equity markets than traditional fixed income investments (see Table 6–2). This result is consistent with the junior ranking in the capital structure.

TABLE 6–2
The First Boston High-Yield Index™ statistical information

	1986–1988
Correlation coefficient between	
First Boston High-Yield Index™ and	
• 10-Year Treasury	0.34
• Salomon Brothers Mortgage Index	0.41
• Shearson Lehman Government/Corporate	0.53
• Standard & Poor's 500	0.65
• OTC Composite	0.68
Correlation coefficient between	
10-Year Treasury and	
• Salomon Brothers Mortgage Index	0.86
• Shearson Lehman Government/Corporate	0.92
• Standard & Poor's 500	0.13
• OTC Composite	0.05
R-square First Boston High-Yield Index versus	
• Standard & Poor's 500	42%
• Shearson Lehman Corporate	17%
• 5-Year/10-Year Treasury	9%

Source: First Boston High-Yield Research Group

However, during periods of relative calm in securities markets, the fixed income characteristics of high-yield bonds produce greater correlations with the bond market. In turbulent markets such as October 1987, the high-yield market tends to have dramatic inverse correlations with bonds and high correlations with stocks. As a result of these conflicting tendencies, hedging high-yield bonds has proven to be a difficult challenge. However, owning high-yield bonds provides incremental diversification for balanced portfolios, lowering total portfolio volatility.

FUTURE SHOCKS?

The rapid growth of the high-yield market in the last decade suggests that performance in future periods may not resemble that of the past. No doubt high-yield securities will experience lower returns during a period of economic uncertainty. However, the relative return may compare surprisingly well to equity securities given the much higher volatility and lower dividend yield of equities. Furthermore, if interest rates rise simultaneously, high-grade bonds may suffer because of their relatively higher volatility (and longer duration). In such a scenario, government bonds would likely outperform as investors move toward higher quality securities. While such a scenario is likely to occur at some point, an accurate model for predicting the timing of such developments remains to be developed. Over longer periods, high-yield bonds should continue to benefit from the wide yield advantage over other security types. And the growth of the sector should continue, until such time as the equity market presents a higher yielding alternative. It is also possible that regulators could attempt to legislate away the high-yield bond market. Such an approach would reduce financing sources, potentially cause stock prices to fall dramatically, and perhaps lead to the development of "high-yield stocks"—a return to capital markets of the early 20th Century.

CHAPTER 7

COMMENTS ON INVESTMENT PERFORMANCE OF FIXED-INCOME SECURITIES[*]

Martin S. Fridson, CFA[†]

This session's papers vividly illustrate the benefits of collaboration between practitioners and academe. Certain of the findings, derived by techniques not yet in common use among investors, are valuable precisely because they are not the intuitive conclusions one might reach solely through the experience of daily trading. In other cases, the findings confirm impressions formed in the marketplace. Providing a more solid intellectual foundation for these inferences aids those of us who seek to interpret the high-yield bond market for the benefit of sophisticated institutional investors.

One result that may surprise many traders and portfolio managers is Blume and Keim's conclusion that the correlation between lower-grade corporates and long-term government bonds was lower during 1985–1987 than in 1982–1984. The common wisdom is that the "go-gos" (large capitalization issues typically arising from restructurings of corporations that enjoy high name recognition) track the Treasury market more closely

[*]This research was produced while the author was a Principal at Morgan Stanley & Co. Incorporated

[†]Martin S. Fridson is Managing Director, Merchant Banking Group, Merrill Lynch Capital Markets, and was formerly Head of High-Yield Research at Morgan Stanley & Co. Incorporated..

than other high-yield bonds do. Given the expansion in the population of go-gos during 1985–1987, when large-scale leveraged buyouts first became common, one might have expected that the overall high-yield market's correlation with government bonds would have increased rather than fallen. A possible extension of Blume and Keim's work would be to segregate the universe in order to test whether the perception is accurate that go-gos are more sensitive to Treasury rate fluctuations than bonds of smaller capitalization companies and acquisition vehicles.

Fons's chapter makes a valuable contribution by explaining a phenomenon that emerges clearly from empirical observation but may seem paradoxical to investors who are more familiar with investment grade corporates. In that market, quality spreads (i.e., yield differentials between higher-rated and lower-rated bonds) tend to be widest when Treasury yields are highest. The speculative grade-versus-Treasuries spread, in contrast, tends to narrow when Treasury yields rise. This pattern, far from being an anomaly, follows naturally from Fons's finding that "the difference between effective and Macaulay duration widens as credit quality falls." The implication is that to a greater extent than is true for a high-rated bond, a speculative grade bond is shorter in effective duration than a comparable-maturity Treasury bond and therefore less volatile in terms of yield in an environment of fluctuating rates. Consequently, as Treasury yields rise, speculative grade yields rise less, so the spread, by definition, narrows.

The mortality rate analysis described in Altman's chapter has already been eagerly embraced by some of the more progressive thinkers in the life insurance industry. It is a technique well suited to the formulation of actuarial assumptions and a significant advance over conventional methods of calculating default rates.

Properly interpreted, Altman's figures have considerable value, but must be used with care. On the surface, his Figure 3–1 (page 45) suggests that Single-B bonds underperform less risky Double-B issues over longer periods. Note however, that these figures represent the performance of particular cohorts, rather than of a portfolio that grows through new cash contributions (such as premium income) each year. Simply buying and holding an unmanaged portfolio may simulate the behavior of a unit trust, but most other types of investors add to their holdings year by year as new cohorts become available for purchase. As a result, they never get to the point of being totally concentrated in eight- or nine-year issues, as the hypothetical one-time-buyer does.

This difference is important because there is likely to be a bias toward lesser credit quality among issues that are not redeemed, prior to maturity, sooner than a half-dozen or so years after issue. (Improving credits are likely either to liquidate debt through surplus cash flow or to refinance their costly high-yield obligations at cheaper rates.) To extend Altman's insurance analogy, owning a single-cohort portfolio is akin to underwriting policies for one year, then relying on the performance of those policies until they all run off. Clearly, as the policyholders grow older, and no new, young policy holders enter the pool, annual claims will rise relative to premium income and underwriting results will deteriorate. Unless one chooses to adopt an equally unwise strategy on the investment side, Figure 3–1's implied underperformance of Single-B bonds is irrelevant, even though the return data are quite useful in an actuarial sense.

Turning finally to Ma, Rao, and Peterson's chapter, the authors provide important evidence about the high-yield market's performance during periods of stress. Since this is an especially controversial subject, I have added my own thoughts in the section below entitled "Resiliency: Real and Imagined."* By concentrating on evidence from the secondary market, it complements Ma, Rao, and Peterson's analysis of primary market data.

RESILIENCY: REAL AND IMAGINED

> "The panic is palpable. Investors have lost over 20% of their principal in a single day. Market makers are failing to support their issues. Critics point their fingers at the government authorities, whom they accuse of having failed to police irresponsible trading practices. As night falls, the world wonders whether the United States is on the brink of a financial crisis that will touch off an economic depression."

This grim scene is not some high-yield hater's apocalyptic vision of the way the speculative grade bond market will behave on the day the next recession hits. Rather, it describes what did happen (in the equity market) on October 19, 1987.

Curiously, nobody responded to Meltdown Monday by saying, "I told you so! Common stocks are not legitimate investments. Their values are

---

*Reprinted from Morgan Stanley's *High Performance*, September 1988, pp. 6–10.

illusory and the market for them is thin. Furthermore, they're designed for suckers—they have all the risk (total loss of principal) but only a fraction of the upside of options." The reader may rest assured that had a comparable panic gripped the high-yield market on October 19, similar denunciations of "junk bonds" would have reverberated all over the airwaves. Indeed, defamation of the high-yield market's character is a popular pastime despite a monumental lack of evidence to support the notion that a calamity is inevitable.

At this point the alert reader may protest, "Wait a minute! The October 19 hysteria did engulf the high-yield sector. Look at the numbers: On October 16, 1987, the spread between the Morgan Stanley High-Yield Composite and 10-year Treasuries was 381 basis points. One week later the spread was at 560, wider than at any other time since Morgan Stanley's series was first tracked. In other words, investors dumped their junk bonds and fled to the safety of Treasuries, exactly as the newspapers reported. Those who didn't sell took a bath, just as they will again when the economy falters or the insider trading scandal widens."

WIDESPREAD CONFUSION

Like so many before him, the reader has erred by looking at yield spreads—the source of perhaps more mistakes and deception than any other technique of bond analysis. A more rudimentary tool—absolute yield—tells a different story. It is true that the high-yield/Treasury spread widened by 179 basis points during the week bracketing October 19. Of that change, however, only 53 basis points (or 27% of the shift) represented an increase in the risk premium on high-yield bonds (from 14.04% to 14.57%.) The remainder, 126 basis points, represented a much more dramatic drop in the 10-year Treasuries yield—from 10.23% to 8.97%.

Is it rational to conclude that a 53-basis-point rise in rates on high yield bonds—supposedly representing an exodus of capital from the sector—produced a 126-basis-point decline in yields on Treasuries? Hardly, for if a given amount of funds flowed directly out of the high-yield sector into a sector nine times its size (i.e., Treasuries), the impact should have been smaller on the receiving sector. Instead, Treasury rates moved more than high-yield rates. The hypothesis of a direct flow of funds from high-yield bonds to Treasuries therefore fails to explain the observed changes in yields. It is about as logical as supposing that emptying half the contents of a Perrier bottle into Lake Michigan would cause that lake's water level to rise by more than the bottle's level would fall.

THE PATH NOT TAKEN

Analysts who relied on market observation, rather than oversimplified notions of yield spread mechanics, saw that there was no direct connection between the rise in speculative grade rates and the fall in Treasury rates following October 19. There was a flight to safety—in fact, there were two separate and simultaneous flights, but neither flight path was from high yield to Treasuries. Within the high-yield sector, investors sold "unseasoned" issues (recent leveraged buyouts and recapitalizations premised on yet-to-be-completed asset sales) and bought "seasoned" issues, which they expected to be less directly affected by the sudden devaluation of assets. High-yield bonds were quoted down as traders braced for massive redemptions of high-yield mutual fund shares, which they feared would trigger dumping by mutual fund organizations. In the end, however, little capital flowed out of the high-yield sector. It was therefore a flight from other financial assets (presumably including equities) that accounted for the drop in Treasury yields, aided by a benign Federal Reserve policy.

Admittedly, high-yield investors were not untouched by the destruction of value on October 19, but neither did they "take a bath," at least not in comparison to the dousing that equity investors received. The Morgan Stanley High-Yield Composite's dollar price fell 2% on October 19, a far cry from the 23% one-day drop in the Dow Jones Industrial Average. In retrospect, the "junk bond" buyer was the Prudent Man who hitched his trousers with both the belt of high current income and the suspenders of a comparatively high ranking in the capital structure, while the common stock investor was the speculator who forwent yield support and bought the most junior paper available.

Actually, it is not at all paradoxical that an investor may be safer in a Single-B bond than in a Triple-A corporation's equity. As analysts must continually remind themselves, a good company is not the same as an attractive security. A group of excellent companies may be recognized as excellent and their stocks may as a consequence be fully priced. Their dividends, representing yields of 2% and subject to reduction or omission with no covenanted penalty to the issuer, do not provide much of a floor. In contrast, a well-diversified portfolio of Single-B debt, supported by contractual obligations to pay interest, is likely to have a fairly steady market value. Certainly, default risk is greater in these lower quality companies than in the blue chips, but default risk is only one component of overall risk, as measured by volatility of returns. Thanks in part to the stabilizing influence of high current income, speculative grade bonds have historically fluctuated less than common stocks. By our measure, the high-yield bond sector is right in line with other classes of securities in a Capital Market Line analysis.[1] Based on these factors, it is not at all surprising that "junk bonds" were a harbor of refuge when common stocks collapsed on October 19, 1987.

Why, then, is owning common stocks considered a patriotic gesture, while investing in high-yield bonds is commonly viewed as at best fool-hardy and at worst a contribution to the nation's moral decay?

AN IMAGE PROBLEM

In part, the explanation lies in the unsavory image that high-yield bonds have in many investors' minds. The press has created the impression that the only issuers available for high-yield buyers are blind pools, personal holding companies of corporate raiders and Rust Belt dinosaurs on the brink of default. In reality, the high-yield market also includes recapitalized corporations with leading positions in healthy industries—e.g., Owens-Illinois, Safeway Stores, Burlington Industries—but these are much less fun to write about.

It is surprising that so many observers fail to recognize the wide differences in quality among high-yield companies, since nobody seems to have that problem when looking at equities. No one confuses IBM, Exxon or Merck with the scores of stock issuers that are every bit as dicey as any company found in the high-yield universe. To cite a few equity standouts of 1987:

- **Philip Crosby Associates** registered a 77% peak-to-trough price decline in 1987, a year highlighted by a company investigation of possible embezzlement.
- **Crazy Eddie,** which fell 89% from its 1987 high to its low for the year, lost $109.1 million on sales of $315.5 million, amidst allegations that the former management falsified financial data and violated federal securities laws.

- **Stars to Go** tumbled 95% from its peak during 1987, which it ended by obtaining a deferment of interest payments from its principal lender.

Despite such hair-raising stories, the equity market is considered safe for widows and orphans. Fiduciaries acknowledge that these examples of capital devastation are quite unlike investors' typical experiences with higher-quality common stocks. Moreover, the risks represented by the more volatile stocks can be largely diversified away.

The record suggests, however, that investment advisors could protect their clients' principal even better by applying the same principles of prudent management to speculative grade bonds.

Not only did the supposedly disreputable high-yield bonds not go into the tailspin observed in common stocks on October 19, 1987, but they rebounded much more quickly than equities. In absolute terms, the yield on Morgan Stanley's High-Yield Composite receded to less than its October 16 level of 14.04% in just three weeks, reaching 13.95%. The spread off 10-year Treasuries was back to within 2.5% of its October 16 level (381 basis points) in just seven months, reaching 390 basis points on May 27, 1988. By way of contrast, it took the Dow Jones Industrial Average more than eight months to rebound to a level 4% below its October 16, 1988 mark—its closest approach to date.

PERSISTENT PROPHETS OF LOSSES

Against this concrete evidence of the high-yield market's resiliency, the junk-bond-haters offer little in the way of facts to support their belief that disaster looms. Instead, they keep sagely repeating, "Wait until the recession. High-yield bonds have not yet been tested."

This statement is not correct, strictly speaking, since there was already $18.5 billion of straight speculative grade debt outstanding in 1982. That year's economic slump (the most severe since the bottom of the Great Depression) pushed the default rate up to 3.1%—a high level but not a catastrophe. Total return for high-yield bonds in 1982 was no catastrophe either, at 32.45%. The low-rated sector underperformed long-term Treasuries that year, but came roaring back in 1983 to outperform Uncle Sam's debt by nearly 2,000 basis points.

Still, the high-yield market's detractors have a valid point when they say that the sector's composition has changed since 1982, with large leveraged buyouts and recapitalizations representing a new element. Until the next recession hits, we cannot prove—nor can the critics disprove—that the high-yield market will be as resilient as in past crises. Nonetheless, the July 28,1988 Chapter 11 filing by Revco, the most prominent LBO failure to date, suggests that the high-yield market can shake off such incidents. The Morgan Stanley High-Yield Composite stood at 391 basis points over Treasuries on July 22, 1988 and at exactly the same spread on July 29, hardly suggesting a domino effect. The debt of Jack Eckerd, which as a drugstore retailer was the credit most likely to be associated with Revco in investors' minds, actually traded slightly higher the day Revco went bankrupt.

Notwithstanding evidence of its resiliency, however, high-yield debt continues to be viewed as too risky by investors who calmly plow millions into common stocks despite their demonstrated ability to decline by 20% in one day. Speculative grade bond issuers must feel like the toddler who gets spanked for the slightest mischief while its sibling's more grievous misdeeds are gushed over as examples of cuteness.

History offers some solace to the less-favored child, however. In 1906, common stocks fell into disrepute among life insurers as a result of practices that sound eerily familiar. Some life companies' directors were simultaneously serving as directors of brokerage firms, for which they were reaping huge profits by stuffing the insurance portfolios with worthless shares. A cry for reform arose and for the next 45 years, U.S. life insurance companies were prohibited from owning common stocks. Even today, equities represent a small portion of insurance companies' portfolios, although the reputation of common stocks has improved dramatically. Perhaps high-yield bonds' image will be similarly rehabilitated some day— maybe even less than half a century from now.

CONCLUSION

The record of high-yield bonds' resiliency stands in sharp contrast to the popular perception. Self-styled experts judge the securities to be, without exception, lacking in substance and therefore certain to collapse at the first hint of trouble. Each time the high-yield market coasts through an event that is supposed to ignite the panic, the doomsayers say that the real test is still to come. Against this sort of argumentation there is no effective rebuttal and, in fairness, there is no way to prove absolutely that the market will behave in the future as it has in the past. All that an investor can do is judge, in light of the record, whether the risks of owning high-yield bonds are tolerable. We submit that one need not be a crazed daredevil to conclude that the record—as opposed to the perception—of high-yield resiliency justifies reasonable confidence about preservation of capital. To be sure, investors will have to continue to buy selectively, but the better-quality issues within the speculative grade universe should not be collectively decimated by any event that we can currently foresee.

NOTES

1. Martin S. Fridson, CFA, and Michael C. Heaney, "High-Yield Bonds versus Common Stocks: Risk Adjustment and Inter-Market Valuation," *High Performance* (June 1987): pp. 4–9.

TABLE 7–1
Yield Spread: High-Yield Composite minus 10-Year Treasuries

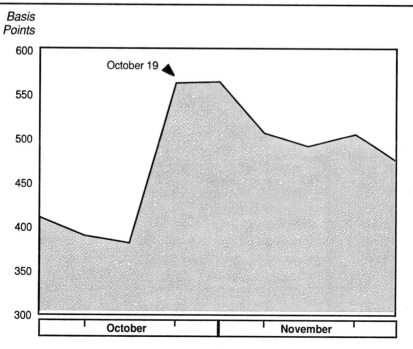

TABLE 7–2
Absolute Yield: High-Yield Composite

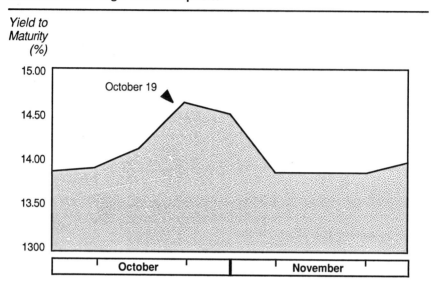

TABLE 7–3
Absolute Yield: 10-Year Treasuries

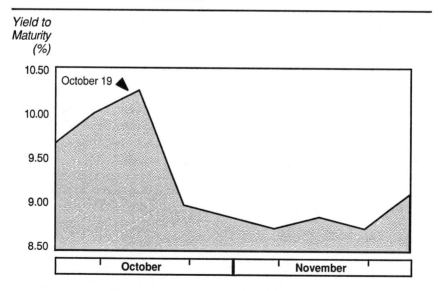

PART 2

REFLECTIONS ON THE HIGH-YIELD DEBT MARKET

CHAPTER 8

A WALL STREET VIEW OF THE HIGH-YIELD DEBT MARKET AND CORPORATE LEVERAGE

Frederick H. Joseph[*]

Recently, the related topics of high-yield debt and leveraged buyouts have become increasingly controversial. Yet both have made important contributions to the U.S. economy, giving American businesses the flexibility and the incentive to remain competitive in global markets. Neither is particularly new. They have been studied extensively and have been found to be valuable tools for corporate growth. In this article, I'll discuss the history of both, briefly cite some of the pertinent academic research on leverage and high-yield debt, then address the policy issues—taxation, international competitiveness, management incentives, employee ownership, and the possible effect of recession.

FORERUNNERS OF THE LBO

Like Moliere's gentleman who was astonished to discover that he had been speaking prose all his life, American companies have been involved in highly leveraged transactions long before terms like "LBO" and "junk bond" became common business language.

[*]Frederick H. Joseph is Chief Executive Officer and Vice Chairman of Drexel Burnham Lambert.

In 1901, the legendary financier J.P. Morgan merged eight steel companies at a cost of $1.4 billion, about $24 billion in today's dollars. U.S. Steel itself took on $570 million in debt in the form of high-yield bonds to finance the merger.

The U.S. Steel transaction was comparable in size to the recent RJR Nabisco leveraged buyout. And, like the RJR Nabisco transaction, it was the focal point for public debate and some skepticism. In February 1901, *The Wall Street Journal* noted "uneasiness over the magnitude of the affair" and added that the U.S. Steel merger supported arguments "against the centralization of industrial power." Critics claimed the debt would destroy the company; yet six years later U.S. Steel emerged as a solid, profitable enterprise with a 75 percent share of the domestic steel market.

From U.S. Steel to RJR Nabisco, the financial markets have been in a constant state of change, creating new opportunities and new ways for companies to raise capital. To put current concerns about leverage and high-yield debt in the proper perspective, one must examine how high-yield debt and leveraged transactions have helped U.S. companies and the U.S. economy.

HISTORICAL PERSPECTIVE ON HIGH-YIELD SECURITIES

High-yield bonds have been with us for a long time. During critical periods in our nation's economic history—especially in cycles of business start-ups and friendly merger activity—new issue high-yield paper has served as an important financing tool.

Many of America's greatest industrial companies owe their existence to high-yield debt issued at some time in their early history. USX, General Motors, IBM, and Goodyear are just some of today's blue chip, investment grade companies that started out by issuing below-investment grade securities.

THE GROWTH OF THE HIGH-YIELD MARKETS

Since the late 1970s, the new issue high-yield market has been evolving into the viable, strong, growing force for companies seeking to raise capital to finance business growth. Since 1977, some 1,000 companies have issued

$174 billion in high-yield bonds as of December 1988. A large, liquid secondary market for these securities has developed as well, attracting a full range of institutional investors and virtually all major investment banking firms as underwriters and market-makers.

The high-yield market's growth has been extraordinary: In 1977, only about $1 billion of straight public high-yield debt was issued; today, annual issuance runs at over $35 billion. The market as of December 1988 overall approximates $185 billion in principal amount outstanding—roughly 25 percent of all publicly traded corporate debt. While this number includes both former investment grade bonds that have been downgraded ("fallen angels") and loans first issued as private placements and subsequently registered, most are new-issue public securities floated by vigorous, growing companies.

HIGH RETURNS, LOW RISK, READY CAPITAL

Academic studies have shown high-yield bonds to be an important financing instrument—both for investors and for dynamic companies. For investors, high-yield bonds are among the highest performing securities in the portfolio and show the least volatility. Edward I. Altman of New York University has calculated that between 1982 and 1987 the yield spread on high-yield bonds averaged about 411 basis points over comparable Treasury bonds. At the same time, the average net loss due to defaults on high-yield was about 135 basis points. Even allowing for default risk, high-yield investors still earned an average 276 basis points more than Treasury bond investors. Marshall Blume and Donald Keim of The Wharton School have also studied the risk-return characteristics of high-yield bonds from 1982 to 1986 and found an annualized compound monthly rate of return of 11.04 percent for high-yield bonds, compared to 9.6 percent for high grade corporate bonds and 9.36 percent for long-term Treasury bonds. They also found that during this period returns from the S&P were 1.7 times as volatile as high-yield bonds, Treasuries 1.4 times as volatile, and high grade bonds 1.4 times as volatile.

Economic studies by Glenn Yago and John Pound have demonstrated that issuers of high-yield securities have experienced higher than average growth in revenues, employment, and productivity after assuming higher levels of debt. Dr. Yago's study found that firms issuing high-yield debt had outperformed industry average in employment growth (6.68 *vs.* 1.38

percent), sales per employee (3.13 *vs.* 2.41 percent), sales (9.38 *vs.* 6.42 percent), capital investment (12.37 *vs.* 9.85 percent), and capital expenditures (10.61 *vs.* 3.83 percent).

Similarly, Dr. Pound's study showed that companies which had increased their debt by 50 percent to finance corporate growth and investment experienced an increase in sales, capital spending, earnings, cash flow, and dividend payments in the year after the high-yield bond issue. In addition, the companies exceeded analysts' forecasts for these five performance measures by significant margins, topping capital spending predictions by 80 percent, sales and earnings by over 15 percent, cash flow and dividends by over 20 percent.

Yet, despite the large body of empirical evidence in favor of high-yield bonds, there has been resistance to the market in certain quarters.

THE LEVERAGE DEBATE

The recent wave of leveraged transactions has raised the hackles of Wall Street's critics. As a result, committees of both the Senate and the House began hearings on financial restructurings and corporate debt in 1989 and debated whether new legislation is in order. Although, as yet, no new legislation has been developed, some suggest that now is the time to reassess the tax code, which it is claimed encourages corporations to take on more debt. The target of proposed legislation is the interest deductibility of corporate debt used to finance takeovers or issued by companies already highly leveraged. Some would like to see the tax deductibility of a company's interest payments determined by its debt-to-equity ratio.

As in the past when there have been major transactions, there is a danger of overzealous legislation. In the long-run, penalizing corporate debt issuance will have a damaging effect on our economy. It will throw the brake on business expansion and blunt our nation's competitiveness at a time when it is predicted that our economy is ripe for a recession.

DEBT AND GLOBAL COMPETITION

America's corporations are already overtaxed and are at a disadvantage against foreign competitors. According to two separate studies by Alan Auerbach of the University of Pennsylvania and Richard Ellsworth of

Claremont College, U.S. corporations are actually underleveraged compared to those in Japan and Germany, two of the most efficient industrial economies in the world. If American companies are further hobbled by a new, stringent tax code that penalizes debt, we are likely to see foreign companies making leveraged acquisitions in the U.S. and buying up large equity stakes in U.S. industry.

A firm's most expensive capital is equity. An underleveraged capital structure with higher capital costs makes it more difficult to compete, especially, as in recent years, when the principal competitors are West German and Japanese concerns. Rigid adherence to traditional debt-equity norms impose hardships that are difficult to overcome considering that capital costs for U.S. industrial companies run more than 80 percent in excess of those of foreign corporations (an average of 16.6 percent versus 9 percent abroad).

In both West Germany and Japan, corporate debt-to-capital ratios are twice that of U.S. companies; adjusted for market-related equity values, the gap could be even wider. Although institutional lenders and corporate borrowers in countries like West Germany and Japan are very different from those in the U.S., the result is that our foreign competitors are able to fund R&D and invest in new plants and programs much more aggressively than their American counterparts.

Clearly, the relationships between financial institutions and corporations are very different in Japan and Germany than they are in the United States. However, even after adjusting for these differences, American companies are underleveraged relative to their international competitors.

LEVERAGE AS A TOOL FOR GROWTH

By definition, leveraged buyouts involve high levels of debt. However, the common perception that American corporations are over-leveraged is inaccurate. Current debt ratios are not outside of historical experience, according to statistics prepared for the Joint Committee on Taxation for the Federal Reserve Board. Debt ratios, with equity measured at book value, were, in 1986, at roughly the same level as they were in 1970. When equity is measured at market value, which better reflects growth in asset values, debt ratios have actually fallen from the levels of a decade ago and now stand at about the same level they were in 1975. In fact, the market value of equities has risen by approximately $2 trillion over the past two decades.

Much of the debt taken on in recent years by corporate America has been used to finance growth. Debt capital has been used to build new plants and equipment, to further R&D, to boost working capital reserves, and to finance mostly friendly acquisitions. While a substantial portion of corporate debt is in the form of commercial bank loans, an increasingly larger share is raised in the capital markets.

CHANGING CAPITAL MARKETS

The amount of corporate debt issued as securities has risen from about 26 percent in the late 1970s to some 44 percent today. Within the corporate bond market, high-yield securities represent a larger portion than ever before, today close to 25 percent.

The tremendous growth of the high-yield bond market has given companies large and small, new and old, the option of increasing the amount of leverage in their capital structures. This increase has given them important advantages and has helped to make American industry more competitive, particularly against foreign companies with higher debt levels in their capital structures—which usually result in lower capital costs.

In that context, opening the public debt markets to less-than-investment grade companies—which represent roughly 95 percent of U.S. companies with sales in excess of $35 million—is helping to change established norms in capital structure. Along the way the high-yield market itself has grown, matured, and evolved into a far more sophisticated entity which now accommodates a wide range of investor needs, facilitating transactions that might have been impossible 15 years ago.

Innovation has been one of the main characteristics of the high-yield market, and investment banks have created a whole menu of securities to fill the needs of both issuers and investors. These include such instruments as:

• **Collateralized bond obligations (CBOs)** which bring securitization of high-yield corporate bond portfolios to a new level of sophistication. Drexel Burnham pioneered two types of CBOs through which high-yield portfolios can be overcollateralized and their credit rating enhanced. In one, the market value of the underlying securities is the source of overcollateralization; in the other, the source is based on cash flow, the future stream of principal and interest payments on the pool of high-yield securities. Both types allow investors to meet diversification requirements.

- **Split coupon securities** accrete interest, like a zero coupon bond, during the first three to five years, after which cash interest accrues at a higher rate. The bonds are issued at a discounted price calculated by using the stated coupon rate in effect on the date from which cash interest begins to accrue. Issuers are attracted to this structure because cash interest requirements are reduced or eliminated during the initial period. Investors enjoy a locked-in rate of return during the deferred interest period and generally higher yields than cash-pay securities.
- **Pay-in-kind (PIK) bonds** pay interest in either cash or additional securities, at the issuer's option, for a specified period, usually one to six years (average maturity is 11 years). Like split and zero coupon bonds, PIKs give issuers flexibility in managing cash flow during the early years. Investors are attracted to PIKs because, unlike cash-paying securities, interest payments are automatically compounded at a stated coupon rate and because interest payments in securities are more tangible than accretion of a discount.
- **Increasing rate notes (IRNs)** are securities with coupons that increase at a pre-determined rate, usually 50 basis points a quarter during the first year and 25 basis points a quarter thereafter. Approximately 40 percent of all IRNs float at an increasing spread over LIBOR. Typically intended to act as bridge financing, IRNs are usually callable at par within six months. Since speedy issuance is important, some 85 percent of IRNs are issued privately. Issuers finance with IRNs because they offer rapid access to capital; investors are drawn by the 300 to 600 basis points IRNs offer over high-yield commercial paper and, in some cases, a 1/4 to 1/2 point commitment fee. Drexel Burnham's recent role in financing the RJR Nabisco transaction involved a $5 billion private placement of increasing rate notes. Within a few months of issuance, the firm refinanced the debt with a public offering.

THE BEATRICE LBO

Until the RJR transaction, the largest leveraged buyout ever was Kohlberg Kravis Roberts & Co.'s (KKR) purchase of Beatrice for $6.2 billion, for which we raised $2.5 billion in subordinated debt. Before the buyout, Beatrice was a $12 billion consumer products company formed via acquisitions; its stock was selling at around $31 a share. The group which eventually successfully bid for Beatrice paid $50 a share in cash and securities, a total of $5.7 billion.

To finance the transaction, the buyers contributed $407 million in equity and borrowed $3.3 billion in bank debt. They also raised $2.5 billion of funded debt in the high-yield market, a record which was only recently eclipsed by the RJR transaction.

The offering included 11 percent senior notes, designed to appeal to banks and insurance companies looking for safety and yield; 12-1/2 percent senior subordinated debentures, sold primarily to pension and bond funds; 12-3/4 percent senior subordinated debentures, sold to yield-oriented investors; and floating-rate junior subordinated debentures for more risk-tolerant investors. There also was an exchangeable preferred, part of the proceeds paid to stockholders in the old Beatrice. The preferred was later exchanged into a debenture, having the same 15-1/4 percent coupon.

As BCI sold off assets, it was able to reduce debt significantly. At last report, BCI had about $1.5 billion in debt, down from almost $6.7 billion at its peak (including around $900 million of assumed borrowings), plus a business with considerable assets—Hunt Foods, Wesson Oil, among others—having annual sales of approximately $4 billion. The value of those assets are estimated at two times its current debt. Operating earnings, before goodwill amortization, exceed $325 million. No less important, BCI bondholders earned more than $250 million in excess of what they would have received if they had purchased Treasury securities with comparable maturities instead of BCI high-yield issues.

If such leveraged transactions as the Beatrice LBO and this year's $25 billion RJR LBO seem excessive, it is only a small part of the landscape. The latter, especially, is something we are not likely to see often, due to limits on the availability of debt, high-yield and otherwise. Although large transactions have produced huge gains for investors, they have also caused serious political repercussions, which may affect banks' ability to provide financing in the future. The RJR Nabisco transaction itself required $11.9 billion in bank financing, and a recent study by Moody's Investors Service noted that 11 of America's largest banks have a total of $21 billion in leveraged buyout loans. Federal Reserve Chairman Alan Greenspan has gone on record saying that he doesn't view LBO financing as a constructive use of capital, and this may put a damper on $20 billion leveraged transactions in the future.

HIGH GRADE LEVERAGED BUYOUTS

Limits on high-yield debt will not put an end to large acquisitions. Philip Morris' $13.1 billion acquisition of Kraft, the largest non-oil merger in history, was completed without resorting to the high-yield bond market and without tapping any equity but its own. Although the transaction raised Philip Morris' outstanding debt to $17 billion, the company is expected to be able to pay down that debt within five years, using more than $2 billion a year in free cash flow from its tobacco sales. The merger allows the two companies to combine their strengths—Kraft's widely recognized brand names and powerful food distribution system with Philip Morris' marketing clout and deep pockets. Together, they are far more competitive with such European giants as Nestle, for example.

While massive transactions are timely and interesting, the majority of leveraged buyouts, management buyouts, and employee buyouts are considerably smaller—some 54.5 percent are under $200 million. For the most part, these transactions are producing positive results. Their value is often misunderstood by the public and the press.

MANAGEMENT INCENTIVES

Attitudes about corporate leverage are slowly changing. Ten years ago, I would have been reluctant to finance a deal with the high debt-to-equity ratios which are typical of LBOs. Today, Drexel Burnham alone has done hundreds of LBOs. Nearly all have shown outstanding performance, and many have provided spectacular returns. Likewise, a recent study by Dr. Glenn Yago at the Harriman School for Management and Policy at SUNY-Stony Brook found that LBOs generally reversed patterns of sales declines or increased low rates of growth, increased rates of growth in sales per employee and capital spending, and reversed patterns of job loss prior to ownership change.

Increased debt has important consequences for management. It reduces discretion in spending free cash flow. Instead of pouring free cash flow into perks or unproductive investments, management is forced to direct cash flow to debt service, effectively returning it to the investing public. "Debt creation, without retention of the proceeds of the issue, enables managers to effectively bond their promise to pay our future cash flows," notes Harvard economist Michael C. Jensen, "Thus, debt can be an effective substitute for dividends...."

Substituting debt for equity actually raises the value of a company. In 1985 and again in 1986, Dr. Jensen and Clifford Smith summarized more than a dozen studies of stock price changes at announcements of transactions which change capital structure. They found that over the two-day period following the announcement, leverage-increasing transactions resulted in common stock price gains ranging from 21.9 percent (where debt replaced common stock) to 2.2 percent (where debt or income bonds replaced preferred stock.) By contrast, in leverage-reducing transactions, he found two-day losses ranging from −9.9 percent (where common stock replaced debt) to −.4 percent (where a call of convertible preferred stock forced conversion to common stock).

As leverage increases, discretionary spending is continually reduced, and management is forced to increase efficiency and profitability to meet debt service. The willingness of managers to take on additional debt burdens is a measure of their confidence in their ability to maintain high levels of productivity. In short, debt binds managers to their promises to produce profitable results. If they fail to make good, control of the corporation will pass to the debt holders.

In leveraged buyouts, where managers hold a substantial equity stake in the company, the incentive to prevent that from happening is particularly strong. For instance, in 1986, the leveraged buyout firm KKR took Safeway Stores private in a $5.7 billion LBO. Safeway sold stores using the approximately $2.4 billion in proceeds to reduce debt. But although this period was painful, the company emerged stronger. By 1987, it had improved the retail divisions' operating profit by 40 percent over 1985 levels, and in 1988 by another 15 percent. Safeway also added service, increasing manhours in its stores by 12 percent in the years after the buyout and creating approximately 3,300 new full-time jobs in its continuing operations.

In a recent speech, Peter Magowan, chairman and chief executive of Safeway, stated, "I believe the LBO process itself caused us to transform the company into a truly excellent one.... The transformation of our operators from being managers to being co-owners of the business may have been the most powerful stimulus of all."

EMPLOYEE OWNERSHIP

The same incentives that motivate managers can also work for employees. Drexel Burnham is among the largest employee-owned companies in the country. In 1988, the firm had close to $4 billion in revenues, over $2 billion in capital, and was 75 percent owned by officer-employees. Despite the pressures the firm has faced over the last couple of years, we've done better than many firms in terms of our ability to generate revenues and profits and keep our clients. Our employees' personal fortunes are tied to the firm's performance. And our people have a vested interest in the firm's continued growth.

Similar ownership incentives are at work in companies that have gone private with employee stock ownership plans, or ESOPs. When every employee has an equity stake in the company, everyone has the same motivation to increase efficiency and profitability. That can work wonders for service businesses like Avis, HealthTrust, or Charter Medical.

WEATHERING RECESSION

In the face of these arguments, critics often contend that leveraged companies have not yet been tested by a general economic downturn. Obviously, increased leverage increases economic risk. And the world markets will face an eventual economic downturn, perhaps even a recession. The important question is: what can leveraged companies do to avoid defaults and bankruptcies?

It's important to consider four key elements: First, the high debt levels incurred in leveraged buyouts are not intended to be permanent. In most cases, the companies plan to return to "normal" capitalization ratios in five to seven years. A recent study by Kohlberg Kravis Roberts & Co. of 17 companies which had undergone LBOs proved this true. KKR found that of $33.6 billion in debt assumed after LBOs, some $20.9 billion had already been retired; the rest had not yet become due. Those that have already paid down substantial portions of their debt may not suffer at all.

Second, no company enters into a leveraged buyout without realistic contingency planning, including a list of assets that can be sold to raise cash and reduce debt service in the event of a cash flow crunch. Divesting non-essential businesses is a natural part of the leveraged buyout process and a sound practice for any company. During an economic downturn, leveraged buyouts may speed up their program of planned divestitures to reduce debt service and concentrate on their core businesses.

Many people mistakenly assume that when assets are sold they disappear into a black hole and can no longer generate profits, create jobs, or contribute to the economy. Nothing could be further from the truth. Divested businesses are generally purchased by companies that feel they can put them to more productive use. Often, the buyers provide business synergies or economies of scale that the original owner could not. As a result, divested units are usually purchased at full market value, and many continue to prosper and grow under the direction of new management.

Tropicana, a former subsidiary of Beatrice Foods, is an example. Since 1986, Tropicana, which is now owned by the Canadian conglomerate Seagram Co. Ltd., has increased capital spending six-fold to cut costs, improve packaging technology, and introduce a new brand called Pure Premium Homestyle.

Tropicana had always been a dominant brand in New York City and other Eastern Seaboard markets because it specialized in nonfrozen juice, which until recently could not be distributed nationally because it was too perishable. A combination of improved packaging technology and Seagram's increased marketing clout has boosted its popularity nationwide. As of December 1989, Tropicana led the industry with a 27.5 percent market share in fresh-pressed or not-from-concentrate orange juice, a product which it introduced. The company has successfully defended against attempted incursions from marketing powerhouses Coca-Cola (Minute Maid) and Proctor and Gamble (Citrus Hill).

In February 1989, the *Financial Times* noted that "Almost singlehandedly, Tropicana has changed a commodity industry into a market where it can establish and defend a price premium.... Tropicana's success has had a lot to do with luck and technology, an experienced workforce and oodles of capital. More than that, it shows what a small and tightly knit management group can do if it really understands its product and loves to fight." Clearly, Tropicana is still a viable, successful company despite the fact that it is no longer part of Beatrice.

EXCHANGE OFFERS TO AVOID DEFAULTS

The third point to consider regarding an economic downturn is that in many cases companies can avoid defaults or bankruptcies through restructuring techniques such as exchange offers. An exchange offer is a refinancing mechanism in which a new security or securities are offered to the holders of an existing security. Exchange offers can provide financially distressed companies with breathing room by reducing cash obligations. Companies can conserve cash by issuing 1) new debt with a longer maturity, 2) new debt that allows interest to be paid in either cash or shares of common stock or 3) new convertible or secured debt which bears a lower coupon than the existing debt. In addition, bonds tendered in an exchange offer can be used to satisfy sinking fund obligations on any bonds which remain outstanding.

High-yield debt investors have enhanced their portfolio returns by understanding and accepting exchange offers. In general, the package of new securities offered in an exchange is designed to create a premium sufficient to convince existing holders to accept the exchange offer. In troubled situations, holders must measure the value of the package of new securities offered in an exchange against the potential values available in bankruptcy, after giving consideration to the delays, costs, and complications of bankruptcy proceedings.

Since 1981, Drexel Burnham has played a leading role in the growth and increasing sophistication of exchange offers. DBL has served as financial advisor or dealer manager for more than 275 exchange offers and recapitalizations seeking over $17 billion principal amount and liquidation value of securities. Although the firm's initial focus for exchange offers was assisting financially distressed companies, the techniques have been successfully modified to assist investment grade and healthy high-yield companies.

THE EXPERIENCE OF THE 1980s

The fourth point about economic downturns is that the high-yield market has been through them before. In the early 1980s, the U.S. experienced its worst recession since the 1930s. The oil service industry was particularly hard-hit. Drexel Burnham worked out exchange offers for a number of oil service clients. Only one of those clients actually went bankrupt. The others shifted ownership or deferred their interest payments. All of them made it through the economic slump.

In answer to fears about recession, yes, leverage increases financial risk. Yes, when there's a recession, defaults will be higher than they have been in the past. But there's no reason to assume that the economic horizon will be littered with bankruptcies. Adversity in one industry generally means opportunity in others. Companies that face difficulties can sell off assets, restructure their balance sheets, or take other steps to stay ahead of their debt service obligations. If necessary, they can seek merger partners to supply what they lack. The result may be substantial reorganization and restructuring. But we're not likely to see problems on the scale people have anticipated, because we have the financial tools and the management incentives to avoid them.

RAISING CAPITAL, BUILDING BUSINESSES

In a period of intense global competition, American companies can't afford to let productivity slide or be overrun by waste and inefficiency. By combining ownership incentives and the motivating power of debt, leveraged transactions provide a natural answer to these economic challenges. They demand efficiency, productivity, and profitable results. And the evidence clearly shows that managers and employees are willing to shoulder these responsibilities, as long as they have an opportunity to share in the rewards.

References and Related Reading

Altman, E. I., and Nammacher, S. A. (1987). *Investing in junk bonds: Inside the high yield debt market.* New York: John Wiley & Sons.

Anders, G. (November 15, 1988). Shades of U.S. Steel: J. P. Morgan paved the way for LBOs. *The Wall Street Journal.*

Auerbach, A. J. (January 25, 1989). Leveraged buyouts, corporate debt, and the role of tax policy. Testimony before the Senate Committee on Finance.

Auerbach, A. J., and Andow, A. (June 1977). *The cost of capital in the U.S. and Japan: A comparison.* Cambridge, MA: National Bureau of Economic Research working paper 2286.

Blume, M., and Keim, D. (December 1984). Risk and return characteristics of lower-grade bonds. University of Pennsylvania, The Wharton School, Rodney White Center for Financial Research.

Blume, M., and Keim, D. (July/August 1987). Lower-grade bonds: Their risks and returns. *Financial Analysts Journal.*

Buchan, J. (February 23, 1989). Marketing and advertising: Putting the squeeze on the juice sector. *Financial Times.*

Ellsworth R. R. (April 1987). U.S. business should take on more debt. Graduate Management Center, The Claremont Graduate School.

Ellsworth, R. R. (September/October 1985). Capital markets and competitive decline. Harvard Business *Review.*

Forde, J. P. (March 15, 1989). Moody's issues warning on leveraged buyouts. *American Banker.*

Hof, R. D. (April, 24, 1989). How two big grocers are bringing home the bacon. *Business Week.*

Jensen, M. C. (1986). Agency costs of free cash flow, corporate finance, and takeovers. *American Economics Association Papers and Proceedings, 76.*

Jensen, M. C., and Warner, J. B. (August 1988). The distribution of power among corporate managers, shareholders, and directors. *Journal of Financial Economics.* Amsterdam: North-Holland/Elsevier Science Publishers.

Joint Committee on Taxation. (January 18, 1989). *Federal income tax aspects of corporate financial structures.* Schedule for hearings before the Senate Committee on Finance (January 24–26, 1989) and the House Committee on Way and Means (January 31 and February 1–2, 1989).

Kaplan, S. (July 1989). Management buyouts: Evidence on taxes as a source of value. *Journal of Finance,* pp. 611–632.

Kaplan, S. (1989). The effects of management buyouts on operations and value. *Journal of Financial Economics* (forthcoming).

Kohlberg Kravis Roberts & Co. (January 1989). Presentation on leveraged buyouts.

Magowan, P. A. (October 11, 1988). Address to the Stanford Business School Alumni Association. (Concerning Safeway Stores, Inc.'s leveraged buyout.)

Pound, J. (April 1988). Debt and corporate performance: New theories and evidence on capital structure. Drexel Burnham Lambert, 1988 Institutional Research Conference.

Pound, J., and Gordon, L. A. (April 6, 1988). High-yield placements and corporate performance: A summary of research in progress. Drexel Burnham Lambert, 1988 Institutional Research Conference.

U.S. General Accounting Office. (March 1989). *High-yield bonds: Issues concerning thrift investments in high-yield bonds.* GAO/GGD-89-48.

Yago, G. (April 1989). Leveraged buyouts in focus: The effects of debt on corporate performance. Economic Research Bureau, W. Averell Harriman School for Management and Policy, State University of New York at Stony Brook.

Yago, G. (November 1988). *The uses and effects of high-yield securities in U.S. industry, 1980–1986.* Economic Research Bureau, W. Averell Harriman School for Management and Policy, State University of New York at Stony Brook.

CHAPTER 9

A VIEW FROM WASHINGTON ON THE HIGH-YIELD DEBT MARKET

Hon. Edward J. Markey *

It is indeed a pleasure to discuss some of the issues that undoubtedly will cause government and private enterprise to intersect during the coming year.

As you know, I am Chairman of the House Telecommunications and Finance Subcommittee. During the past session, we have had more than a few small items on our plate—items such as tender offer reform, the stock market crash, Glass-Steagall reform, insider trading, the role of institutions in the marketplace and in corporate governance, securities industry arbitration, and the list goes on

ACCOMPLISHED LEGISLATION

On some of these issues we passed legislation—such as the Insider Trading and Securities Fraud Enforcement Act of 1988. We worked closely with the securities industry and other groups in preparing this legislation and, as a

---

*Congressman Edward J. Markey is Chairman of the Subcomittee on Telecommunications and Finance, House Committee on Energy and Commerce.

result of the close and open negotiating process, passed the bill by a vote of 410-0 in the House and without opposition in the Senate.

This is the toughest and most comprehensive insider trading legislation ever to emerge from the Congress. It (1) substantially increases the penalties for insider trading, (2) provides for private rights of action for contemporaneous traders who are injured by insider trading, (3) enhances the SEC's authority to cooperate with foreign governments to investigate international securities law violations, (4) authorizes what will be a major study of the adequacy of our nation's securities laws, and (5) authorizes the SEC to award bounties of up to 10% of the amount recovered for information leading to the settlement or fine.

Finally, the centerpiece of the law is that for the first time, broker-dealers and investment advisers may be held derivatively liable if they fail to establish and enforce an internal system designed to prevent and detect the misuse of material, non-public information by the firm or its employees. This is not a strict liability standard. It is not expected that firms can or will prevent and detect all instances of insider trading. The law does provide, however, that firms will be liable if they "knowingly or recklessly" fail to take reasonable steps to prevent these abuses.

DEFERRED LEGISLATION

There are other areas of the Subcommittee's jurisdiction where we determined that the timing or circumstances, or both, made legislation inappropriate. Included here was tender offer reform.

John Dingell, Chairman of the Energy and Commerce Committee, and I introduced the Tender Offer Reform Act in April 1987, and my Subcommittee then held six comprehensive hearings on that bill. Indeed, on Monday morning, October 19, 1987, we were in a conference determining how best to revise portions of that bill in light of those hearings. Well, the events of October 19 caused us to defer further legislative action on tender offers.

I am convinced now more than ever that was the right decision. First, the markets were in too delicate a condition to experience the effect that tender offer legislation at that time might have caused. Second, the Supreme Court had decided the CTS case, which gave the states enhanced rights in the tender offer area. The states were taking advantage of that decision by passing their own tender offer-related laws. Some of these laws were being litigated and the whole issue of federal versus states' rights in this area had not percolated sufficiently to make Congressional action appropriate. Third, our bill did not deal directly with matters relating to corporate debt and LBOs. Some of us have believed for well over a year now that these are issues that should be addressed by Congress and we will be doing so in the coming session.

Issues Related to Junk Bonds

Now, you might note that our Subcommittee did not deal directly last Congress with issues relating to junk bonds. That too was a careful and deliberate decision. In part, that decision may change in the coming Congress. What may cause it to change is the RJR transaction and the use of what some people view as excessive leverage in the takeover or going private of some of our major American corporations.

Sometimes all of us are given to oversimplification. For years, Congress was bogged down on the question of whether corporate takeovers are "good" or "bad." Congress even produced a 300-page report on the issue. Predictably, the report was inconclusive, but it determined that the issue needed further study!

Well, since becoming Chairman, the "good or bad, up or down," approach is one that I have rejected. Some takeovers have yielded excellent results—for both the companies involved and for our nation—while others have been failures.

Another oversimplification is that corporate managers would be more productive if they could concentrate on running their businesses rather than having to look over their shoulders for someone who wants to take over the business. Well, if the latest wave of management buyouts does not put that argument to rest, nothing will. Pogo's apothegm was never more true, "We have met the enemy, and it is us."

Also, I've gotten a little religion when it comes to corporate management needing additional discipline. Tim Metz of *The Wall Street Journal* has just written a book entitled *Black Monday*. In it, he has compiled some telling statistics. In the ten-year span ending in 1987, the salary and bonuses of American CEO's rose an average of 12.2% per year, as compared to:

- average inflation rate of 6.5%,
- average increase in the wages of hourly workers of 6.1%, and this is the fascinating figure,
- *average increase in firm's earnings of 0.75%.*

So the need to discipline management in one form or another exists, but this discipline should not come at the expense of America's competitive posture or the stability of our corporate economy.

Congressional Involvement

So, to what degree will Congress become involved in this issue? Well, certainly the House Ways and Means Committee will examine the MBO/LBO phenomenon from the standpoint of the tax laws, especially as they relate to the deductibility of interest on MBO-related debt.

Congress should not become involved in the morass of selecting "good" debt, whatever that may prove to be, from "bad" debt. Debt, in and of itself, is neutral. There is, nevertheless, a perception within Congress and within the population at large that some types of debt are *more obviously* productive that others.

In an era where "competition" or "international competitiveness" is the bottom line of every economic argument, people can understand American companies going into debt to fund new plants and equipment, to develop new product lines, to enter new markets, and the like. People have a harder time relating, however, to a management that undertakes a $3 billion restructuring in the face of an attempted takeover, so it can distribute the proceeds of the bribe to its shareholders as "increased value" for their shares. Sure the present-day shareholders of the company get an economic boon. And, for its part, management remains independent and often gets a chunk of the company. And the bankers and the lawyers do just fine. But is the company really any stronger—in the parlance of the day, is it any more competitive—because it is now an additional $3 billion in debt?

A few years ago, Harcourt Brace Jovanovitch undertook just such a restructuring to escape a takeover by Robert Maxwell. First Boston handled the transaction for them. When the representative from First Boston who handled that transaction testified on takeovers before our Subcommittee, I asked him whether taking on such a debt load was good for the company. He said that it was wonderful for Harcourt Brace and that it would make it a much stronger, more competitive company.

Well, to be kind, I will say that the jury is still out on this optimism. In the second quarter of 1986, before the restructuring, Harcourt Brace had revenues of $312 million and net income of $11 million. Lackluster, but still on the plus side of the ledger.

In the second quarter of 1987, after the restructuring, Harcourt Brace's revenues increased to $409 million, but it had a net *loss* of $71 million. So while revenues increased nearly $100 million, the company turned an $11 million gain into a $71 million loss. Why? Interest payments on its debt.

And this trend is continuing. For the second quarter of 1988, Harcourt Brace had revenues of $446 million, and a net loss of $40 million. This does not strike me as the picture of a revitalized company. It doesn't strike the market as one either—its stock is languishing between $8-9 a share.

So although I am loathe to make judgments about the value of this debt versus that debt, the fact is some uses of debt financing will move you toward a given goal—say competitiveness within a given sector—than will other uses. Building a new plant with innovative technology to make widgets is more likely to result in a better widget more efficiently produced than is using that same money to throw a party for your shareholders.

FUTURE CONGRESSIONAL ISSUES

In the next session, our Subcommittee will deal with some of these admittedly complex issues from the viewpoint of the securities laws. Some of the issues we will deal with include:

• How fair are fairness letters? These letters are prepared by investment banks attesting that the price offered by management for the shares is a fair one. The investment bank, however, relies almost exclusively on the limited information supplied by management, and typically states in the letter that the firm has made no independent verification of the information. Moreover, two-tiered pricing still exists with regard to some fairness letters. For example, the investment bank receives $1 million to prepare the letter, but $1.5 million if the deal goes through.

If management is truly undertaking these transactions to maximize value for shareholders, it would be beneficial for all buy-out proposals to be accompanied by at least one fairness opinion, prepared by reputable independent financial advisers, who are paid without regard to the success of the buy-out and who have no financial stake in the buy-out itself. For example, the adviser should not also be a source of bridge financing or an underwriter of the junk bonds used to finance the deal.

Let's be direct about this. What we are really trying to get at is the problem of Ross Johnson, a fiduciary for his shareholders, low-balling the company at $75 a share to get a better deal for himself and his six management buddies, and then see him raise his offer by nearly 50% in the next few weeks.

• Also with regard to fairness letters, the principle of full disclosure would be served by providing that the investment bank that prepares the letter has appropriate access to the books, records, premises and so forth, of the company so that it can provide a realistic appraisal of all of the company's holdings, including real estate which may be carried on the books at below current market value. Sometimes these letters are nothing more than five paragraphs of caveats and two paragraphs of valuation.

• We should require that all studies, analyses and projections prepared by management, or by anyone else on behalf of managment, at least be disclosed to the Board of Directors and the Special Committee.

• Some commentators have also suggested that when management makes a bid for a company, it should be required to explain in writing to the Board and/or the Special Committee why the business plan that it intends to adopt after the MBO cannot be pursued while the company is publicly held.

• Some commentators have proposed that there be a time period of somewhere between 45-90 days between announcement of the MBO/LBO and its consummation to give other parties an opportunity to bid on the company.

• Consider possible civil penalties for failure to file under Rule 13e-3 or for making a material misstatement in a 13e-3 filing.

• Require all parties trying to do an LBO — not just the issuer and its affiliates — to make Rule 13e-3 filings.

• Consider the advisability of requiring that firm financing be in place prior to announcement of an LBO or MBO.

• We need to determine whether there are adequate protections afforded bondholders in these transactions. This will include disclosure vis-a-vis bondholders. Are bonds sometimes issued so close to the date of a subsequent MBO that management had to have been considering the buyout, but failed to disclose it to the bond purchasers?

All of these issues fall squarely within our Committee's jurisdiction and we will pursue them vigorously during the 101st Congress. In addition, there are other issues that will be examined within Congress. These include:

• Should we restrict or prohibit federally insured institutions—and possibly other publicly backed institutions such as pension funds—from investing in highly leveraged transactions? Where the taxpayer can be looked to as the ultimate guarantor, the government must undertake its own risk analysis and limit its own financial exposure. We should be very careful not to put the full faith and credit of the United States behind these investments.

• Should the tax law be amended to provide progressively lower rates the longer an investment is held, with a relatively minimal tax payable on securities and other assets held more than 5 years? Thus, the tax on investments held for less than a year might be substantial, e.g., 50 percent.

• Should Congress consider changing the tax treatment of institutions, e.g., pension funds, charitable trusts, investment companies that participate in highly leveraged transactions? Possibly they could be taxed like any corporation with respect to capital gains resulting from their participation in these transactions, or be taxed at a rate based on the length of time they hold the investment. The purpose of such a provision should be to encourage pension funds to invest in secure, long-term investments. Any change in the tax law must be carefully written to avoid double taxation. If pension funds are taxed now on the returns from these transactions, we should avoid taxing this money again once the pension funds are distributed to the pensioners. This would be analogous to the double taxation of dividends.

• Congress should look closely at eliminating the double taxation of dividends. This is one of the principal reasons why debt is preferred to equity by many companies. We should look toward putting debt and equity at least on parity.

• Congress should consider limiting the percentage of outstanding securities that can be purchased with debt financing in an MBO, LBO, or related restructuring. This would be similar to the fed's margin requirements. The average American has a hard time understanding why he has to put down 50 percent when he buys 100 shares of RJR/Nabisco, but when an LBO firm buys 100 percent of the entire company it need put down only one-sixth of one percent. Congress should not be against corporate takeovers, rather it should be for pay-as-you-go takeovers.

• Should we consider limiting the deductibility of corporate debt, possibly after the debt reaches a certain percentage of equity. I understand this is an option currently under consideration within the Treasury Department.

• Finally, there is a school of thought that concludes with regard to MBOs that the conflict of interest for management is intolerable. Management has access to more information concerning the company, the markets for its products, future plans and expectations, etc., than anyone outside the company. Management is given access to this information on the assumption that it will be used to benefit shareholders. If management determines on the basis of this proprietary information, that the long-term value of the company is significantly greater than the market price of the stock indicates, and if it acts to appropriate any part of that value to itself, it breaches its duty to shareholders. The bottom line is that there may be an intolerable conflict between management's fiduciary duty to maximize value for shareholders while it tries to minimize the amount it pays for their shares.

These are some of the issues that Congress will be considering in the coming session. We welcome your comments concerning them.

CHAPTER 10

A VIEW FROM WASHINGTON
ON THE HIGH-YIELD DEBT
MARKET

U.S. Rep. Carroll Hubbard *

I want to extend my thanks and appreciation to Dr. Edward I. Altman, Max L. Heine Professor of Finance, Graduate School of Business Administration at New York University, for his very kind invitation for me to participate in the Conference on Financial-Economic Perspectives on the High-Yield Debt Market. Indeed, I am grateful to be here with you this afternoon and am pleased to have the opportunity to participate on the panel entitled "View from Washington" with such a distinguished group of panelists.

I have been a member of the House Committee on Banking, Finance and Urban Affairs for fourteen years and have the privilege of serving as chairman of its Subcommittee on General Oversight and Investigations.

Our General Oversight and Investigations Subcommittee is charged with assisting the Banking Committee in appraising the administration of the laws and regulations under the jurisdiction of the committee and presenting such recommendations as deemed necessary. By way of background, during the 99th Congress on September 19, 1985, our subcommittee held a hearing entitled "Issues Relating to High-Yield Securities

*Congressman Carroll Hubbard, Jr., is Chairman of the Subcommittee on General Oversight and Investigations, House Committee on Banking and Urban Affairs.

(Junk Bonds)." We were honored that day to have Dr. Edward I. Altman as one of our witnesses. We also heard the views of then-Chairman of the Federal Reserve Board Paul A. Volcker, the views of Federal Home Loan Bank Board Associate General Counsel Julie Williams, the views of G. Chris Anderson in behalf of Drexel Burnham Lambert, and the views of Richard T. Pratt in behalf of Merrill Lynch Mortgage Capital, Inc., of New York.

Allow me to briefly share with you several statements that I made during my opening remarks at the beginning of the September 19 hearing:

> The junk bond market is rapidly changing from the 'fallen angels' of yesteryear.

> But the dramatic growth in the junk bond market recently has come from bonds issued by young emerging companies—successful companies, I might add—which include Humana, Inc., of Louisville, Kentucky, the noted heart transplant hospital, and MCI Communications.

> The growth of the high-yield bonds market has given rise to enormous controversy. One primary area being increasingly scrutinized involves the role of high-yield financing as a tool to aid corporate raiders in hostile company takeover attempts.

> Through deregulation (the passage of the Depository Institutions Deregulation and Monetary Act of 1980 and the Garn-St Germain Act of 1982), many financial institutions have seen fit to invest in high-yield bonds in an effort to diversify their portfolios and maximize their profits.

> However, the very nature of these bonds coupled with the uncertainty of how issues may fare in a time of economic downturn are sources of legitimate concern, inasmuch as these bonds may possess a foreseeable likelihood of default, and thus could possibly contribute to the failure of those financial institutions which have invested in them.

> In this time of increasing failures of our financial institutions and because of the strain on our federal deposit insurance systems which result from these failures, our subcommittee is vitally interested in knowing precisely what dangers, if any, exist for financial institutions which choose to invest in these securities.

Over two years have passed since these remarks were made at our hearing, but they are indeed still timely today. The topics of whether these high-yield bonds have a favorable or unfavorable impact upon our federally insured financial institutions and their overall impact upon our economy are certainly of great interest.

What you call these debt securities depends upon who is doing the talking and depends entirely upon how the speakers feel about them. Investment bankers, investment managers, and academicians are among those who favor the "high-yield bonds" label, but many financial market participants and others use the more colorful "junk bond" designation.

As we know, a junk bond is a debt security which has not been rated as "investment quality." Because high risk and low quality are often thought to be the same, and because high risk usually calls for a high return as an offset, these bonds are also known as "high-yield" debt.

Until recently, junk bonds have been one of many noncontroversial sources of finance for U.S. corporations in the area of U.S. corporate finance. They have been in existence since the early 1900s and have been a significant source of corporate funds since then. Their usage has been drawing increased criticism, though, because of the changes which have occurred in recent years.

Prior to 1977, the high-yield market was relatively small and consisted of "fallen angels," bonds issued by blue-chip companies that fell on difficult financial times and had been downgraded. Beginning in 1977, though, a new type of high-yield bond entered the market. These bonds were rated below investment grade when first issued, and were issued either by relatively new companies for financing leveraged buyouts.

For the nontakeover usage of high-yield bonds, it has been proven that they have been a most important source of raising capital and they have been a major contributor to our economy. Indeed, the use of these bonds is a known fact. Companies in the Northeast and Midwest have used high-yield bonds to retool their factories and diversify the economies of their states. In the South, they have been critical to the textile and energy industries, and in the sun belt, companies from real estate development to movie making to biotechnology to glass manufacturing have used these bonds to finance their growth.

In 1983, though, the use of high-yield debt changed and they were first used at that time in a hostile takeover attempt. Since then, most media and congressional attention has been focused on what in reality is a very small proportion of the high-yield bond market. The change in usage of high-yield bonds to finance takeover defenses, either through a management-led or a recapitalization plan, as well as to finance hostile acquisitions has been the source of growing concern these days.

The high-yield bond phenomenon is relatively recent for federally insured institutions. With the passage of the Garn-St Germain Depository Institutions Act of 1982, Congress for the first time allowed federal thrifts to make commercial loans and expanded the amount of assets a federal thrift could invest in corporate debt securities such as bonds. Although regulations adopted by the Federal Home Loan Bank Board to implement this corporate debt investment authority generally limit corporate bond investments to those in the four highest grades, investment of up to one percent of assets in unrated debt securities is permitted. In addition, the general commercial lending authority granted federal thrifts is broad enough to allow investment of another 10 percent of their assets in corporate debt securities, including high-yield bonds. What this means is that federal thrifts may place up to 11 percent of their assets in such bonds and direct commercial loans.

The law differs for commercial banks. Federally insured commercial banks are discouraged from investing in high-yield bonds because of restrictions imposed by the Comptroller of the Currency, the Federal Reserve Board, and the Federal Deposit Insurance Corporation. The law also prohibits national banks and stated-chartered members of the Federal Reserve System from acquiring below investment-grade securities for their portfolio. State banks which obtain federal deposit insurance but do not become members of the Federal Reserve System, however, are permitted to purchase high-yield bonds.

As I stated earlier, though, questions are raised about whether federally insured institutions should be restricted from using these high-yield securities. The following questions are among those heard most often in this regard. First, how adequate are state laws and regulations governing federally insured institutions, which in some states are granted even greater authority to make commercial loans or invest in corporate securities. Should state-chartered institutions have the same limitation of assets (11 percent) as federal institutions? Second, how can we protect the FSLIC and the FDIC from unreasonable risk as a result of investment in high-yield bonds? Third, should federally insured institutions be prohibited from purchasing high-yield bonds issued in connection with the financing of a hostile takeover or a leveraged buyout? Should these institutions be restricted from these activities? The questions are difficult, and unfortunately the answers are difficult as well.

Federal regulators are increasing their surveillance of bank loans that are used to finance leveraged buyouts (or LBOs) and similar transactions. The Office of the Comptroller of the Currency, which regulates national banks, plans to issue guidelines requiring more scrutiny of bank handling of all loans to finance highly leveraged takeovers, recapitalizations, or management-led LBOs. The purpose of these guidelines is to urge banks to scrutinize such loans and guard against providing too many of them.

To help improve their monitoring of such loans, both the comptroller and the Federal Reserve Bank of New York are working to broaden their definitions of loans derived from highly leveraged transactions. These changes illustrate the growing concern among regulators about the risks to banks of debts created by these highly leveraged transactions. Federal Reserve Board Chairman Alan Greenspan has said that the Federal Reserve has warned banks to look at the prospects for leveraged buyout loans "under a range of economic and financial circumstances."

Tightened scrutiny of these loans may result in banks curbing their participation in LBOs. It is predicted that banks will take a closer look at them if the federal regulators are urging their examiners to watch out for various risks associated with this type of financing.

The comptroller also wants banks to watch their level of loans to highly leveraged companies. Many banks look at their loan portfolios to see whether they are carrying too much exposure to reverses that might happen in a single industry or region. The comptroller is urging banks to monitor whether their entire portfolios of loans to debt-burdened companies are too large. Some believe these changes will ultimately change the participation of banks in this type of lending, and they believe this will be a favorable change in the long run.

Although a supporter of high-yield bonds, the free market place and limited government regulation, naturally I am concerned that the banks, savings and loans, insurance companies, and pension funds are putting too much of their own money into high-yield bonds and highly leveraged loans used to pay for these risky corporate restructurings.

This takeover boom of the 1980s has indeed led businesses to make more and larger acquisitions, paying for these takeovers with almost entirely borrowed money. This has been favorable to lenders, though, who have been willing to finance these corporate buyouts because they can charge higher interest rates, thereby collecting two or three percentage points more on these buyout loans than on other business loans. The fear today, however, is that in time of recession or sudden increases in interest rates, these financial institutions would face heavy losses because the highly leveraged businesses (their loan clients) would have a difficult time in paying their debts, thereby leaving the banks with massive loans that would not be repaid.

On November 28, it was reported in *The Washington Post* that state and federal regulators are "stepping up their scrutiny of the financial institutions providing the financing for today's megadeals." The biggest share of high-yield bonds is held by insurance companies which hold about 30 percent of all junk bonds outstanding. Pension funds have about 15 percent and 7 to 8 percent of these bonds is held by federally insured savings and loans. Banks are increasing their investment in junk bonds, "a disturbing trend," said FDIC Chairman L. William Seidman, who reported that federally insured banks have $150 billion in buyout loans and nearly 10 percent of big banks' new business loans are for buyouts.

The debate continues in Congress, in financial circles, and at the regulatory agencies. It has been reported that various House and Senate committees will be taking a close look at the implications of these corporate megadeals during the 101st Congress. Our General Oversight and Investigations Subcommittee will be holding a follow-up hearing to the one previously held on issues relating to high-yield securities as they apply to federally insured financial institutions. In the meantime, though, I would like to close with several ideas. First, undue risk should not be placed on the deposits of financial institutions that are federally insured. We have a commitment in this regard. However, risks cannot be avoided entirely. I believe the emphasis should be to combine adequate capital reserves and prudent diversified investing as well as the best possible management. A combination of these factors will, indeed, go a long way toward ensuring the health of our federally insured financial institutions.

Thank you for the opportunity to participate in this forum. I appreciate your attention and look forward to working with you during the upcoming months on these matters of concern to all of us.

CHAPTER 11

NEW DEVELOPMENTS IN REGULATION OF THE HIGH-YIELD BOND MARKET AND JUNK BOND INVESTMENTS*

Michael A. Burnett †
Frank Philippi ‡

As some of you know, the General Accounting Office [GAO] has been conducting a review of the high-yield bond market since August of 1987. We have published two documents since that time and are close to issuing a final report on our work. Because our final report is not yet complete and our conclusions and recommendations have not been finalized, we will not talk specifics here today. However, we will talk about some of the work we have done to date and what it has revealed. First, let me tell you briefly about GAO.

*The remarks contained herein are those of the authors and do not necessarily reflect the views of the U.S. General Accounting Office.

†Michael Burnett is Assistant Director, U.S. General Accounting Office, Financial Institutions and Markets Issues Group.

‡Frank Philippi is Evaluator, Information Management and Technologies, General Accounting Office.

A LITTLE ABOUT GAO

The Washington Post likes to describe us as the auditing and investigative arm of Congress, and that's as good a description as any, although we call ourselves evaluators. Supporting the Congress is GAO's fundamental responsibility. We do this by providing a variety of services—the most prominent of which are audits and evaluations of federal programs and activities. Most of our reviews are made in response to specific requests of congressional committees. Sometimes we independently study government programs in accordance with our basic legislative responsibilities. GAO examines virtually every federal program, activity, and function. Our goal in meeting the needs of the Congress is to furnish useful, objective, accurate information.

The types of questions GAO answers are usually the following:

- Are government programs being carried out in compliance with applicable laws and regulations, and are data furnished to the Congress on these programs accurate?
- Do opportunities exist to eliminate waste and inefficient use of public funds?
- Are funds being spent legally and is accounting for them accurate?
- Are programs achieving desired results or are changes needed in government policies or management?
- Are there better ways of accomplishing the programs' objectives at lower costs?
- What emerging or key issues should the Congress consider?

GAO has staff expertise in various disciplines—accounting, law, public and business administration, the social and physical sciences, economics, and others. We are organized so that staff members concentrate on specific subject areas, enabling them to develop a detailed level of knowledge. For example, out of the approximately 4,000 professional staff GAO has to cover all functions of the government, we spent about 100 staff years looking at the financial institutions and market area. On key assignments our staff go wherever necessary, working on-site to gather data, test transactions, and observe first-hand how federal programs and activities are carried out.

CONGRESSIONAL CONCERNS

Congress became interested in junk bonds about four years ago when some of the big hostile takeover deals first came to their attention: the Pantry Pride takeover of Revlon, Carl Icahn and T. Boone Pickens' attempt to take over Phillips Petroleum, and Ted Turner's attempt to take over CBS. Hostile takeover hearings convened by Congressional Committees in 1985 and 1986 indicated considerable concern in Congress about what junk bonds were, how they were being used, and whether they should be regulated in some way. Congressional interest seemed to focus on two main issues: (1) the role of junk bonds in enabling corporate raiders to carry out hostile takeovers, and (2) whether federally insured thrifts, which are permitted to invest in junk bonds under the deregulation provisions of the Garn-St Germain Act, should limit their investments in junk bonds or not invest in them at all. Committee members expressed concern about junk bonds as an appropriate investment for thrifts because of the perceived higher risk as well as their connection to hostile takeovers.

During the legislative give-and-take before the passage of the Competitive Equality Banking Act of 1987 [CEBA], several proposals were introduced which would have restricted thrift investment in junk bonds. However, Congress heard testimony from Dr. Ed Altman of New York University, as well as from Merrill Lynch, Drexel Burnham Lambert, and others that the primary use of high-yield bonds was to finance growing companies—not takeovers—and that these securities provided a good investment for thrifts as long as some precautions were taken.

Faced with this kind of conflicting information and deciding that it needed more information from an independent source, Congress did what it sometimes does in these cases—have the GAO study the issue.

What GAO's Study Covered

Section 1201 of the CEBA required GAO to study the high-yield bond market. The Act called on us to determine several things:

- in general, who issues and who buys high-yield bonds;
- who issues and who buys takeover-related high-yield bonds;
- what percentage of high-yield bonds are issued for takeovers, and for other reasons;

- how do state laws govern high-yield bond investments by state-chartered thrifts (some members of Congress seem to suspect a lack of regulation in certain states), and
- how risky are these bonds, what kinds of returns do they provide, and do they seem to be riskier than other investments that thrifts make.

What We've Done So Far—Our First Report

We reported in February 1988 on the statistical information requested by the Congress. We issued a second document in May which provides a transcript of a public hearing on the high-yield bond market we held on March 1. Soon we will report our analysis of thrift investments in high-yield bonds, and present our final conclusions and recommendations.

In our first report we talked about who issues high-yield bonds, who buys them, and to what extent they have been used to finance hostile takeover deals. The data on issuers should be well known to many of you—we found that over 600 different companies from a wide range of industries issued publicly traded, nonconvertible high-yield bonds between 1982 and 1987. The face value of bonds issued during this time period was over $108 billion. These figures would increase if you included data on privately placed debt which can only be estimated. Some say this market is as large as the public market.

Who *buys* high-yield bonds proved to be harder to determine. The brokers we contacted told us their customer lists were proprietary information which could not be disclosed, but they could tell us, in general, the purchasers of junk bonds. For example, Drexel estimated that 32 percent of high-yield bonds are bought by mutual funds, 30 percent by insurance companies, 10 percent by pension funds, 7 percent by thrifts, with the remaining 21 percent broken down among individuals, corporations, foreign investors, and others. Estimates obtained from other brokers were similar to Drexel's.

We approached the question about the use of high-yield bonds to finance hostile corporate takeovers in two ways. First, we examined 54 takeovers in 1985 and 1986 where the SEC and industry observers identified the initial tender offer as hostile, and the takeover was completed by either the unwelcome bidder, a "white knight," or the target firm's management. After reviewing tender offer filings, bond prospectuses, and annual reports, we determined that high-yield bonds accounted for about 12 percent of the value of the initial financing for these takeovers. The bulk of the financing came from bank loans—an estimated 42 percent—and privately placed debt, as best we could determine, accounted for about 9 percent. We made a distinction between *initial* financing and the final picture because we found that after bank and bridge loans were refinanced and privately placed bonds were registered, high-yield debt accounted for about 22 percent of the financing of the deals we reviewed. The other approach we used was to review the "use of funds" section of a sample of bond prospectuses filed with the SEC. This showed that 13 percent of high-yield bonds were issued for the purpose of carrying out an acquisition, another 15 percent were for future acquisitions, and 23 percent were to retire debt of previous mergers and acquisitions. Whether this level of high-yield bond use in corporate takeover financing indicates high-yield bonds encourage takeovers depends on your point of view.

Current Work

Since February we have concentrated on reviewing thrift investment in high-yield bonds, the risks and returns of these investments relative to other thrift investments, and the extent of oversight of thrift high-yield bond investment by the Federal Home Loan Bank Board [FHLB]. At our public hearing we obtained opinions from interested parties—academics, the rating agencies, investment bankers, and the thrifts themselves—on the subject of thrift investment in high-yield bonds.

RISKS AND RETURNS OF HIGH-YIELD BONDS AND OTHER INVESTMENTS

One of the unfortunate side effects of deregulation of the thrift industry by the 1982 Garn-St Germain Act has been the failure of thrifts due to mismanagement. Some of the notorious cases have involved thrifts entering into investments, such as commercial real estate, windmill farms, racehorses, and other areas, which were risky and about which the thrift management knew little. Because of the stories that were surfacing about thrifts getting into risky areas and because of concerns about junk bonds being not only risky but a primary tool of the corporate raiders, Congress wanted to know the risks and returns of these bonds, and how these risks and returns compare to other thrift investments.

Data available from Dr. Altman, First Boston, and others shows that the yield on junk bonds has been more than enough to compensate for measurable risks (i.e., default risk), between 1977 and 1987. In certain years risk-adjusted returns on high-yield bonds have been exceeded by returns on Treasuries and investment grade bonds because of declining interest rates. However, over the last ten years, yields and total returns of high-yield bonds have exceeded other fixed income investments.

We discovered that it would be difficult to answer the Congress' question, "How do the risks and returns of junk bonds compare to other investments thrifts make?" for a number of reasons. First of all, neither the Bank Board nor the thrifts maintain the type of data we needed to make this comparison. Second, from a safety and soundness perspective it is most useful to view returns on junk bonds in a total portfolio context and not in isolation—a difficult task in view of current data limitations. Third, because the number of thrifts that invest in junk bonds is few, it is very hard to generalize to the entire industry for purposes of regulatory rulemaking.

However, we were able to obtain some data from two sources which compare the risks and returns of various thrift investments. The first source was a study by Wharton Econometric Forecasting Associates. The second was data generated by the Federal Reserve's Functional Cost Analysis program. Both show comparative data on gross and net returns of various types of assets that are held by thrifts and others. Our analysis of the data showed that high-yield bonds have provided thrifts attractive risk-adjusted returns compared to their other activities, such as home mortgage, commercial, or consumer lending. The credit loss on high-yield bonds appears to be about the same as commercial and consumer loans, but the returns have been higher because of lower servicing costs and higher yields.

THRIFT INVESTMENT IN HIGH-YIELDS

Since the end of 1985, thrift investments in high-yields have more than doubled, from less than $6 billion to over $12 billion in March 1988. However, the number of thrifts which invest in high-yields is relatively small—only about 4 percent of the 3,100 thrifts nationwide have any high-yield investments at all.   The number of thrifts which are significant investors is even smaller—in March 1988 only 10 institutions held about 77 percent of the $12 billion invested in high-yields by the thrift industry. The thrifts which have been big players in the market tend to be concentrated in a few states—California, Texas, and Florida—and most are state-chartered rather than federally chartered institutions.

We visited eleven of the largest thrift investors in high-yield bonds to determine what their investment objectives were, what results they have had from their high-yield portfolios, and what investment policies they were following.   The thrift officials told us that their main reason for investing in high-yield bonds was the high risk-adjusted returns these bonds provide compared to other investments. One thrift also told us about capital appreciation—selling bonds at a profit—which helped keep its head above water. Other reasons for investing included (1) high-yield bonds are an easy, inexpensive way to get into commercial lending, and (2) they allow thrifts to geographically diversify their assets. So far, the thrifts we visited have had default experience similar to what Dr. Altman calculates—2 percent of book value defaulted, but recoveries of about 60 percent, reducing the loss rate to less than one percent.

All of them established policies in the areas of loss reserve allowances, diversification, and type and extent of credit analysis, but these policies varied somewhat. Loss reserve allowances, for example, ranged from zero to more than three percent of the portfolio's book value. Most thrifts had diversified portfolios, but in a couple of cases the portfolios did not meet the diversification guidelines Dr. Altman has espoused. Credit analysis at some thrifts was done in-house, while others used outside investment advisors. In a number of cases, the FHLB examiners criticized some aspect of the institution's credit analysis.

REGULATION AND OVERSIGHT

Over the years, a number of regulatory questions have surfaced regarding thrift investment in high-yield bonds. These have included

- whether thrifts should be allowed to invest in high-yield bonds at all (commercial banks generally are not),
- whether state-chartered thrifts should be capped at the federal limit of 11 percent, and

- whether (a) the classification of assets regulation and (b) risk-based capital requirements rules should be extended to high-yield bonds.

Bank Board regulations permit federally chartered thrifts to invest up to 11 percent of their assets in high-yield bonds. State-chartered thrifts may invest either more, the same amount, or none at all, depending on the laws of their individual states. Of the 32 states which allow thrifts to invest in high-yield bonds, 7 allow thrifts to invest more than the 11 percent maximum allowed for federally chartered thrifts.

From time to time the Bank Board has considered further regulating junk bond investments. Each time they have concluded that there is no evidence to support banning junk bond investments or, for that matter, capping state-chartered thrifts at 11 percent of assets. The Board has cited the numerous studies showing returns exceeding risk and the absence of any negative effect from high-yield bond investment as reasons for no further regulation. However, there have been some recent changes. CEBA established rules which enable the Bank Board to classify assets in the same way commercial bank assets are classified: substandard, doubtful, and loss. When its assets are classified by a Bank Board examiner, a thrift has to specifically set aside reserves as an allowance for possible loss. The classification rule applies to high-yield bonds, but high-yield bonds are not automatically classified. The examiner makes this determination based on a number of factors, such as rating of the bond, financial health of the issuer, and future income potential.

Currently, the Bank Board is developing a system for uniformly classifying high-yield bonds. One reason the Board wants a uniform classification system is to prevent a situation in which an examiner in one district would classify a bond "doubtful" while one in another district would classify the same bond "substandard." Another reason is to assure that classification is done by a committee of knowledgeable persons.

The Board is also planning to issue a new supervisory memorandum which would establish minimum underwriting and investment practices for thrifts that choose to invest in high-yield bonds. This memorandum provides a basis for examiners to judge whether thrifts are applying sound principles in their high-yield bond investing. This memorandum will include guidance for establishing investment policies, diversification standards, underwriting criteria, credit analysis practices, and loss reserve allowances.

We believe the Bank Board efforts are a step in the right direction. At our hearing on the high-yield bond market, several experts testified that an adequately diversified portfolio, prudent loss reserves, and thorough credit analysis are the keys to sound high-yield bond investment by the thrift industry. We believe this is good advice.

In a more general regulatory vein, we are not aware of any specific initiatives at this moment to impose restrictions on high-yield bonds. We do know, however, that Congressional staffers are concerned about LBO debt. Though these concerns are not focused, we expect renewed interest in LBOs and high-yield bonds when Congress reconvenes in January.

CHAPTER 12

A VIEW FROM WASHINGTON ON LEVERAGED BUYOUTS

Kenneth Lehn[*]

After a year in which the SEC and its congressional oversight committees have been concentrating largely on policy issues related to the October 1987 stock market crash, it appears that the issue of leveraged buyouts (LBOs) will be occupying center stage in 1989. The recently announced acquisition of RJR Nabisco by Kohlberg Kravis Roberts & Co. has rekindled public interest in LBOs, in part, because of the size of this transaction (approximately $25 billion) and, in part, because of the notoriety of RJR Nabisco's products (e.g., Oreo cookies, Winston and Salem cigarettes). Numerous congressional committees and subcommittees, with jurisdiction over tax, banking, securities, and labor issues, have already announced that they will hold hearings on LBOs in early 1989.

The term "leveraged buyout" is used to describe a wide variety of corporate control transactions that substitute debt for equity, including highly leveraged going private transactions, hostile tender offers, mergers, and recapitalizations. During the 1980s, LBOs have created significant wealth gains for stockholders in U.S. corporations. Numerous studies have documented that, on average, takeover premiums paid to stockholders in

[*]Kenneth Lehn is Chief Economist, Securities and Exchange Commission. The views expressed here are those of the author and do not necessarily reflect the views of the SEC or the author's colleagues on the staff of the SEC.

target firms range from 30-50%. Jensen (1988) estimates that shareholders received approximately $346 billion in takeover premiums during 1977-1986. A preliminary SEC staff report finds that more than $37 billion in premiums have been paid to stockholders in going private transactions alone during the 1980s.

Notwithstanding the beneficial effects of LBOs on stockholder wealth, these transactions have raised numerous public policy questions concerning the source of these stockholder gains. For example, do the stockholder gains derive from improved operating efficiencies following the buyouts? Or do these gains "simply" represent the reduced tax liability of companies following the buyouts? Do the stockholder gains in leveraged buyouts represent the creation of wealth, or do these transactions "simply" redistribute wealth from other corporate stakeholders, including employees and bondholders? In addition to concern about the source of stockholder gains in leveraged buyouts, concerns have been raised about the effects of LBOs on research and development, the exposure of federally insured deposit institutions to LBO debt, the adequacy of present disclosure rules in LBOs, and the macroeconomic effects of increased levels of corporate debt, especially if the U.S. economy experiences a recession during the next couple of years.

Although many of these questions remain unresolved empirically, the body of academic evidence on corporate takeovers strongly suggests that these transactions have been healthy for the U.S. economy. In short, there are three major potential sources of value in corporate takeovers. First, mergers of two firms in the same industry, or LBOs that result in subsequent asset sales that have the same effect, can create value by allowing the combined firms to exploit economies of scale (i.e., to lower unit costs by spreading fixed costs over larger levels of output). This potential source of value is likely to be especially important in industries with declining growth rates. Second, takeovers can create "synergistic" value by combining two firms with complementary assets (e.g., combining a firm that has a good product and a weak distribution system with a firm that has a good distribution system). Finally, and perhaps, most controversially, takeovers can discipline managers who operate firms inefficiently. Since this third source of value evokes considerable controversy, it is appropriate to elaborate on it.

Since Berle and Means' (1932) classic work, *The Modern Corporation and Private Property,* it has been widely recognized that a potential conflict exists between managerial incentives and stockholder interests in publicly traded corporations that are characterized by diffuse ownership structures and relatively small shareholdings by corporate managers. This potential conflict arises because managers in these firms do not bear the entire wealth consequences associated with their managerial decisions. If the equity is diffusely owned, then monitoring by outside shareholders is "incomplete," since no individual shareholder receives the full value created by his costly monitoring activity. Although Berle and Means' discussion of these potential "agency problems" is rich, they ignored numerous institutional arrangements, including corporate takeovers, that may arise to mitigate these problems.

The type of managerial "inefficiency" that is often referred to in the takeover controversy concerns the consumption of perquisites by top-level managers in large corporations. Although there undoubtedly are cases where managers have overindulged in the consumption of these perks, it is hard to believe that the premiums paid in takeovers largely derive from a reduction in the value of these perks. Rather, it seems that a much more important source of value in LBOs is the discipline that these transactions impose on managers who pursue strategies that diminish the value of their firms, however well-intentioned these strategies may be. Jensen (1986) has suggested that takeovers, in part, discipline managers in firms that have abundant free cash flow (i.e., cash flow in excess of what is required to finance positive net present value projects), since managers may prefer to invest the excess cash flow in value-reducing projects that expand firm size (e.g., value-reducing acquisitions), rather than pay out the excess cash flow to stockholders in either dividends or stock buybacks.

Mark Mitchell, an economist at the SEC, and I recently have completed a study that provides empirical support for the "free cash flow" theory of takeovers. Specifically, it appears that many takeovers in the 1980s have been attempts to undo value-reducing acquisitions made by the target firms. For example, consider the case of Goodyear Tire and Rubber Co. In the fall of 1986, Sir James Goldsmith unsuccessfully attempted a hostile takeover of Goodyear. At the time, Goldsmith indicated that if successful, he would sell off Goodyear's oil and aerospace assets, and focus its managerial attention on Goodyear's tire and rubber assets. Interestingly, when Goodyear made its first major energy acquisition (Celeron Oil for $850 million in 1983), its stock price fell approximately 15%, presumably reflecting the market's disenchantment with Goodyear's diversification strategy. Hence, the approximately one billion dollar premium offered by

Goldsmith, at least in part, would have recaptured equity value that stockholders of Goodyear had previously lost when Goodyear management embarked on a major acquisition program.

Mitchell and I find that the "Goodyear result" generalizes to a large sample of firms. Specifically, firms that subsequently became takeover targets during the period from 1982 through mid-1988 had been making acquisitions that were systematically diminishing their stock prices, whereas firms that did not become takeover targets during this same period had been making acquisitions that were systematically increasing their stock prices. Hence, consistent with the free cash flow theory, we find that "bad bidders become good targets." The results suggest that, in addition to benefiting target stockholders, takeovers during the 1980s have benefited the economy at large, since they have facilitated the redeployment of assets to more profitable uses.

In addition to mitigating agency problems associated with the use of free cash flow, other studies suggest that LBOs during the 1980s have increased the profitability and operating efficiency of target firms. Smith (1988) and Kaplan (1988) find that one source of increased profits appears to be a significant reduction in resources that are tied up in working capital following these transactions. Specifically, Smith (1988) finds a significant reduction in both the inventory holding period and receivables collection period following these transactions; Kaplan (1988) finds similar results with respect to a shortened inventory holding period.

Several academic studies also shed empirical light on many of the concerns that have been expressed about leveraged buyouts. One study (Kaplan, 1988) finds that, on average, employment is not cut following leveraged buyouts. In fact, controlling for subsequent divestitures, the study actually finds a slight increase in employment following LBOs. Parenthetically, it is worth mentioning that concomitant with the significant increase in LBO activity has been a significant reduction in the U.S. unemployment rate. Although I am not suggesting that LBOs have caused the unemployment rate to decline, this observation is generally inconsistent with the argument that these transactions have created widespread layoffs of employees in the U.S.

Several studies have examined the effect of LBOs on bond prices (Travlos and Millon, 1988; Cook and Martin, 1988; Marais, Schipper, and Smith, 1988; Lehn and Poulsen, 1988). Although the evidence is mixed, and suffers from severe data limitations, it generally shows that, on average,

LBOs have a small negative effect on bond prices. Although these bond price effects should concern bondholders, in my view, they do not require public policy changes. Bondholders can insure against this "event risk" with negative pledge clauses, restricted sale-leaseback agreements, and other covenants that restrict the issuance of secured debt. Undoubtedly, bondholders pay a price for this protection in the form of lower coupon rates than they otherwise would receive. Hence, bondholders who forgo this protection presumably receive a premium in exchange for bearing some increased risk of a leverage-enhancing transaction. Unless transaction costs impair the efficiency of the market for this protection, there appears to be no justification for a public policy "remedy" to this "problem." Furthermore, it is noteworthy that the stockholder gains in leveraged buyouts far exceed the losses sustained by bondholders, indicating that these transactions involve much more than simply a redistribution of wealth from bondholders to stockholders.

Several academic studies (Lowenstein, 1985; Schipper and Smith, 1988; and Kaplan, 1988) also have examined the extent to which the stockholder gains in leveraged buyouts are financed by a reduction in the effective tax liability of corporations following the transactions. These studies generally conclude that a large part of these gains are related to tax advantages associated with LBOs, including the tax deductibility of interest payments on corporate debt, the tax advantages associated with the use of employee stock ownership plans (ESOPs), and prior to tax law changes in 1986 and 1987, increased depreciation deductions associated with the "step-up" of assets in these transactions.

Although these studies indicate that a large part of the stockholder wealth gains in leveraged buyouts derive from reduced tax liability at the corporate level, the net effect of these transactions on tax revenues is unclear. First, stockholders pay capital gains taxes on the wealth gains they receive in leveraged buyouts. Second, tax-paying owners of the debt used to finance leveraged buyouts pay income taxes on the interest income they receive. Finally, to the extent that corporate profitability is increased following leveraged buyouts, additional taxes may be paid on the increased profits. A priori, the net effect of leveraged buyouts on tax revenue is ambiguous. If it is determined that the existing tax code should not favor debt over equity, this bias can be eliminated in at least two ways: either removing the interest deduction on debt, or eliminating the double taxation on dividends by allowing corporations to deduct dividend payments. There are, of course, difficulties associated with both proposals. The former would adversely affect corporate investments in capital projects and research and development, and may put U.S. firms at a competitive disadvantage vis-à-vis foreign companies. The latter proposal might adversely affect tax revenues at a time when we have a large federal budget deficit.

Many critics of leveraged buyouts have argued that the high interest expenses following these transactions require firms to significantly cut expenditures on research and development and capital projects following leveraged buyouts. Concerning research and development expenditures, most leveraged buyouts have not occurred in industries that are research-intensive. For example, SEC data reveals that during 1980-1987, the industries with the highest value of going private activity were grocery and convenience stores, food processing and beverages, broadcasting and cable operators, and department stores and catalog showrooms, four industries that typically do not expend much on research and development. Furthermore, Smith (1988) finds that of 58 management buyouts during 1977-1986, only five companies had research and development expenditures that were significant enough to be reported in their SEC filings. It should be noted that in these five cases, Smith (1988) found significant reductions in expenditures on research and development following the management buyouts. Similarly, two studies (Kaplan, 1988; Smith, 1988) have examined the effect of leveraged buyouts on capital expenditures; both studies find significant reductions in capital expenditures following these transactions.

Although the evidence on reductions in capital expenditures following leveraged buyouts is consistent with a critical view of these transactions, it also is consistent with a more favorable view of these transactions. As discussed above, some have argued that a principal reason for leveraged buyouts is the mitigation of managerial incentive problems associated with overinvesting in capital projects and acquisitions. Leveraged buyouts effectively "disgorge" the excess cash flow to stockholders, and the subsequent reduction in capital expenditures may reflect the elimination of value-reducing capital projects. Since the premiums typically are reinvested in the securities markets, these transactions free up capital for more valuable uses, which enhances the productive efficiency of the economy.

In short, corporate takeovers generally, and leveraged buyouts in particular, have created significant wealth gains for stockholders in U.S. corporations during the 1980s. In addition to increasing stockholders' operation of firms following these transactions. To the extent that LBOs facilitate the redeployment of assets to more profitable uses, and strengthen managerial incentives to maximize profits, these transactions benefit the U.S. economy, and promote, rather than retard, the international competitiveness of U.S. firms.

References and Additional Reading

Berle, A., and Means, G. (1932). *The modern corporation and private property.*

Cook, D. O., and Martin, J. D. (1988). The co-insurance and leverage effects on target firm bondholder wealth. Unpublished manuscript.

Jensen, M. C. (May 1986). Agency costs of free cash flow, corporate finance, and takeovers. *American Economic Review,* 323–339.

Jensen, M. C. (Winter 1988). Takeovers: Their causes and consequences. *Journal of Economic Perspectives,* 21–48.

Lehn, K., and Poulsen, A. (1988). Leveraged buyouts: Wealth created or wealth redistributed? In Murray L. Weidenbaum and Kenneth Chilton (eds.), *Public policy towards corporate takeovers.* New Brunswick, NJ: Transaction Publishers.

Lowenstein, L. (1985). Management buyouts. *Columbia Law Review,* 730–784.

Marais, L., Schipper, K., and Smith, A. (June 1988). Wealth effects of going private for senior securities. Unpublished manuscript.

Mitchell, M. L., and Lehn, K. (August 25, 1988). Do bad bidders become good targets? Office of Economic Analysis, U.S. Securities Exchange Commission.

Schipper, K., and Smith, A. (June 1988). Corporate income tax effects of management buyouts. Unpublished manuscript.

Smith, A. (January 1989). Corporate ownership structure and performance: The case of management buyouts. Unpublished manuscript.

Travlos, N., and Millon, M. H. (August 1986). Going private buyouts and determinants of stockholder returns. Unpublished manuscript.

CHAPTER 13

THRIFT INSTITUTIONS AND HIGH-YIELD BONDS

*James R. Barth **

The Federal Savings and Loan Insurance Corporation (FSLIC) has taken action against hundreds of thrift institutions in recent years. In 1988 alone, the FSLIC resolved and stabilized 223 thrifts at an estimated present value cost of nearly $40 billion. Despite this flurry of activity, there are still hundreds more institutions that will require financial assistance. As the costs of resolving troubled thrifts mount, it is understandable that efforts are well underway to be sure that this situation does not recur.

In this regard, it is appropriate to examine investments by FSLIC-insured thrift institutions in below-investment-grade corporate debt securities, commonly known as junk bonds. Although these bonds did not cause the many thrift failures that have occurred in recent years, there is nonetheless concern by some that such investments pose a significant threat to the thrifts that invest in them and to the FSLIC. How concerned one should be depends in part on the extent to which thrifts invest in high-yield bonds and the regulatory treatment of such investments. Both of these issues will be addressed in this chapter.

*James R. Barth is Lowder Eminent Scholar in Finance at Auburn University and was formerly Director, Office of Policy and Economic Research, Federal Home Loan Bank Board.

THRIFT INVESTMENT IN HIGH-YIELD BONDS

Of the 3,024 FSLIC-insured thrift institutions operating at the end of September 1988, only 161 held investments that are unrated or rated below the four highest investment grades. Table 13–1 presents information on all thrifts that have held high-yield bonds since the Federal Home Loan Bank Board (Bank Board) began collecting data on such investments in 1985. As may be seen, relatively few institutions invest in high-yield bonds, only 5.3 percent of all thrifts in September 1988. However, these thrifts held 24.9 percent of the industry's total assets. As regards the amount of high-yield bonds held by the 161 thrifts, it is $13.2 billion or less than one percent of all thrift assets. In terms of just the assets of those thrifts holding these bonds, the figure is 4 percent. These thrifts have an average GAAP capital-to-assets ratio of 3.2 percent, up sharply from 1.8 percent in June 1988. The corresponding ratio for the entire industry is 3.0 percent.

More detailed information on thrifts holding high-yield bonds is presented in Table 13–2, with those institutions whose holdings are less than 2 percent excluded. The institution holding the most high-yield bonds holds $3.7 billion or 2.8 percent of all such holdings by thrifts. Although 32 percent of its assets are in high-yield bonds, this thrift does have a GAAP capital-to-asset ratio of 5.8 percent. Of the remaining 45 thrifts, only 5 are insolvent. This suggests that insolvent thrifts that were still operating in September 1988 were not heavily into high-yield bonds since so few of them appear on this list. One also observes that the biggest investors in these bonds—based on high-yield bond-to-asset-ratios—are typically state-chartered, stock institutions.

Table 13–3 presents information on the 31 institutions holding high-yield bonds that have been liquidated or merged by the FSLIC. Three thrifts held more than 5 percent of their assets in these bonds. Yet, the estimated resolution costs for each of these thrifts far exceed their holdings of high-yield bonds. This means that even if the bonds were worthless—an extremely unlikely event—the resolution costs can only partially be accounted for by investments in these bonds. The same situation exists for the remaining thrifts on the list. High-yield bond holdings, therefore, clearly cannot be blamed for the large costs imposed upon the FSLIC in recent years, not even those for failed thrifts having displayed a relatively high propensity for such investments.

TABLE 13–1
High-yield bond holdings by FSLIC-insured thrift institutions,
June 1985 to September 1988

Year/Month		Number of Institutions	High-Yield Bonds ($ millions)	Assets ($ millions)	High-Yield Bond-to-Asset Ratio (%)	GAAP Capital-to-Asset Ratio (%)
1985	June	111	5,741	161,688	3.6	3.1
	September	120	5,170	171,968	3.0	3.1
	December	121	5,587	178,422	3.1	3.2
1986	March	125	6,038	175,852	3.4	3.4
	June	129	6,582	176,359	3.7	3.2
	September	127	7,221	193,426	3.7	3.1
	December	129	7,572	175,915	4.3	2.8
1987	March	140	8,278	256,756	3.2	3.5
	June	133	9,971	237,313	4.2	3.4
	September	149	11,364	267,369	4.3	3.2
	December	145	12,294	270,806	4.5	2.9
1988	March	148	12,392	275,786	4.5	2.2
	June	149	13,136	293,532	4.5	1.8
	September	161	13,210	329,801	4.0	3.2

Note: These figures may include, for some thrifts, certain below-investment grade or unrated bonds that are not considered junk bonds. Despite this limitation of the data, it is the best available and does undoubtedly display a reasonably accurate picture of this type of investment for the industry. One must be cautious, however, about drawing strong conclusions about individual institutions without first determining the type and importance of unrated securities.

The distributions of return-on-assets for thrifts holding high-yield bonds compared with those thrifts holding no bonds are shown in Figures 13–1 and 13–2. As may be seen, the distributions are quite similar, suggesting no noticeable difference can be attributed to high-yield bonds. Figures 13–3 and 13–4 show the distributions of GAAP capital-to-asset ratios for thrifts holding high-yield investments and those thrifts holding no such investments, respectively. Once again, there are no noticeable differences in the two distributions, suggesting that these bond holdings do not account for differences in capital levels among thrifts.

The last two tables contain information on the portfolio composition of thrifts holding high-yield bonds compared with those without any such

TABLE 13–2
Financial characteristics of FSLIC-insured thrift institutions with high-yield bond-to-asset ratios exceeding 2 percent (ranked by high-yield bond-to-asset ratio)—September 1988

Institution	District	Charter	High-Yield Bonds ($ millions)	High-Yield Bond-to-Asset Ratio (%)	GAAP Capital-to-Asset Ratio (%)	1-4 Family Mortgages-to-Asset Ratio (%)	Multi-Family Mortgages-to-Asset Ratio (%)	MBS-to-Asset Ratio (%)
1	11	State-Stock	3,687	32.2	5.8	10.0	5.5	30.2
2	5	State-Stock	205	15.9	6.4	43.5	1.9	4.8
3	11	State-Stock	801	15.2	4.7	1.1	0.5	9.1
4	12	State-Stock	47	12.4	2.8	50.4	0.9	14.2
5	4	State-Stock	1,173	12.1	4.2	18.3	0.1	30.2
6	9	State-Stock	536	11.5	-4.4	17.2	2.4	26.9
7	11	State-Stock	1,397	11.2	2.3	37.4	6.3	9.7
8	4	State-Stock	3	10.8	10.8	25.0	0.0	0.0
9	11	Federal-Stock	5	8.8	6.7	25.3	1.2	33.7
10	8	Federal-Stock	15	8.7	5.8	27.5	8.3	4.6
11	9	State-Stock	236	8.6	-2.6	23.7	3.9	2.9
12	9	State-Stock	550	8.5	1.2	13.5	0.1	24.2
13	11	State-Stock	55	8.1	5.1	48.4	3.2	2.7
14	2	Federal-Stock	745	6.9	3.2	39.0	4.1	16.5
15	4	State-Stock	123	6.8	1.0	29.1	1.1	9.7
16	8	Federal-Stock	161	6.6	4.8	15.1	0.9	53.9
17	1	Federal-Stock	250	6.4	5.7	20.0	0.3	25.3
18	8	Federal-Mutual	197	5.4	-1.8	32.4	2.1	26.5
19	1	Federal-Stock	413	5.0	3.5	30.2	0.4	34.5
20	11	State-Stock	103	4.4	5.1	29.7	17.3	1.5
21	2	Federal-Stock	86	4.4	2.5	23.0	4.6	10.3
22	10	Federal-Stock	68	3.9	2.4	30.8	5.6	28.9
23	11	State-Stock	493	3.8	0.8	15.3	10.1	41.7

TABLE 13–2, continued

Institution	District	Charter	High-Yield Bonds ($ millions)	High-Yield Bond-to-Asset Ratio (%)	GAAP Capital-to-Asset Ratio (%)	1-4 Family Mortgages-to-Asset Ratio (%)	Multi-Family Mortgages-to-Asset Ratio (%)	MBS-to-Asset Ratio (%)
24	6	Federal-Mutual	4	3.7	0.0	62.7	2.2	0.4
25	7	Federal-Stock	29	3.7	2.4	38.3	7.8	15.3
26	5	Federal-Mutual	20	3.6	0.4	56.7	9.2	0.3
27	5	Federal-Mutual	2	3.4	3.9	56.8	0.1	3.7
28	9	Federal-Mutual	5	3.2	3.2	38.2	0.8	16.9
29	4	State-Stock	3	3.1	8.7	47.5	3.5	8.1
30	9	State-Stock	10	2.9	3.1	29.5	1.0	18.0
31	12	Federal-Stock	74	2.9	6.8	20.9	3.6	41.2
32	7	Federal-Mutual	10	2.9	-0.1	26.1	0.8	33.0
33	9	Federal-Stock	2	2.9	5.7	12.9	2.6	9.5
34	9	Federal-Mutual	9	2.8	-3.4	29.6	1.3	20.2
35	7	Federal-Stock	10	2.6	3.3	10.0	8.1	40.6
36	5	State-Stock	21	2.6	5.1	18.3	17.6	5.8
37	11	State-Stock	2	2.6	7.8	18.4	18.1	0.0
38	9	State-Stock	97	2.6	5.4	9.3	9.9	0.0
39	5	State-Stock	3	2.4	1.6	53.9	5.0	16.2
40	10	Federal-Stock	48	2.4	2.7	3.9	8.2	27.2
41	6	Federal-Stock	2	2.4	2.5	67.4	8.9	3.2
42	2	Federal-Stock	181	2.2	5.6	41.8	3.9	7.6
43	11	State-Stock	70	2.2	2.8	18.3	7.6	21.1
44	12	Federal-Stock	60	2.1	0.9	37.3	5.4	15.7
45	5	Federal-Mutual	53	2.1	7.7	26.8	5.3	13.3
46	6	Federal-Stock	45	2.0	5.0	27.4	1.5	31.5

TABLE 13–3
FSLIC-insured thrift institutions holding high-yield bonds that were liquidated or merged with FSLIC assistance—June 1985 to December 1988

Docket	District	Name	High-Yield Bonds ($ millions)	High-Yield Bond-to-Asset Ratio (%)	Estimated Resolution Cost ($ millions)	Resolution Date (Year-Qtr.)	Data Date (Year-Qtr.)
55	9	GIBRALTAR SA	550.1	8.5	1,504	88 IV	88 III
1280	5	OHIO VALLEY SLA	1.7	0.8	77	88 IV	88 I
2599	9	FIRST FSLA	0.1	0.2	31	88 IV	87 III
4430	9	UNITED SA OF TEXAS	535.6	11.5	1,372	88 IV	88 III
5001	10	COLUMBIA FSLA	20.5	0.7	74	88 IV	88 III
5684	9	HOME SA	0.1	0	391	88 IV	86 IV
7637	4	BROWARD FSLA	0.6	0.1	151	88 IV	85 IV
8257	11	BEVERLY HILLS SAVINGS, FSLA	8.8	0.5	983	88 IV	86 IV
7572	9	CENTRAL ARKANSAS SLA	2.8	15.9	4	88 IV	86 III
8438	9	TWIN CITY SAVINGS, A FSA	4.3	3	177	88 IV	87 IV
2603	9	FIRST FSB	4.8	3.2	24	88 III	88 III
8068	9	GUARANTY FSLA	22.7	1.1	1,194	88 III	88 II
6202	9	RICHARDSON SLA	3.4	0.5	215	88 III	88 II
7505	11	HOMESTATE SLA	0.3	0.2	40	88 III	88 II
7564	5	COMMERCE FSB	0.4	1	17	88 III	88 II
3926	7	GALVA FSLA	0.3	1.7	2	88 II	87 I
7753	12	LYNNWOOD SLA	0.8	1.2	6	88 II	85 II
8375	11	NORTH AMERICA SLA, A FSLA	0.3	0.2	133	88 II	87 I
2268	11	EUREKA FSLA	0.6	0	303	88 II	85 II
5673	9	BRIERCROFT SA	38.6	4.5	68	88 II	88 I
4660	7	CITIZENS SLA	0	0	6	88 I	88 I
7641	12	TRI-CITIES SLA	0.3	0.6	16	88 I	87 I
2321	8	FIRST FSB	1.5	1	58	88 I	87 IV

TABLE 13–3, continued

Docket	District	Name	High-Yield Bonds ($ millions)	High-Yield Bond-to-Asset Ratio (%)	Estimated Resolution Cost ($ millions)	Resolution Date (Year-Qtr.)	Data Date (Year-Qtr.)
3166	3	TRADERS FSLA	0	0	10	88 I	88 II
3179	3	MAGNET BANK, FSB	0	0	60	88 I	87 IV
7100	9	FIRST FSB	0.1	0.2	11	87 IV	87 III
6186	11	CENTRAL SLA	3.1	0.2	290	87 II	87 I
1342	12	UMPQUA FS&LA	0.5	0.4	11	87 I	86 IV
2827	9	FIRST SOUTH, FA	0.2	0	657	86 IV	86 III
3820	12	GUARANTY FEDERAL BANK FSB	1.1	1.6	30	86 IV	86 III
7654	12	PENINSULA FS&LA	0.3	0.6	4	86 III	86 II

FIGURE 13–1
Institutions holding high-yield bonds

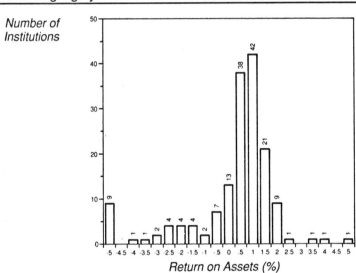

Note: Two quarters annualized income.

FIGURE 13–2
Institutions holding no high-yield bonds

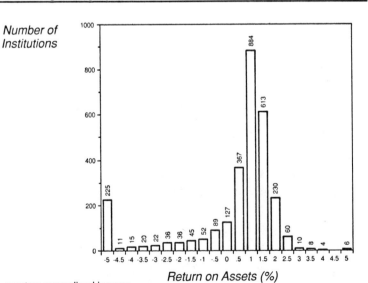

Note: Two quarters annualized income.

FIGURE 13–3
Institutions holding high-yield bonds

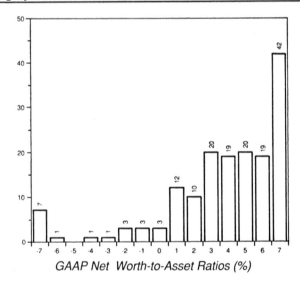

Number of Institutions

GAAP Net Worth-to-Asset Ratios (%)

FIGURE 13–2
Institutions holding no high-yield bonds

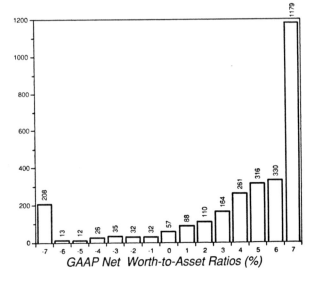

Number of Institutions

GAAP Net Worth-to-Asset Ratios (%)

TABLE 13–4
Financial comparison of FSLIC-insured thrift institutions holding high-yield bonds vs. all other FSLIC-insured thrift institutions—September 1988

	Group A		Group B	
	Amount	Ratio	Amount	Ratio
Number of Insitutions		158		2,827
Assets:	316,181	Asset %	946,848	Asset %
1-4 Family Morts	89,687	28.4	423,045	44.7
Mort-Backed Sec	64,660	20.5	131,036	13.8
Multifamily	19,505	6.2	62,307	6.6
Non-Res Morts	24,537	7.8	77,472	8.2
Land Loans	8,482	2.7	16,334	1.7
Commercial	8,283	2.6	15,738	1.7
Consumer	16,355	5.2	43,450	4.6
R E Owned	4,620	1.5	14,549	1.5
R E Investment	1,907	0.6	3,946	0.4
Cash & Investments	56,465	17.9	114,308	12.1
Eligible Liq	18,886	6.0	71,821	7.6
Fixed Assets	3,280	1.0	12,336	1.3
Goodwill	7,836	2.5	16,097	1.7
Service Corp	9,015	2.9	14,202	1.5
Purchased Servicing	539	0.2	1,215	0.1
Other Assets	1,012	0.3	812	0.1
Liabilities:	302,833	Liab %	909,574	Liab %
Deposits =< 100K	179,516	59.3	626,018	68.8
Deposits > 100K	34,466	11.4	93,433	10.3
Advances	32,501	10.7	84,595	9.3
Repos	27,526	9.1	53,714	5.9
Other Borrowings	22,161	7.3	33,568	3.7
Other Liabs	6,664	2.2	18,245	2.0
Thousands of Accounts	22,046		86,174	
Net Worth:		Asset %		Asset %
RAP	14,725	4.7	40,408	4.3
GAAP	10,586	3.3	29,027	3.1
Tangible	2,750	0.9	12,930	1.4
Profitability:		Avg A %		Avg A %
Operating Income	6,913	9.1	21,242	9.2
Non-Operating Inc	489	0.6	729	0.3
Non-Int Oper Exp	1,330	1.8	4,513	2.0
Non-Operating Exp	642	0.8	1,967	0.9
Cost of Funds	5,756	7.6	16,314	7.1
Taxes	97	0.1	484	0.2
Net Income	(350)	-0.5	(1,239)	-0.5

Note: Dollars are in millions of dollars and income and expense ratios are annualized. Also, this analysis is based upon the inclusion of three merged thrift institutions.

TABLE 13–5

Financial comparison of GAAP-solvent FSLIC-insured thrift institutions holding high-yield bonds vs. all other GAAP-solvent FSLIC-insured thrift institutions—September 1988

	Group A		Group B	
	Amount	Ratio	Amount	Ratio
Number of Insitutions		140		2,419
Assets:	293,886	Asset %	834,345	Asset %
1-4 Family Morts	84,302	28.7	387,994	46.5
Mort-Backed Sec	60,021	20.4	117,623	14.1
Multifamily	18,228	6.2	55,964	6.7
Non-Res Morts	22,433	7.6	65,639	7.9
Land Loans	8,047	2.7	12,207	1.5
Commercial	7,834	2.7	13,497	1.6
Consumer	15,374	5.2	37,761	4.5
R E Owned	3,818	1.3	6,345	0.8
R E Investment	1,785	0.6	2,602	0.3
Cash & Investments	52,537	17.9	98,221	11.8
Eligible Liq	17,638	6.0	62,783	7.5
Fixed Assets	3,091	1.1	10,667	1.3
Goodwill	7,183	2.4	13,246	1.6
Service Corp	7,974	2.7	11,332	1.4
Purchased Servicing	536	0.2	834	0.1
Other Assets	724	0.2	412	0.0
Liabilities:	279,701	Liab %	784,050	Liab %
Deposits =< 100K	164,193	58.7	531,599	67.8
Deposits > 100K	33,165	11.9	86,723	11.1
Advances	29,563	10.6	70,729	9.0
Repos	24,956	8.9	48,847	6.2
Other Borrowings	21,490	7.7	29,977	3.8
Other Liabs	6,334	2.3	16,174	2.1
Thousands of Accounts	20,239	75,408		
Net Worth:		Asset %		Asset %
RAP	15,334	5.2	52,153	6.3
GAAP	11,845	4.0	44,894	5.4
Tangible	4,662	1.6	31,648	3.8
Profitability:		Avg A %		Avg A %
Operating Income	6,495	9.2	19,123	9.4
Non-Operating Inc	480	0.7	632	0.3
Non-Int Oper Exp	1,238	1.8	3,849	1.9
Non-Operating Exp	379	0.5	786	0.4
Cost of Funds	5,286	7.5	13,937	6.9
Taxes	98	0.1	487	0.2
Net Income	34	0.0	759	0.4

Note: Dollars are in millions of dollars and income and expense ratios are annualized. Also, this analysis is based upon the inclusion of three merged thrift institutions.

bonds. Tables 13–4 and 13–5 also contain information on the capital levels of the two groups of thrifts as well as the corresponding income and expense figures. Briefly, institutions holding high-yield bonds held 28.4 percent of their assets in 1-4 family residential mortgages and 20.5 percent of their assets in mortgage-backed securities. Institutions holding no high-yield bonds held 44.7 percent of assets in 1-4 family residential mortgages and 13.8 percent of assets in mortgage-backed securities. Approximately the same percentages hold when the sample is limited to just GAAP-solvent institutions (see Table 13–5).

Institutions holding high-yield bonds held 17.9 percent of their assets in cash and investment securities, while those holding no high-yield bonds held 12.1 percent of assets in cash and investment securities. Approximately the same percentages hold when the sample is limited to GAAP-solvent institutions (see Table 13–5).

The average GAAP capital-to-assets ratio at institutions holding high-yield bonds is 3.2 percent compared with an average ratio at institutions holding no high-yield bonds of 3.1 percent. The ratios change to 4.0 and 5.4, respectively, when the sample is limited to GAAP-solvent institutions (see Table 13–5).

THRIFT REGULATORY TREATMENT OF HIGH-YIELD BONDS

Federally chartered institutions may invest up to one percent of assets in high-yield bonds through their authority to invest in corporate debt securities. Furthermore, based upon the Garn-St Germain Depository Institutions Act, the Bank Board's Office of General Counsel ruled that corporate debt securities are classified as commercial loans. As a result, federally chartered institutions are permitted to invest up to 10 percent of assets in high-yield bonds through their commercial lending authority. Thus, federally chartered institutions may invest up to 11 percent of assets in high-yield bonds.

While investment authority for state-chartered institutions varies depending on the state, in general, most states limit high-yield bond holdings to less than 10 percent of assets. However, state-chartered thrifts often have broader investment authority in their service corporations that allows greater consolidated holdings of high-yield bonds.

Two supervisory memoranda address thrift investment in high-yield bonds. R-60, issued in August 1984, advises prudent underwriting practices. Institutions that fail to adhere to such practices may be cited for an unsafe and unsound practice. R-63, issued in July 1985, provides general guidelines for implementing a safe and sound investment policy for commercial loans. Thrift investment in high-yield bonds is also subject to the loans-to-one borrower limitations of 15 percent of capital.

Investment in high-yield bonds by savings and loan associations must conform to new guidelines, which sharply restrict such investment by troubled institutions. These guidelines are spelled out in a thrift bulletin, TB-15, issued by the Office of Regulatory Activities on January 30, 1989. The bulletin provides minimum standards designed to ensure that all thrift institutions that invest in below-investment-grade corporate debt securities understand the risks involved, adopt appropriate controls, and are competent to manage those risks. The bulletin says any thrift institution that is under special supervisory attention may have its use of high-yield bonds restricted by its principal supervisory agent (PSA). Insolvent institutions are prohibited from making any new investment in high-yield bonds and generally will be required to divest such investments unless approved by their PSA as in the best near-term interest of FSLIC. Solvent but undercapitalized savings institutions may make new investments in high-yield bonds only with prior approval of their PSA, and only after a thorough review of the association's business plan, investment policy, and management controls by the institution's Federal Home Loan Bank.

On November 28, of 1988, the staff of the Bank Board presented the Board with a proposal that would significantly change the minimum capital requirements for thrift institutions. Similar to the proposal put forth by the banking regulators, the staff's proposal would require different capital levels for different assets. Under the staff proposal, high-yield bonds would require six percent capital. This is the same capital level as would be required for commercial and consumer loans and twice as much capital as would be required for mortgage loans. In addition, to the extent that high-yield bonds increase the interest-rate risk of a thrift, the institution would be required to hold additional capital.

SUMMARY AND CONCLUSIONS

Some individuals have expressed concern about thrift investment in high-yield bonds. As the data presented here indicate, such investments have neither caused the recent wave of thrift failures nor the associated heavy costs imposed upon the FSLIC. Furthermore, relatively few thrifts invest in high-yield bonds, and even these institutions display return and capital characteristics not unlike those for thrifts with no such investments. Recent regulatory actions, in any event, should minimize the risk exposure to the FSLIC from thrift investment in high-yield bonds.

CHAPTER 14

THE IMPACT OF DEBT ON MANAGEMENT INCENTIVES

Sheridan Titman[*]

Corporate debt among nonfinancial firms has increased from close to one trillion to over 1.8 trillion dollars since 1983. The growth in the amount of high-yield debt has been even more dramatic and has created a great deal of controversy. Policy makers have expressed particular concern about the impact of this increase in debt on the economy in the event of a recession.

A recent study by Bernanke and Campbell (1988) suggests that over 10 percent of all major corporations will be insolvent if we go into a major recession similar in magnitude to the 1973-74 recession. While most policy makers find this a cause for alarm, a number of economists have argued that this bankruptcy threat creates very few problems. Indeed, bankruptcies can weed out inefficient firms, and bankrupt firms that are efficient can in many cases be reorganized without great expense. These arguments, however, ignore some of the less-direct costs and benefits of debt financing that arise, among other reasons, because of the impact of debt on the incentives of a firm's management. Before we can conclude whether or not this increase in debt is good or bad for the economy, these incentive issues must be sorted out.

[*]Sheridan Titman is Professor of Finance, University of California–Los Angeles, as well as serving with the U.S. Treasury Department.

THE IMPACT OF DEBT ON PRODUCTION EFFICIENCY

A number of authors, [e.g., Grossman and Hart (1982)], have suggested that debt can have the effect of motivating management to cut costs and in other ways increase efficiency. The rationale for this argument is straightforward; the added debt forces management to produce higher operating income to avoid bankruptcy and the probable loss of their jobs. Evidence in Kaplan (1988) indicates that there are efficiency gains in firms that take on a great deal of high-yield debt in leveraged buyouts. However, it is not clear whether the increased efficiency occurs because of the high leverage or from the substantial increase in the portion of the management's compensation in these firms that is tied to the firm's performance.

THE IMPACT OF DEBT ON INVESTMENT CHOICES

The impact of leverage on corporate investment decisions is particularly important. A highly leveraged firm has very little financial slack, and as a result, is likely to invest less than a less highly leveraged firm. Jensen (1986) argues that this can be beneficial, suggesting that managers often take on unproductive investments solely because they have funds available. Myers and Majluf (1984), on the other hand, argue that a lack of financial slack can cause firms to pass up profitable investment projects. This will be especially true for firms that for one reason or another believe that they are undervalued. These firms may prefer to pass up additional new investments rather than issue what they believe to be undervalued stock or by borrowing at unattractive rates. If they were initially financed with very little debt, they could probably finance new investments by borrowing at favorable rates in such situations.

The excessive use of debt financing can also distort managements' risk-preferences [Jensen and Meckling (1976)]. In some cases, it can provide a tendency for them to select very risky investments, while in other cases it can make managers overly cautious. Our recent experiences with savings and loan institutions provides evidence on the tendency of individuals to take risks when gambling with other peoples' money. Similarly, managers may wish to increase risk since equity holders, whom the managers represent, enjoy most of the gain if their investments pay off, but share the risk with the firm's creditors if the investments do not turn out well. Offsetting this inclination to increase risk is the tendency of managers to invest conservatively to avoid bankruptcy. It is not clear which of these two offsetting effects will predominate in any given case, but it is clear that the type of investment that firms choose can be adversely affected by large amounts of debt financing.

In addition to influencing the risk profile of a firm's investments, debt financing can also affect whether management selects short horizon or long horizon investment projects. A firm with large debt obligations may, in the near-term, find it advantageous to pass up a higher NPV, long-term investment project, in favor of a lower NPV project that allows it to meet its upcoming debt obligations without additional borrowing. This will be the case whenever the firm's credit rating is such that it cannot borrow at favorable terms. In this case, raising funds internally by speeding up the payoffs of existing projects may be preferable to borrowing externally. One way to understand this is to think of raising funds internally as being equivalent to issuing senior debt; the firm's other debtholders are not protected from the reduction in future cashflows that occur as a result of the increase in the earlier cashflows. As with issuing senior debt, value is created for the firm's equity holders only by expropriating wealth from the firm's existing bondholders.

Since research and development is generally considered a long-term investment project the relation between R&D spending and leverage has been of interest. The relation between R&D spending and debt levels is in fact strongly negative [see, for example, Titman and Wessels (1988)], but the causation very likely runs in the opposite direction. For a variety of reasons, firms in industries that have a need for research and development tend not to be highly leveraged. It would be interesting to examine a sample of firms in R&D intensive industries that were involved in LBOs or have financed investments with high-yield debt. But to date, very few firms in high technology industries have been involved in leverage-increasing restructurings.

THE EFFECT OF DEBT ON THE ABILITY OF FIRMS TO DO BUSINESS

A second factor that may be of importance is the effect of debt on a firm's ability to deal with its various business associates. A number of authors [e.g., Altman (1984)] have noted that financial distress, or more generally, high leverage, can make a firm's customers and other business associates reluctant to do business with it. My research, [Titman (1984) and Maksimovic and Titman (1989)], has suggested two reasons why this might be the case.

Because both stockholders and management have strong incentives to avoid bankruptcy and liquidation, management may take actions under the threat of financial distress that they would not otherwise take. For example, they may cut quality on their products to save money or in some other ways break implicit contracts with their business associates. Under normal situations, the long-run value of maintaining a reputation provides a strong incentive to carry out these implicit contracts. However, under the threat of bankruptcy, these long-term considerations become secondary, and the incentive to temporarily increase cashflows by lowering product quality and by breaking implicit contracts arises.

Potential customers and other business associates of the firm anticipate this change in incentives and, as a result, become reluctant to do business with highly leveraged firms. Hence, leverage can adversely affect a firm's sales as well as its operating costs.

There is a second reason why potential customers and other business associates may be reluctant to do business with a highly leveraged firm. This relates to the incentives of a firm to stay in business. Both management and shareholders generally have a bias toward keeping a firm in business, even if its liquidation value exceeds its operating value. Managers generally want to keep their jobs, and equityholders will not necessarily do well in the event of a liquidation since debtholders and preferred stockholders must be paid in full before the common stockholders receive anything. Indeed, the full gain associated with the liquidating of a firm's assets is likely to accrue to these senior claimants.

For this same reason, bondholders have a bias towards liquidation. Hence, the bankruptcy process, which gives a greater voice to bondholders, does have an effect on whether or not a firm will stay in business. As a result, customers of firms who, for example, have a need for spare parts in the future, will be reluctant to do business with a firm in financial distress. For similar reasons, any individual that must rely on the long-term existence of the firms with which it does business will, therefore, be reluctant to do business with a highly leveraged firm.

ARE THESE LEVERAGE RELATED COSTS
RELEVANT FOR ALL FIRMS?

The foregoing discussion suggests that the magnitude of the costs that arise because of high leverage is not the same for all firms. In high technology industries, such as computers, these costs could be quite large. Computer makers rely on long-term relationships, in their dealings with customers and producers of complementary products as well as with their employees. The nature of their products also requires a great deal of research and development and long-term investments. Financial distress for such firms could create a number of problems.

Perhaps, because of these leverage related costs, high technology firms include relatively little debt in their capital structures. This is especially apparent if we look at leveraged buyouts; the industries that accounted for 84 percent of the industry-sponsored research and development in 1986 experienced only 17 percent of the recent LBO activity.

POLICY IMPLICATIONS

Most economists would agree that unless the private costs and benefits of a particular decision differ from the social costs and benefits, the government should neither encourage nor discourage it. For the most part, the various costs and benefits associated with financial policy and the use of high-yield debt affect only the firm and, therefore, are not suggestive of a need for government intervention. Possible exceptions relate to externalities that arise with certain kinds of investments that may be either discouraged or encouraged by debt financing, and problems that arise when a firm's leverage is unobservable.

There seems to be the presumption in much of government policy that, in general, investment is good and should be encouraged. People have made the argument that debt financing should be subsidized since it promotes investments [see John and Senbet (1988)]; however, as was discussed earlier, it is equally plausible that high debt levels discourage investments. Moreover, if debt does promote investment, it is not clear that it promotes the kind of innovative investment that creates spinoffs and other externalities. As I mentioned previously, debt financing may lead to a bias towards shorter-term investment projects, which probably are the least likely to produce spinoffs that benefit the entire economy.

There is another kind of externality that can arise when a firm's financial condition is not perfectly observable. This is especially important when the main deterrent to high debt levels is the reluctance of customers to do business with highly leveraged firms. If customers don't observe which firms are having financial problems, their actions can no longer serve as a deterrent to increasing debt. This of course does not eliminate the problem; it makes it worse since it provides an incentive for firms to be overly leveraged. Customers would rationally, in this case, assume the worst about firms' financial conditions because the incentive for a firm to have a low level of debt is less in this case. It follows that if the federal government can add its own discouragement to the use of debt financing, customers will be able to anticipate that firms will be less highly leveraged and will, therefore, be less suspicious about the quality of the firm's products and their intention to stay in business in the future. Hence, discouraging the use of debt financing could conceivably increase productivity and increase firm values.

Do the preceding arguments suggest that we should be subsidizing equity and penalizing the use of debt financing? Probably not, but that really isn't the relevant question. The relevant question is whether or not there is justification for our current tax policy that subsidizes the use of debt financing. Given the lack of external benefits associated with debt financing, a subsidy on debt financing is likely to lead firms to increase their use of debt until, on the margin, the costs that arise because of the various inefficiencies associated with debt financing equal the tax benefits. The elimination of this policy to subsidize debt financing might, therefore, lead to a reduction in debt financing and a subsequent increase in productivity.

There are a number of ways the tax bias favoring debt financing can be reduced. One could reduce the deductibility of interest payments, institute a tax deduction for dividend payments, or reduce the tax on capital gains. Revenue considerations, as well as the effects on the corporate cost of capital, should determine which of these alternatives is preferable.

POLICY CONSIDERATIONS RELATING TO
LEVERAGED BUYOUTS

Much of the controversy associated with the growing use of high-yield debt relates to the recent increase in the size and the number of leveraged buyouts. In response to this increase, there has been a number of proposals to limit the tax deductibility of the interest payments in these deals, while keeping the deduction for firms that maintain the traditional corporate form. I think such a policy may be seriously misguided.

LBOs create an institutional structure that minimizes many of the leverage related costs discussed above. People have argued that Japanese firms can prudently be more highly leveraged than U.S. firms because bankers are also stockholders and thus have an incentive to work things out if the firm cannot meet its interest payments. KKR and others that structure LBOs can probably play a similar role in the event that things don't work out. Hence, even though insolvency is much more likely with these firms, the consequences of a financial shortfall and the incentive problems that arise, are not necessarily very important.

Empirical evidence suggests that for many firms LBOs offer a more efficient organizational form (in addition to the tax effects) than traditional corporations, (eg. Kaplan (1988)). In general, it makes sense to initially subsidize successful innovations that can be copied by other firms and used to increase productivity in general. Penalizing LBOs will not necessarily limit the use of debt in general if the tax benefits in the more traditional corporate sector are unaffected, however, the use of this innovative organizational structure will certainly subside.

CONCLUSION

In conclusion, corporate debt, and in particular high-yield debt that carries a high probability of default, can potentially have negative effects on the economy. The costs associated with debt could be quite large in high technology industries, but are probably less relevant in industries such as retail sales, where research and development and long-term capital expenditures are less important, and the need for long-term business relationships is not as critical. Since the recent increase in leverage is concentrated mainly in the latter industries, the recent concern may be a bit premature. Moreover, leveraged buyout firms are generally structured in a way that minimizes the conflicts of interest between bondholders and stockholders. This is likely to have the effect of mitigating many of the above mentioned costs associated with debt financing.

As the market for high-yield debt continues to develop, it is likely that with a tax bias in favor of leverage, the trend toward increased leverage is likely to continue. Since firms will in the long run increase their debt levels until the marginal cost of increased leverage equals the marginal benefits, it is likely that some of the debt-related costs discussed in this paper will become more relevant if the current tax subsidy of debt is not eliminated.

Bibliography

Altman, E. (September 1984). A further investigation of the bankruptcy cost question. *Journal of Finance*, 1067–1089.

Bernanke, B., and Campbell, J. (1988). Is there a corporate debt crisis? *Brookings Papers on Economic Activity, 1*, 83–125.

Grossman, S., and Hart, O. (1982). Corporate financial structure and managerial incentives. In J. McCall (ed.), *The economics of information and uncertainty.*

Jensen, M. (May 1986). Agency costs of free cash flow, corporate finance, and takeover. *American Economic Review*, 323–329.

Jensen, M., and Meckling, W. (October 1976). Theory of the firm: Managerial behavior, agency costs and ownership structure. *Journal of Financial Economics*, 305–360.

John, K., and Senbet, L. (July 1988). Limited liability, corporate leverage, and public policy. New York University working paper.

Kaplan, S. (1988). Management buyouts: Efficiency gains or value transfers. University of Chicago working paper.

Maksimovic, V., and Titman, S. (January 1989). Financial policy and a firm's reputation for product quality. UCLA working paper.

Myers, S., and Majluf, N. (June 1984). Corporate financing and investment decisions when firms have information that investors do not have. *Journal of Financial Economics*, 187–221.

Titman, S. (March 1984). The effect of capital structure on a firm's liquidation decision. *Journal of Financial Economics*, 137–152.

Titman, S., and Wessels, R. (March 1988). The determinants of capital structure choice. *Journal of Finance*, 1–19.

PART 3

CORPORATE FINANCE AND CAPITAL MARKET ISSUES

CHAPTER 15

DEVELOPMENT OF THE JUNK BOND MARKET AND ITS ROLE IN PORTFOLIO MANAGEMENT AND CORPORATE FINANCE

Kevin J. Perry
*Robert A. Taggart, Jr.**

The recent growth of the junk bond market has been one of the most controversial capital market developments in recent years. To some observers (e.g., Grant, 1988; Forstmann, 1988), junk bonds have come to symbolize an era of perceived financial excess. The role of junk bonds in giant leveraged buyouts and hostile takeovers and their purchase by mutual funds, insurance companies, and other financial institutions are seen by critics as evidence of a prevailing recklessness in financial dealings. Supporters, on the other hand, have extolled what they prefer to call "high yield bonds" for their indispensable contribution to the revitalization of American industry.[1]

Rather than jumping directly into this heated controversy, the current paper seeks to offer some perspective on the development of the junk bond market and its role in corporate finance. It is argued that the same forces of increased competition, volatile interest rates, and "securitization" that have

*Robert A. Taggart, Jr., is Professor of Finance at Boston College. The authors are grateful to Kimberly Haynes for valuable research assistance.

spawned a host of capital market changes in the 1970s and '80s have also been conducive to the growth in junk bond issuance. Given this background, the factors that corporate treasurers should consider in deciding whether to issue junk bonds are then discussed.

RECENT GROWTH OF THE JUNK BOND MARKET

Junk bonds are those rated below Ba by Moody's or below BBB– by Standard & Poor's. That is, they are bonds with below investment grade ratings. Unrated corporate bonds are usually included in the junk bond category as well.

Under their broadest definition, junk bonds include private placements and public issues, convertible and straight debt, low-rated municipal bonds, and even low-rated preferred stock. For the most part, however, this chapter focuses on the largest segment of the market: public, straight debt issued by U.S. corporations.

Junk bonds have existed ever since the first bond ratings were published by John Moody in 1909. In fact, junk bonds were a significant source of corporate funds throughout the prewar period, accounting for 17 percent of total rated, publicly issued straight corporate debt during the years 1909 to 1943. Downgradings during the Depression swelled the supply of junk bonds so that they grew from 13 percent of total corporate debt outstanding in 1928 to 42 percent in 1940 (Atkinson, 1967).

Junk bonds were less widely used as a source of corporate funds in the early postwar years. Between 1944 and 1965, for example, they accounted for only 6.5 percent of total corporate bond issues (Atkinson, 1967), and from the mid-sixties to the mid-seventies they were used even less frequently. By 1977, junk bonds accounted for only 3.7 percent of total corporate bonds outstanding and most of these were "fallen angels" or bonds initially issued with investment grade ratings and subsequently downgraded (Altman and Nammacher, 1986).

In 1977, however, the market began to change, as newly issued junk bonds started to appear in larger volume. Although this has been widely heralded as the birth of the new issue junk bond market, it is perhaps more accurately viewed as a resurgence of the flourishing market of the prewar years. In either case, the growth of new issues, as documented in Table 15–1, has been impressive, particularly since 1983. Even in the wake of the

TABLE 15–1
New issues of junk bonds (billion $)

Year	Newly Issued Public Straight Junk Bonds [a] (1)	Exchange Offers and Private Issues Going Public [a] (2)	Total Junk Bond Issuance [(1) + (2)] (3)	Total Public Bond Issues by U.S. Corporations [b] (4)	(1) as Percentage of (4) (5)	(3) as Percentage of (4) (6)
1988[c]	19.2	n/a	n/a	175.0	11.0	n/a
1987	28.6	7.2	35.8	219.1	13.1	16.3
1986	34.3	11.3	45.6	232.5	14.8	19.6
1985	15.4	4.4	19.8	119.6	12.9	16.6
1984	14.8	0.9	15.8	73.6	20.1	21.5
1983	8.0	0.5	8.5	47.6	16.8	17.9
1982	2.7	0.5	3.2	44.3	6.1	7.2
1981	1.4	0.3	1.7	38.1	3.7	4.5
1980	1.4	0.7	2.1	41.6	3.4	5.0
1979	1.4	0.3	1.7	25.8	5.4	6.6
1978	1.5	0.7	2.1	19.8	7.6	10.6
1977	0.6	0.5	1.1	24.1	2.5	4.6

[a] From Drexel Burnham Lambert (1988), except 1988 figure from *Investment Dealer's Digest*.
[b] From *Federal Reserve Bulletin,* except 1988 figure from *Investment Dealer's Digest*.
[c] (first three quarters)

stock market crash of October 1987 and the ongoing investigations by the SEC and U.S. Attorney's office of Drexel Burnham Lambert, the primary underwriter in the market, junk bond issuance has fallen only slightly during 1988 as a proportion of total corporate debt issuance.

Between cumulative new issues and additional fallen angels, the total amount of junk bonds outstanding has been estimated at about $159 billion by the end of 1987 (Drexel Burnham Lambert, 1988) and at about $170 billion by mid-1988. This represents more than 20 percent of the entire corporate bond market. Approximately one-quarter of total junk bonds outstanding consisted of fallen angels as of year-end 1987 (Drexel Burnham Lambert, 1988).

On the investor side, the junk bond market is primarily institutional. More than 50 mutual funds now specialize in holding junk bonds and these, together with other nonspecialized mutual funds, hold nearly one-third of junk bonds outstanding. The estimated ownership distribution of junk bonds as of December 1987 is shown in Table 15–2.

TABLE 15–2
Estimated ownership of junk bonds at December 1986

Type of Investor	Estimated Holdings ($ billion)	Percent of Total
Mutual funds and money managers	48	30
Insurance companies	48	30
Pension funds	24	15
Individuals	8	5
Thrift institutions	13	8
Other (foreign investors, corporations, securities dealers, etc.)	19	12
Total	159	100

Source: Drexel Burnham Lambert, 1988.

INVESTMENT CHARACTERISTICS OF JUNK BONDS

Presumably, the attraction that junk bonds hold for investors is a high expected return. Expected returns are impossible to measure, and realized returns are an imperfect proxy because of their substantial variation from year to year. Over longer periods, however, junk bonds seem to offer higher average, realized rates of return. For the period January 1977 to December 1986, for example, Blume and Keim (1987) calculated an annualized compound monthly rate of return of 11.04 percent for an index of junk bonds, compared with 9.6 percent for an index of AAA– and AA– rated corporate bonds and 9.36 percent for an index of long-term Treasury bonds.[2]

The performance characteristics of junk bonds during various economic scenarios are also of great interest. As can be seen in Table 15–3, high yield bonds outperformed stocks but underperformed investment grade bonds during periods of recession. However, junk bonds substantially outperformed investment grade bonds while underperforming stocks just prior to and just following recessions. Junk bonds outperform investment grade bonds just prior to a recession because interest rates are usually rising at this time, pushing down the value of investment grade debt. However, financial conditions are generally improving during such periods, improving the creditworthiness of lower grade issues. Because high yield securities have a much greater percentage of their total volatility attributable to company and sector factors, the effect of credit improvement swamps the interest rate effect. The net result is that junk securities have a positive return during such periods. These securities have characteristics of both debt and equity. The performance results in Table 15–3 are thus in line with expectations when viewed in this light.

In exchange for these returns, investors in junk bonds can expect to bear higher levels of risk. Their lower ratings, of course, suggest a high risk of default.[3] In addition, junk bonds tend to have fewer restrictive covenants than other bonds, and they are frequently subordinated. Thus, junk bondholders have less flexibility to accelerate the bankruptcy process in the event that the borrower's condition deteriorates, and they stand lower in the line of creditors if bankruptcy does occur.

TABLE 15–3
Portfolio performance around recession periods

Portfolio [a]	Comparative portfolio return during		
	Recession Quarters [b] (32 Observations)	Four Prerecession Quarters (28 Observations)	Four Postrecession Quarters (28 Observations)
Overall capital market	2.04%	1.60%	3.37%
Stocks	1.74	2.75	4.65
Investment grade bonds	2.65	−0.28	0.98
High-yield bonds	1.88	0.26	3.50

[a]Portfolios are constructed as follows:
Stocks: Standard & Poor's 500 Stocks Index
Investment Grade Bonds: Shearson Lehman Government/Corporate Bond Index
High-Yield Bonds: Salomon Brothers High-Yield Bond Index
Overall Capital Market: Market value-weighted average of three preceding portfolios
[b]The seven post-World War II recession periods are: 1953II-1954II, 1957III-1958II, 1960II-1961I, 1970I-1970IV, 1973IV-1975I, 1980I-1980III, 1981III-1982IV.

Measured default rates are, in fact, higher for junk bonds than for corporate bonds generally. For the period 1970 through 1986, Altman (1988) calculates the junk bond default rate (that is, par value of defaulting junk bonds divided by total junk bonds outstanding) as 2.2 percent, compared with 0.2 percent for all straight, public corporate debt. Influenced by the LTV and Texaco bankruptcies, the same calculation yielded junk bond default rates of 3.39 percent of 1986 and 4.69 percent for 1987 (through August 31).

However, the default rate is probably not the best measure of junk bond risk. Losses on defaulting bonds are rarely equal to their entire par value. For the period from 1974 to 1986, for example, the weighted average default loss was 1.10 percent, compared with a default rate of 1.6 percent for the same period. In addition, a variety of factors beside defaults influence the total variability of junk bond returns. These include interest rates, the state of the economy, and factors specific to both industry sectors and individual firms.

If we first examine the broadest measures of risk, the standard deviation of returns and the security "beta" relative to a capital market portfolio that includes both stock and bonds, we find that junk bonds occupy an intermediate position on the risk spectrum. This is indicated in Table 15–4, which gives standard deviations and betas computed for the period from January 1982 to December 1986. Junk bonds have greater total risk than investment grade bonds but less than common stocks, and they move more closely with the market than investment grade bonds, but less so than stocks. The ranking in terms of total risk, however, can change over time, depending on the relative importance during a given period of different risk components. Since junk bonds have higher coupon rates, they have shorter "durations" than investment grade bonds. That is, the weighted average of the times at which cash is received over the life of the bond is shorter for a junk bond.[4] This in turn implies that junk bond values are less sensitive to interest rate fluctuations, and during periods when interest rates are very volatile, junk bonds as a group may even exhibit lower total risk than long-term Treasury bonds or high-grade corporates. This is what Blume and Keim (1987) found for the period 1977–86, a time of substantial interest rate fluctuations.

At the same time, junk bonds are typically protected by smaller equity cushions than investment grade bonds and, thus, are more sensitive to fluctuations in the value of the issuing firm's assets. The value of the assets

TABLE 15–4
Comparative portfolio risk measures

Portfolio [a]	Beta [b]	Standard Deviation of Monthly Returns
Overall capital market	1.000	3.844%
Investment grade bonds	0.269	1.849
High-yield bonds	0.354	2.336
Large stocks	1.086	4.332
Small stocks	1.123	4.232

[a]Portfolios are constructed as follows:

Investment grade bonds: Shearson Lehman Government/Corporate Bond Index

High-yield bonds: Salomon Brothers High-Yield Bond Index through October 1984; Merrill Lynch High-Yield Bond Index thereafter

Large stocks: Standard & Poor's 500 Stocks Index

Small stocks: Wilshire 5000 Index

Overall capital market: Market value-weighted average of four preceding portfolios

[b]Betas and standard deviations estimated from monthly data for the period from January 1982 through December 1986

in turn reflects the present value of the operating cash flows they generate. As a result, the variability of junk bond returns is more heavily influenced by sector and firm-specific factors than is that of investment grade bonds. This point is graphically illustrated in Figure 15–1.

It might be said, then, that junk bonds are hybrids of both bonds and stocks. However, they also have characteristics all their own. If monthly high-yield bond returns are regressed successively against investment grade bond returns and common stock returns for the period 1982–86, 50.2 percent of the variance in total junk bond returns is attributable to movements in the investment grade bond market. Movements in the general stock market explain 27.1 percent of the variance of junk bond returns. The remaining variability is that portion not explained by either the investment grade bond market or the stock market. This portion is unique to the high yield market, adding to its diversification potential as an asset category.

In summary, the investment characteristics of junk bonds are unlike those of either high grade bonds or common stocks. Their lower sensitivity to interest rate changes and the diversifiability of a substantial portion of

FIGURE 15–1
Components of Risk

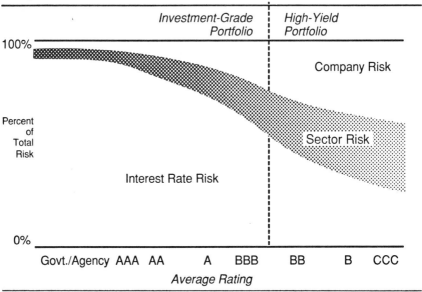

their risk make them unlike high grade bonds. Like common stocks, junk bond values move up and down with the value of the issuing firms' assets. Unlike common stocks, however, this upward movement is truncated for junk bonds beyond a certain point. This is because most junk bonds are callable, and if the issuing firm's creditworthiness improves dramatically, it will find it advantageous to call the bonds and refinance at a lower rate.

In the final analysis, investing in junk bonds may be most akin to a covered call option strategy, whereby a portfolio manager buys common stocks but also writes call options on those stocks. If the stocks fail to appreciate, the portfolio manager still receives the premium income from having written the call options. If the stocks do appreciate, however, the portfolio's upside potential is limited, because the stocks will be called away.

In a similar fashion, junk bonds' high current yield affords the investor some protection against the possibility that the firm's assets will decline in value. If the firm's fortunes improve substantially on the other hand, the junk bond holders participate in some degree, but that participation is limited by the fact that the firm will ultimately call the bonds away.

The summary statistic that is perhaps most relevant to a sophisticated investor is the return per unit of risk from investing in the high-yield market. On this score, junk bonds have performed quite well in recent years. Table 15–5 shows that, for the period, junk bonds had the highest return per unit of risk of any major market segment. Using Sharpe's and Treynor's risk adjusted performance measures, the high-yield market had substantially greater return per unit of risk than the stock market during this period and marginally more return per unit of risk than the investment grade bond market.

CAPITAL MARKET CONDITIONS AND THE RISE OF THE JUNK BOND MARKET

Capital Markets in the 1970s and '80s

It is natural to wonder why junk bonds suddenly regained a significant share of the total corporate debt market after having been relatively dormant for a number of years. Several key factors emerged in the 1970s and '80s that brought about fundamental changes in the overall capital market environment. These same factors were conducive to the growth in junk bonds.

The first factor has been increasing competition on an international scale. Industry boundaries and firms' market shares have become more fluid, and the financial services, transportation, communication, and energy industries, as well as major segments of the U.S. manufacturing have all undergone extensive restructuring. Deregulation has been a factor in several of these industries. In banking, for example, the erosion of interest rate ceilings has forced banks to compete on a broader scale in financial markets. It could be argued that these and other moves toward deregulation have often come as a response to, rather than a cause of, increased competitive pressure. Whatever their source, these pressures have generated substantial capital market activity in the form of mergers and divestitures, issues and repurchases of securities, and the start-up of new firms and liquidation of old ones. Regulatory changes that have given financial institutions greater flexibility should also be mentioned. For example, the

TABLE 15–5
Risk-adjusted portfolio return measures[a]

Portfolio [c]	Excess Returns Per Unit of Risk [b]	
	Sharpe Measure	Treynor Measure
Overall capital market	0.210	0.810
Investment grade bonds	0.373	2.565
High-yield bonds	0.410	2.712
Large stocks	0.203	0.792
Small stocks	0.185	0.712

[a]All measurements are made for the period from January 1982 through December 1986.
[b]The risk-adjusted return measures are defined as:

$$\text{Sharpe: } \frac{R_j - R_f}{\sigma_j} \qquad \text{Treynor: } \frac{R_j - R_f}{b_j}$$

where

R_j = average monthly return on portfolio j

R_f = average monthly risk-free rate of return

σ_j = standard deviations of monthly returns for portfolio j

b_j = estimated beta for portfolio j

[c]Portfolios are constructed as follows:

Investment grade bonds: Shearson Lehman Government/Corporate Bond Indes

High-yield bonds: Salomon Brothers High-Yield Bond Index through October 1984; Merrill Lynch High-Yield Bond Index thereafter

Large stocks: Standard & Poor's 500 Stocks Index

Small stocks: Wilshire 5000 Index

Overall capital market: Market value-weighted average of four preceding portfolios

ERISA standards of 1973 for pension fund investments essentially replaced the "prudent man" rule with a rule of reasonable compensation for risks incurred. This allowed pension funds to compete more broadly for investment opportunities.

A second important factor has been uncertain inflation and interest rate volatility. As exemplified by the response to the Federal Reserve's switch from interest rate to money supply targets in October 1979, the prices of fixed income securities have become more variable. This has spurred investors to seek protection against sudden changes in rates and has induced them to increase their portfolio turnover. For corporations, changing inflation rates have contributed to sharp fluctuations in the availability of internal funds relative to total financing needs. Thus many firms have found themselves moving in and out of the capital markets more frequently and facing highly variable conditions when doing so.

The third important factor in changing capital market conditions is at least partially motivated by the first two. Securities issuers have greatly expanded the range of their potential sources of funds. In part, the increasingly global nature of competition in many industries has led to raising funds on an international scale as well. This is exemplified by the growth of the Eurobond markets, in which U.S. corporations raised an average of $28.4 billion in both 1986 and 1987, up from just $300 million in 1975. In addition, the need to move in and out of markets more frequently has led to an emphasis on reducing the costs of external financing. Since 1982, corporations have taken advantage of the shelf registration rule (Rule 415) to cut their underwriting costs. They have also sought to raise funds in public markets, where possible, circumventing more costly borrowing through financial intermediaries.

This has been especially apparent in recent years, as indicated in Table 15–6. As the corporate bond market has expanded, the share of corporate debt financing accounted for by bank loans has declined. In particular, issuance of bonds and commercial paper by the most creditworthy corporations has eroded banks' traditional lending relationships with their prime customers. These developments, combined with competition from foreign banks and other financial institutions, have turned prime lending into more of a low-margin commodity business. The banks have thus been forced to turn to lower grade credits in an attempt to maintain their profitability.

The Influence of Capital Market Conditions on the Junk Bond Market

The same factors that have molded capital market developments more generally have been important contributors to the recent growth of the junk bond market. Let us consider in turn the impact of these factors on investors, underwriters, and issuers of junk bonds.

TABLE 15–6
Composition of credit market debt raised by U.S. nonfinancial corporations

	Period	
	1977–83	*1984–87*
Total credit market debt raised ($ billion)	$473.9	$640.3
Proportion of credit market debt accounted for by		
Bank loans	36.6%	18.0%
Commercial paper	5.2	4.6
Finance company loans	7.8	9.0
Tax-exempt bonds	14.7	5.0
Corporate bonds	30.5	53.3
Mortgages	−4.4	5.1
Other	9.6	5.1
Total	100.0	100.0
Note: Credit market debt as a percentage of total sources of funds	20.6	32.9

Source: Federal Reserve Flow of Funds Accounts

Hurt by unexpected inflation during the 1970s, investors have sought higher returns and greater flexibility. Thus junk bonds, with their premium yields and shorter durations, grew more attractive by the late 1970s. This attractiveness was enhanced by the widely noticed performance of Keystone's B4 Fund, a pioneer junk bond fund that inspired the start-up of other such funds.

Investors also found that traditional loss-protection measures were inadequate in a rapidly changing environment. High credit quality, for example, offered little protection against volatile interest rates. Similarly, restrictive covenants in bond indentures proved insufficient to guard against the losses imposed by massive corporate restructurings (Prokesch, 1986). As a result, investors have increasingly emphasized liquidity relative to credit quality or contractual provisions. Despite their higher default risk and fewer restrictive covenants than other corporate bonds, junk bonds' attractiveness to investors has been greatly enhanced by the development of a liquid secondary market.

In this sense, the rise of the junk bond market has paralleled the "securitization" phenomenon more generally. Because little or no secondary market existed, mortgages, auto loans, and other receivables were formerly held to maturity by their originators or by specialized intermediaries. Increasingly, however, they have been packaged as asset-producing securities, and a more active secondary market has developed. In a similar vein, junk bonds are akin to medium- to long-term loans that might formerly have been originated and held by commercial banks and insurance companies. With the development of a secondary market, however, they are now more widely traded.

Changing capital market conditions have also rapidly eroded the stigma that was formerly attached to junk bond underwriting and trading. As in commercial banking, prime quality underwriting has become more of low margin business as worldwide competition, shelf registration, and issuer pressure have all combined to squeeze profits. This has in turn sparked a search for new opportunities. Merger and acquisition advising is one such opportunity that has been pursued by many securities firms. Providing investment banking services to below-investment grade companies, which comprise about 95 percent of all U.S. corporations, is another natural target.

The latter opportunity was especially attractive to the firm of Drexel Burnham Lambert in the late 1970s, since it did not have a strong investment grade client base. It did, however, have a well-established junk bond trading operation under the direction of Michael Milken. Thus it had already developed a network of investors and an expertise in secondary market-making.

When Drexel Burnham began underwriting junk bonds in 1977, therefore, it was able to provide investors with the liquidity they needed to make these securities attractive. Drexel quickly became—and remains today—the leading underwriter of junk bonds, but other firms have recognized the potential profitability of the business and have entered the market as well.

Junk bonds also afforded Drexel Burnham a way to enter the lucrative merger and acquisition business and thus to participate in the restructuring boom. The firm began financing leveraged buyouts with junk bonds in 1981 and hostile takeover bids in late 1983. Drexel was able to capitalize on its established investor network to mobilize large amounts of funds within very short periods. Again, competitors have either followed suit or come up with alternative means of raising cash quickly, such as committing their own capital in the form of "bridge loans.'

Finally, capital market conditions of recent years have also enhanced the appeal of junk bonds for issuers. Junk bond underwriting spreads are high, typically falling in the three to four percent range, compared to less than one percent for investment grade issues (Sender, 1987). Still, there are reasons to believe that junk bond financing can offer cost advantages to issuers.

Investors appear to be willing to accept lower expected returns in exchange for greater liquidity, for example (Amihud and Mendelson, 1986). Hence, investors' ability to trade their bonds in a secondary market can lower the cost of junk bond financing relative to negotiated debt, for which secondary trading is thin or nonexistent. This should be particularly the case in recent years, as volatile market conditions have dictated increased investor emphasis on liquidity.

In addition, rapidly changing financing needs and competitive situations have necessitated flexibility for issuing corporations. In this respect, the implicit cost of junk bond financing may have been less than that of other sources in recent years. For example, junk bonds have allowed lower grade firms to raise larger amounts of money in a shorter period than would be possible from negotiated sources. Junk bonds also tend to have fewer restrictive covenants and more liberal call provisions than many types of negotiated debt. Recent market conditions have apparently created a willingness on the part of some investors to make these concessions in exchange for greater liquidity. In fact, it could be argued that investors' demand for liquidity has greatly facilitated the placement of junk bonds from the largest leveraged buyouts.

THE ROLE OF JUNK BONDS IN CORPORATE FINANCIAL POLICY

Given that junk bonds have established a solid position in the corporate debt market, we now examine their role in corporate financial policy. When should a corporation consider issuing junk bonds?

Stewart Myers' (1984) "pecking order" theory provides a useful starting point. Myers notes that a firm's managers typically know more about its true value than other capital market participants. If the managers act in the interests of their existing shareholders, they will thus try to issue securities at times when they know them to be overvalued. Realizing this incentive, however, market participants will then interpret securities issues as a sign that they are overvalued. That in turn reduces the amounts they are willing to pay for the securities.

This problem of information gives rise to a pecking order of sources of funds. Internally generated funds are unaffected by the problem, since their use entails no new securities issues. The closer a company's debt securities are to being riskless, the less severe is this problem as well. This is because the value of riskless securities will be unaffected by revisions in the estimated value of the company's assets. Riskier securities such as equity will clearly be affected by investors' perceptions of firm value. Since the mere fact of their issuance is likely to lead to downward revisions in their value, managers will be reluctant to issue these securities. The pecking order, then, implies the following rules for financial policy:

1. Use internal funds first, until these have been exhausted.

2. To the extent that external funds must be relied upon, issue debt first, the less risky the better.

3. Issue common stock only as a last resort, after all debt capacity has been exhausted.

Junk bonds occupy an intermediate position in this pecking order. They are more susceptible to the investor information problem than investment grade debt, but less so than common stock. For a firm that needs large amounts of external financing for its current investment plan, junk bonds can allow the firm to fully use its available debt capacity and thus avoid an equity issue.

At what point is debt capacity used up? While it is difficult to identify a given firm's optimal debt ratio with any precision, finance theory does suggest certain characteristics that will lead some firms to have higher debt capacities than others.[5]

The first of these is the firm's tax paying status. The tax deductibility of interest is one of the potential advantages of debt. However, firms pay for this advantage, because the more debt they issue in the aggregate, the more they bid up the returns on debt securities relative to equity. Thus firms that already have large tax shields (e.g., from depreciation and loss carry-forwards) relative to their cash flow would find little tax benefit from additional debt, even though they would be implicitly paying for this benefit. For such firms, debt capacity is likely to be relatively low.[6]

A second important determinant of debt capacity is the riskiness of the firm's assets. The costs of bankruptcy and of resolving conflicts of interest among security holders are closely related to the perceived probability of default. The fact that a company's bonds are rated below investment grade is, of course, itself an indication that perceived default is relatively high. Hence, issuers of junk bonds should carefully weight the potential costs of bankruptcy and claimholder conflicts against the dilution that might be entailed by an equity issue. In particular, a firm that plans to return to the debt markets on a regular basis in the future should be wary of increasing its debt ratio suddenly and sharply through the issuance of junk bonds today. To the extent that this undermines the value of its already outstanding bonds, the firm can expect investors to extract a penalty yield or more stringent covenants the next time it returns to the market. Indeed, bondholders have become increasingly sensitive to this issue in the wake of numerous recent restructuring transactions.

A third factor affecting a firm's debt capacity is the composition of its assets. A firm whose value stems largely from assets already in place is likely to have a greater debt capacity than one for which future investment opportunities comprise a substantial portion of current market value. This is because debt that is issued now can weaken the firm's incentive to undertake those future investments. The riskier the firm's currently outstanding debt, the more the future projects will tend to bolster the bondholders' position. Because they must share the value of these projects, however, equity holders' willingness to undertake them will be less than if they captured the entire value themselves. In the face of this potential problem, firms with significant future growth opportunities will tend to rely less heavily on debt financing today.

The foregoing analysis suggests that the ideal junk bond issuer is a firm that can take full advantage of the interest tax shield, that does not have a potential for severe bankruptcy costs or conflicts among security holders, and that has a total market value that is largely attributable to assets in place. One such firm would be the prototypical leveraged buyout candidate: a firm with a mature business that generates a high but relatively steady level of cash flows. Another might be a younger firm that has already cleared the hurdles of developing its product and establishing a market position but that now needs capital to finance its major expansion phase.

One other factor should also be considered by the potential junk bond issuer. The arguments advanced above concerning debt capacity and the pecking order of funds sources do not distinguish between public and private debt. Hence the issuer must decide whether it is better to rely on the public market or to negotiate a private agreement with a financial institution. The more highly the issuer values the flexibility entailed by call provisions and fewer restrictive covenants, the more the choice will tend toward public debt. The public market will also be favored the more investors are willing to make yield concessions in exchange for the possibility of secondary trading.

PUBLIC POLICY ISSUES

If junk bonds are simply one possible choice in an entire spectrum of funds sources, why have they aroused such controversy in public policy circles? The general economic conditions described above—especially worldwide competitive upheaval and uncertain inflation combined with interest rate volatility—have been accompanied by many painful dislocations. Although total employment has expanded, the wave of restructurings has brought plant closings and loss of jobs in a number of industries and localities. Changes in control have extended the threat to job security to the most senior executive ranks. Competition and volatile market conditions have also aroused fears over the safety of the financial system. These developments have in turn generated heated debate over such issues as industrial policy and the regulation of financial institutions. And because they are a highly visible product of the same economic forces that have caused these dislocations, junk bonds have become enmeshed in the same policy debates.

However, the true contribution of junk bonds to these perceived policy problems may be more symbolic than real. Their very label tends to surround junk bonds with the unsavory aura that makes them a convenient target. Their real influence is less easy to detect.

Consider, for example, the role of junk bonds in financing mergers and acquisitions. This has been the subject of several congressional hearings, and various restrictions on junk bond financing of hostile takeover bids have been proposed.[7] Sometimes lost amid the furor, though, is the fact that junk bonds do not account for the bulk of merger and acquisition or leveraged buyout financing. Firm statistics are difficult to come by, but it is estimated that in 1986 junk bond issues were related to 7.8 percent of the

$190 billion in total merger financing (*Mergers and Acquisitions*, 1987). This was up from 4.3 percent in 1985 and 2.6 percent in 1984. Merger and tender offer transactions accounted for approximately 41 percent of public junk bond issue proceeds in 1986. Moreover, even the giant leveraged buyouts proposed in recent weeks do not rely predominantly on junk bond financing. In Kohlberg Kravis Roberts' proposed $20 billion buyout of RJR Nabisco, it is estimated that one-quarter of the required financing will come from junk bonds while one-half will come from bank loans (Burrough, 1988). It cannot be denied that the availability of the junk bond market has strengthened the credibility of takeover threats, allowing larger amounts of funds to be raised in a shorter time period than was previously thought possible. Nevertheless, merger-related activity does not absorb a majority of the proceeds from junk bond issues, and bank loans are a bigger source of merger financing than junk bonds.

The junk bond market has also been discussed frequently in conjunction with the recent insider trading scandals and the ongoing SEC investigation into other alleged securities violations. However, as with mergers and acquisitions generally, the issue is broader than junk bonds. Tender offers can create opportunities for insider trading or other violations, but it is not clear why offers that will be financed with junk bonds are more susceptible to such opportunities than others.

Consider finally the connection between junk bonds and the safety of the financial system. Some have argued that junk bonds represent part of a general weakening of corporate financial strength in recent years. However, it is at least debatable whether such weakening has in fact occurred.[8] When measured in market value terms, the ratio of debt to total capital for U.S. nonfinancial corporations has actually declined by more than 20 percent since 1974, even in the wake of last year's stock market crash. Moreover, if it were conceded that U.S. corporations have relied too heavily on debt financing, it should be noted that junk bond issues account for less than ten percent of the total credit market debt that they have raised during the period from 1977 to 1987.

It has also been argued that junk bond investments can weaken the safety of financial institutions. Acting on these arguments the state of New York has recently moved to limit unapproved junk bond investments by insurance companies (Roberts, 1987). Given their default risk, it is of course true that an ill-conceived junk bond investment program can lead to trouble. But the number of ways to make risky investments is almost unlimited. They include, for example, issuing short-term debt and investing in long-term Treasury securities that are free of default risk. Limiting junk bond investments, but not other investments, is unlikely to significantly enhance the safety of financial institutions.

CONCLUSION

The rapid growth of the junk bond market has been impressive, but controversial. Most of the controversy stems from the fact that the market's development has coincided with the rise of such emotional policy issues as industrial restructuring and corporate control. It has been argued here, however, that the market is a product of the same forces—international competition, volatile capital market conditions, and the search for new fund sources—that have given rise to these policy issues. It is a symptom rather than a cause of those forces.

For the corporate treasurer, the development of this market represents a significant financial innovation. It allows companies that do not qualify for investment grade bond ratings to tap the public market and thus to take advantage of investors' willingness to pay for liquidity. For such firms, access to the junk bond market can be an important alternative to privately negotiated debt.

Notes

1. Because of its more widespread popular usage, the term junk bonds is used throughout this article.
2. A similar return relationship even prevailed during 1987, even though junk bonds were hurt by the October stock market crash. The return on the Drexel Burnham Lambert Composite Index of high-yield bonds was 5.41 percent for all of 1987, as opposed to –0.35 percent for comparable-duration Treasury bonds (for the fourth quarter alone, analogous return figures were 2.73 percent for junk bonds versus 6.73 percent for Treasuries).
3. In the Blume and Keim return calculations, default losses are already recognized to the extent that bonds in default are retained in the index as long as they have quoted market prices.

4. Over the period 1978–83, for example, Altman and Nammacher (1987) calculated an average duration of 8.53 years for bonds in the Shearson Lehman Long-Term Government Bond Index versus 6.64 years for their junk bond index. For further discussion and applications of the duration concept, see Schaefer (1984).
5. See Myers (1983) for a discussion of these characteristics.
6. Since the new tax law reduces nondebt tax shields by eliminating the Investment Tax Credit and lengthening allowable depreciation schedules, it may tend to increase debt capacity for many firms.
7. To date, the only restriction actually imposed has been the Federal Reserve Board's 1986 determination that a shell corporation, set up for the purpose of making a takeover bid, is subject to margin requirements under Regulation G. The impact of this ruling is limited, however, by numerous stated exceptions (Langley and Williams, 1986).
8. See, for example, Taggart (1986).

References

Altman, E. I. (July/August 1987). The anatomy of the high-yield bond market. *Financial Analysts Journal, 43*, 12–25.

Altman, E. I. (1988). Analyzing risks and returns in the high-yield bond market. *Financial Markets and Portfolio Management.* (Forthcoming).

Altman, E. I., and Nammacher, S. A. (1987). *Investing in junk bonds.* New York: John Wiley & Sons.

Amihud, Y., and Mendelson, H. (December 1986). Asset pricing and the bid-ask spread. *Journal of Financial Economics, 17,* 223–249.

Atkinson, T. R. (1967). *Trends in corporate bond quality.* New York: National Bureau of Economic Research.

Blume, M. E., and Keim, D. B. (July/August 1987). Lower grade bonds: Their risks and returns. *Financial Analysts Journal, 43*, 26–33.

Brancato, C. K. (October 1986). Corporate mergers and high-yield (junk) bonds: Recent market trends and regulatory developments. Washington, DC: Library of Congress, Congressional Research Service.

Burrough, B. (October 25, 1988). Offers for RJR pit KKR and Shearson in a battle for turf. *The Wall Street Journal.*

Drexel Burnham Lambert, Inc. (1988). *1988 annual high-yield market report.*

Forstmann, T. J. (October 25, 1988). Violating our rules of prudence. *The Wall Street Journal.*

Grant, J. (October, 25, 1988). Corporate finance, 'leveraged to the hilt': Will history repeat itself? *The Wall Street Journal.*

Langley, M., and Williams, J. D. (January 9, 1986). Fed board votes 3–2 to restrict the use of 'junk' bonds in takeovers. *The Wall Street Journal.*

Loeys, J. (November/December 1986). Low-grade bonds: A growing source of corporate funding. Federal Reserve Bank of Philadelphia *Business Review,* pp. 3–12.

Mergers & acquisitions. (May/June 1987). The growth of junk bonds. Vol. 21, p. 16.

Myers, S. C. (Spring 1983). The search for an optimal capital structure. *Midland Corporate Finance Journal, 1,* 6–16.

Myers, S. C. (June 1984). The capital structure puzzle. *Journal of Finance, 39,* 575–592. Reprinted (Fall 1985) in *Midland Corporate Finance Journal, 3,* 6–18.

Prokesch, S. (January 7, 1986). Merger wave: How stocks and bonds fare. *The New York Times.*

Rasky, S. F. (December 7, 1986). Tracking junk bond owners. *The New York Times.*

Roberts, J. L. (June 10, 1987). New York limits assets insurers put in junk bonds. *The Wall Street Journal.*

Rohatyn, F. G. (April 18, 1985). Junk bonds and other securities swill. *The Wall Street Journal.*

Schaefer, S. (Fall 1984). Immunization and duration. A review of theory, performance, and applications. *Midland Corporate Finance Journal, 2,* 41–58.

Sender, H. (March 1987). Don't junk the high-yield market yet. *Institutional Investor, 21,* 163–166.

Smith, R. (December 4, 1986). Junk bonds lag market since Boesky case, but exact gap proves difficult to measure. *The Wall Street Journal.*

Smith, R. (February 18, 1987). Junk bonds retain strength and discount latest fallout from insider trading scandal. *The Wall Street Journal.*

Taggart, R. A., Jr. (May/June 1986). Corporate financing: Too much debt? *Financial Analysts Journal, 42,* 35–42.

Taggart, R. A., Jr. (1988). The growth of the 'junk' bond market and its role in financing takeovers. In A. J. Auerbach (ed.) *Mergers and acquisitions,* Chicago: University of Chicago Press.

CHAPTER 16

HIGH-YIELD DEBT AS A SUBSTITUTE FOR BANK LOANS[*]

Arie L. Melnik[†]
Steven E. Plaut[‡]

INTRODUCTION

In recent years, American corporations have been expanding their use of debt financing. The increasing role of debt has manifested itself in both traditional instruments, such as bank loans, and also in newer types of securities. In particular, the market for low-grade bonds has expanded dramatically. Over the last decade, this market has grown more than 20-fold. Today there are about $150 billion of low-grade bonds outstanding, representing about one sixth of all corporate debt securities.

The rapid growth in the market share of low-quality, high-yield bonds has important implications. First, there is growing concern that very large quantities of high-risk debt may threaten financial stability. As noted by Bernanke (1983), this danger would be particularly acute during periods of macroeconomic slowdown. Second, the growth of the high-risk bond

[*]The authors are indebted to Ed Altman for valuable discussions, insights, and advice.
[†]Arie L. Melnik is Adjunct Professor of Economics, Haifa University and New York University.
[‡]Steven E. Plaut is affiliated with the University of California, Berkeley.

market may be associated with an increase in the riskiness of the portfolios of many institutional investors including thrifts, pension funds, etc. While recent studies by Altman and Nammacher (1985, 1987) and Blume and Keim (1987) suggest that this has not become a serious problem due to portfolio diversification, it continues to attract public attention. Another issue of major policy concern, discussed recently by Taggart (1986), is the role of high-yield bonds in financing mergers and acquisitions.

The expansion of the high-yield bond market represents a marked diversion from traditional methods of corporate debt financing. Specifically, such bonds have to a large extent replaced bank loans for some categories of borrowers. This debt-debt substitution has not received much attention in the academic literature and is the focus of this paper.[1] It has two important implications. First, as noted by Loeys (1986), this substitution has meant that large groups of smaller and riskier borrowers have gained access to previously closed markets. Second, the move towards directly issued low-grade debt securities reduces the market role of commercial banks.

In this chapter, we develop a model that explains how the debt market is segmented between bank lending and directly issued high-yield securities. We show that asymmetric information and regulation together create a market equilibrium, where the lower quality borrowers raise funds through issuing securities rather than borrowing from banks. This adverse selection of debt security issues implies that these will be higher-risk instruments paying a higher yield than comparable bank loans. We show that changes in regulation can explain shifts in the market shares of the two financing methods. In particular, we show that the recent growth of high-yield bonds may be due to the increase in regulatory costs imposed upon banks. Higher regulatory costs offset some of the informational advantage of bank loan processing. As banks lose competitive advantage, bank loans are replaced by high-yield bonds.

In the next section, we review the changing structure of the American corporate debt market. Following that we construct a model of alternative debt financing systems. The model is then used to derive propositions about the segmentation of the market between bank loans and high-yield bonds. The effects of bank regulation on market segmentation are then examined. Finally, the effect of shifts in market segmentation on default incidence is explored.

THE CHANGING STRUCTURE OF CORPORATE DEBT

Traditionally the bulk of corporate financing was done through bank lending. The direct issuing of securities by corporate borrowers was limited to only a small subsegment of the market. These were generally the large, well-known corporations with investment-grade ratings. In recent years, however, a process of increasing disintermediation and securitization has been observed for different segments of the borrower spectrum. In particular, this has been manifested in the growing role of low-grade corporate securities.[2] The growth of this market has been accompanied by a reduction in the financial market share of bank loans.[3] This shift has important implications with respect to the profitability of financial institutions, corporate capital structure, and the stability of the financial system.

While low-grade bonds have expanded rapidly over the past decade, they have in fact existed for a long time. Corporate financing through high-yield debt was common in the 1910s and 1920s. In the 1930s, many high-grade bonds were downgraded as the financial stress associated with the economic depression spread and default rates increased. From then on and until 1977, low-quality bonds consisted mostly of "fallen angels," or bonds with initially high investment ratings that deteriorated over time. Since 1977, annual new issue volume of low-quality bonds has risen from $1.1 billion to $34 billion in 1986. The total stock of these outstanding bonds was about $140 billion in 1987. Low-rated debt grew from 3.7% of all public straight debt in 1977 to 18.0% in 1986.

According to Altman and Nammacher (1986), the high-yield market at the end of 1985 included 1,170 issues with an average issue size of 63.7 million dollars. That paper documents changes that have transpired in the identity of these bond issuers. The typical (median) new issuer in 1985 was a firm 26 years old with $410 million in assets. The average yield to maturity that year was 14.7%. The investor side of the market is heterogeneous. According to Taggart (1986), institutional holders of low-grade bonds include pension funds, insurance companies, commercial banks, thrifts, and investment banking firms. Financial institutions are estimated to hold over 80% of all issues. In 1986, there were 67 mutual funds, with total assets of 32 billion dollars, specializing in high-yield bonds.

While outside the U.S. high-yield bond markets are less developed, they nevertheless exist. For example, in the international bond market during July and August of 1988, approximately 6% of the U.S. dollar and

Deutsche mark bonds were high-yield. The yields on these averaged 13.48% and 9.27%, respectively, compared with average yields of 9.81% and 6.61%, respectively, for these bond markets as a whole. Similarly, about 3 percent of the international Swiss franc bonds were high-yield; the yields on these averaged about 140 basis points above the market average. In contrast, we found no high-yield yen-denominated international bonds. In addition, there are high-yield governmental and government-backed international bonds which represent about 2.7% of all such bond issued during the period 1983-1987. According to the General Accounting Office (1988), about 3% of U.S .domestic high-yield debt is held by foreigners.

Following the rapid expansion of the high-yield bond market, attention is increasingly directed at a number of issues. One major line of inquiry concerns the risk-return characteristics of the market. Altman and Nammacher (1985, 1986) have analyzed the default characteristics of high-yield bonds in great depth. In general, they find that high-yield bond returns adjusted for default risk have compared favorably with those of higher grade bonds. Blume and Keim (1987) reached similar conclusions using a different methodology. A second issue of concern deals with the role of high-yield bonds in the financing of mergers and acquisitions. The expansion of the high-yield bond market has often been said to be the cause of the recent wave of hostile takeover attempts. Taggart (1986), however, notes that their role in financing mergers and acquisitions relative to the total scope of such activity is very small. Alternative forms of financing can and have been used for the same purposes.

An alternative set of issues involves the possible impact of high-yield bonds on the capital structure of firms. Here, there is concern that increasing corporate leverage could lead to financial instability. It has sometimes been argued that low-grade bond financing causes higher corporate leverage due to the substitution of debt for equity. A highly significant related issue concerns the role of high-yield bonds as an alternative to more traditional bank lending as a source for financial corporate borrowing. Jensen (1986), Loeys (1986), and Taggart (1986) have pointed out that high-yield bonds represent a substitute for bank loans and private placement. As such, the growth of the high-yield bond market constitutes an important form of securitization.

The reasons for the outstanding growth in the high-yield bond market have been debated in recent years. Some possible causes for this growth are reductions in the costs of issuing and trading of securities, better and more accessible information about borrowers and issuers, and changes in operating costs of financial intermediaries. These factors may explain the general trend towards securitization and expansion of the population of issuers for securities of all kinds. Other factors which may be relevant specifically for the high-yield bond market are discussed by Loeys (1986). These include changes in the demand (by lenders) for contractual restrictions, changes in information costs for smaller corporations, and changes in the perception of the riskiness of high-yield bonds.

In this chapter, we will argue that high-yield bonds function also as a substitute for traditional bank lending. Accordingly, the operating costs of banks — and in particular regulatory costs — represent a causal factor in the growth of the low-grade bond market. In the following model, the corporate debt market is assumed to be partitioned between two sets of transactions: commercial bank loans and securities. In reality, some corporations tap both markets. For purposes of simplicity, however, we will assume that every borrower is restricted to a single market.[4]

THE INSTITUTIONAL SETUP

In order to analyze the growth of the high-yield bond market, we will assume that the market for corporate debt consists of financial transactions that may take two alternative forms. In the first, corporate borrowers place their debt issues directly (or via underwriters) with portfolio managers or primary investors. In this case, banks do not play any intermediary role. In the second, primary investors lend to banks through deposits, and banks then lend to corporate borrowers. The first paradigm represents a form of securitization and will be referred to as SEC financing. In the second, which will be called INT financing, banks operate as financial intermediaries and traditional asset transformers.

Primary investors in our model are representative of real world institutional investors. They could include mutual funds that specialize in bond portfolios as well as individual investors. For simplicity, these investors will be characterized by risk neutrality. Their choice set for portfolio allocations includes a risk-free security such as a government bond, bonds issued by nonfinancial corporations that carry some default risk, and fully insured bank deposits.

Banks issue insured deposits and make commercial loans that carry default risk. They must comply with a set of regulations that are captured

FIGURE 16–1

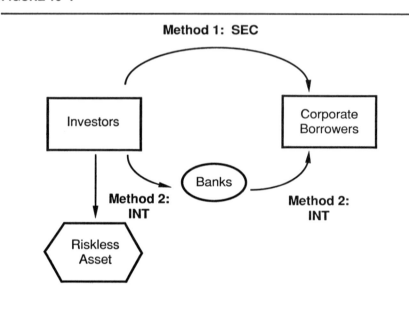

in our model by a minimum zero-interest reserve requirement. The reserve requirement, q, may be thought to represent all regulations that impose costs on the bank (such as capital requirements).[5] As in Fama (1985), these regulations will affect the market in the same way as a tax borne by commercial banks. We assume that banks never hold excess nor deficient reserves.

Banks are also assumed to be risk neutral. Bank equity plays no role in our model and therefore is assumed to be zero. Banks have a competitive advantage as lenders compared with primary investors. They are able to assess the default risk of corporate borrowers accurately while primary investors cannot. This advantage may stem from the maintenance of continuing bank-customer relationships. Because bank deposits are insured, they may be raised at the same interest as that paid on risk-free bonds, r_s. Since all lenders are risk neutral, borrowers must always provide them with an expected return of at least r_s or else they would refuse to lend.[6]

The markets for securities, deposits, and bank loans are perfectly competitive.   Corporate borrowers are highly heterogeneous, differing from one another with respect to default risk. Each borrower i is characterized by a parameter, π_i, which is the probability that a loan will be repaid. Hence, $1 - \pi_i$ is the probability of default. In the case of default, borrowers pay back zero to lenders, but also end up with zero profits. Default is viewed as a kind of "catastrophe" that occurs; it is not "chosen" rationally by the borrower. The probabilities, π_i, therefore are assumed to be exogenous, and unaffected by loan size or loan terms.[7]

Borrowers are distributed in such a way that a proportion, $f(\pi_i)$, is characterized by repayment probability, π_i. It is assumed that i, f, and π are continuous variables. π and f are continuously differentiable with respect to i. It therefore follows that $\int_0^1 f(\pi)d\pi = 1$. Aside from their π values, all corporate borrowers are indistinguishable in all other senses. For now they all seek to borrow exactly the same amount, say \$1, in all situations. (Below, they will have downward-sloping demand curves.)

Borrowers have no way to signal nor communicate their identity (or π value) to those who lack the prescience to "observe" it directly. In the real world, there are duration and maturity differences between bank loans and corporate bonds. We abstract from these differences for reasons of tractability. For simplicity we assume that all corporate borrowing, when it occurs, is for one period only, at the end of which the loan is either fully repaid with interest or complete default occurs.

Recall that banks are capable of assessing π values accurately and costlessly for all potential borrowers. Primary investors are incapable of doing so. They *are* capable of assessing the average group π value for their entire set of corporate borrowers, but cannot distinguish among individual borrowers. In effect, they form unbiased rational "forecasts" of the mean π value for these borrowers.[8] This group value would of course be taken into consideration when advancing loans to members of that group.

THE PRICING OF CORPORATE DEBT

We will consider loan and debt pricing under three sets of circumstances. First, we will consider what happens when all corporate borrowing is financed by banks (INT). We then consider what happens when all debt is placed directly with primary investors (SEC). Finally, we consider what happens when the two forms of funding coexist.

INT Financing

We assume for now that all corporate borrowing is from banks. Because deposits are insured, banks must pay depositors a rate of interest, r_s, compensating them for the opportunity cost of not holding the riskless government security. For each dollar borrowed, the bank is required to bear regulatory costs, q. This means that the total cost to the bank of obtaining funds necessary to advance \$1 in credit is $(1 + r_s)/(1 - q)$. That is because the bank must actually borrow $1/(1 - q)$ dollars in deposits in order to lend \$1, and must pay interest of r_s on its deposits.

Since the bank is risk neutral and is capable of assessing each borrower's π value accurately, bank loans to the ith customer must carry an interest rate, R_i, where

$$[1 + R_i]\,\pi_i = \frac{1 + r_s}{1 - q}\,. \tag{1}$$

On the right-hand side is the cost of funds to the bank and on the left is the expected return to the bank. There is a π_i probability of receiving the promised repayment of $(1 + R_i)$ and a $(1 - \pi_i)$ probability of receiving zero. Equation (1) must hold as a strict equality. This is because if the left-hand side were less than the right, banks would refrain from intermediating and from making the loans. If the left-hand side were strictly greater than the right, then competing banks would have motivation to underbid, driving down R_i. It is noted that R_i is an inverse convex function of π_i, where $\partial R_i / \partial \pi_i < 0$ and $\partial^2 R_i / \partial(\pi_i)^2 > 0$. That is, the cost of bank loans declines with the repayment probability, but at a diminishing pace.

SEC Financing

We now assume that all corporate borrowing is through direct SEC placement of debt with investors without financial intermediation. These investors, it is recalled, cannot assess the π values of borrowers accurately. They can only ascertain the mean value of π for a set of corporate borrowers. This mean value would be

$$\bar{\pi} = \int_0^1 \pi f(\pi)\,d\pi \tag{2}$$

for the entire population of borrowers.

Investors will offer this group of borrowers loans at interest $\bar{R}$, where

$$[1 + \bar{R}]\,\bar{\pi} = 1 + r_s. \tag{3}$$

The left-hand side of (3) is the average rate of return on corporate lending and the right-hand side is the opportunity cost of funds lent. As in the previous case, the equality in (3) follows from risk neutrality and competition. It is emphasized that investors suffer losses on funds advanced to poor credit risks (those with low π values), but make excess profits on funds advanced to good risks. Since borrowers cannot be distinguished from one another, lenders "break even" for the group of borrowers as a whole. All SEC borrowers would receive loans at identical terms. This follows from our simplifying assumption that SEC lenders have no information about individual borrowers.[9]

Coexistence of INT and SEC Financing

We now allow both INT bank lending and SEC direct placement of corporate debt to coexist. Once borrowers may choose between issuing debt to portfolio managers and borrowing from banks, they will use the source of funds that is cheapest. It follows from the above assumptions that the market described will be segmented in such a way that the better borrowers obtain funds from banks, and the worse issue their own securities.

The reason for this is that there exists a problem of adverse selection for the SEC financing paradigm. The worst credit risks, i.e., the borrowers with the lowest π values, will always use the SEC method rather than the INT method of borrowing from banks. They know that banks can discern borrower risk better and hence would charge them very high interest rates, whereas under SEC financing they can borrow at the same terms as all other SEC borrowers. Formally, if the going interest rate for SEC borrowing were some R, then all corporate customers who can borrow from banks at a lower rate will do so. From (1), these will include all borrowers for whom

$$\pi_i \geq \frac{1 + r_s}{(1 + R)(1 - q)}.$$

All other borrowers with *smaller* π values will use SEC financing.

This means that the market for corporate debt will be partitioned or segmented. If borrowers are arranged according to repayment probability from the lowest to the highest as in Figure 16–2, then the lowest-quality, highest-risk borrowers will use SEC financing. Safer borrowers will use INT financing. Since borrowers are partitioned in this way, we will refer to the "cutoff" borrower as that whose repayment probability is π^*. This borrower is indifferent between the two forms of financing. All borrowers with π values between 0 and π^* will use SEC financing and all others will borrow from banks. The average repayment probability for all SEC borrowers is now

$$P = \int_0^{\pi*} \pi f(\pi)\, d\pi\ . \tag{4}$$

SEC lenders assess this P accurately. The average repayment rate for SEC borrowers, P, must be lower than the average across *all* corporate borrowers, $\bar{\pi}$ [as seen in equation (2)]. When the partition point π^* shifts, it alters P but not $\bar{\pi}$.

FIGURE 16–2
Segmentation of the market for corporate debt

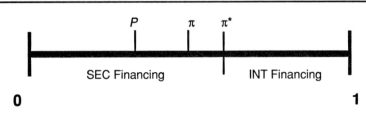

In order for expected profits to be zero, the equilibrium interest rate in SEC financing, denoted R^*, must satisfy

$$(1 + R^*)P = 1 + r_s. \tag{5}$$

It is noted that since P rises (falls) with π^*, R^* falls (rises) when the partition cutoff increases (decreases). That means SEC borrowers become a less risky class when the partition shifts to the right.

Now the partition is formed by the marginal "cutoff" borrower who is indifferent between the two methods of financing. This means that this cutoff borrower would be charged the same rate, R^*, by banks under INT financing and by primary lenders under SEC. R^* must satisfy (5) and [from equation (1)]:

$$[1 + R^*]\pi^* = \left[\frac{1 + r_s}{1 - q}\right]. \tag{6}$$

Combining (4), (5), and (6), we obtain

$$P = \int_0^{\pi^*} \pi f(\pi)\, d\pi = (1 - q)\pi^*. \tag{7}$$

Equation (7) is a necessary condition for π^* to be an equilibrium partition value. It can be shown that a sufficient condition is for (7) to hold together with

$$1 - q > \pi^* f(\pi^*). \tag{8}$$

In general, there need not be a unique equilibrium partition; there could be none, one, or many. It can be shown that there is at most one equilibrium partition whenever $[\partial f(\pi_i)] / [\partial \pi_i] < 0$ for all i. If there are no values for π that satisfy (7) and (8), then there is no internal equilibrium partition. In that case the market will be completely dominated by INT financing; no SEC financing at all will take place. In the discussion below, it will be assumed that there exists exactly one equilibrium partition point.

The above discussion leads to the following:

Proposition I: The market for securitized bonds will consist of high-yield, high-risk instruments, compared with bank loans.

Proof: It should be noted that the interest rate on SEC financing, which involves lending to the borrower segment of $0 < \pi_i < \pi^*$, carries an interest rate, R^*, that is *necessarily* higher than those rates charged by banks for INT loans. The reason is that the cutoff INT borrower would be charged R^*, but all INT borrowers whose π values exceed π^* would be charged [from (1)] less than R^*. Since INT finance is restricted to these borrowers, SEC securities will have high risk and high (promised) yield compared to bank loans   Q.E.D.

To summarize, whenever both SEC and INT forms of financing short-term corporate debt coexist, SEC securities will consist of high-risk, high-(promised) yield bonds. The market will be segmented so that safer corporate borrowers take bank loans. SEC financing will be restricted to low-quality bond issuers.

THE EFFECT OF REGULATION ON MARKET SEGMENTATION

We now wish to address the question of how changes in the bank regulatory environment affect market segmentation. Recall that such changes are captured in the reserve requirement ratio, q. While q is defined as the required reserve ratio, it can capture any increase in bank operating costs caused by regulatory changes. In particular, to the extent that the phasing out of Reg Q and the introduction of capital requirements caused bank cost of funds to rise in recent years, these cost increases may be analyzed in our model through increases in q. Indeed, according to Baer and Pavel (1988), regulatory taxes on American commercial banks have grown steadily since 1981, primarily due to capital requirements (but also due to changes in the tax treatment of municipal securities).

It is recalled that the first-order condition that describes the partition cutoff point that segments the market is equation (7), which can be rewritten

$$P = \int_0^{\pi^*} \pi f(\pi)d\pi - (1-q)\pi^* = 0 . \qquad (9)$$

It will be assumed that the second-order condition holds and that the partition is unique. Note that since r_s does not enter equation (9), market-wide changes in interest rates (as captured by r_s) have no effect on the partitioning. Therefore, the market share of high-yield bonds is independent of the general level of interest rates.

Proposition II: Increases (decreases) in the regulatory cost variable, q, cause the market share of directly issued bonds to increase (decrease) relative to bank lending.

Proof: Totally differentiating (9) yields

$$\pi^* f(\pi^*)d\pi^* - (1 - q)d\pi^* + \pi^* \, dq = 0$$

or

$$\frac{d\pi^*}{dq} = \frac{\pi^*}{(1 - q) - \pi^* f(\pi^*)}. \tag{10}$$

The second-order condition (8) ensures that (10) is positive. Therefore the partition cutoff value of π^* rises (falls) when the reserve level q rises (falls). In effect, when q rises, the cost disadvantage of INT financing becomes more severe. Banks lose market share to SEC financing when q increases, represented by a shift of the partition value π^* to the right, reducing the share of INT financing (see Figure 16–3).   Q.E.D.

FIGURE 16–3
Shift in market segmentation from increasing reserve requirements

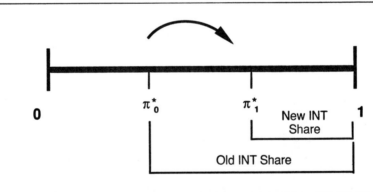

Proposition III: As q rises (falls), the average riskiness of directly issued bonds falls (rises).

Proof: P would shift in the same direction as π^* [which changes as in equation (10)], and so the *average* risk of SEC borrowers would fall when q rose. Low-grade bonds would become somewhat less "junky." Q.E.D.

Corollary: As q rises (falls), the interest rate on high-yield bonds falls (rises).

Proof: The impact of changes in reserve requirements on the SEC interest rate can be found by total differentiation of equation (5), applying the chain rule, and making use of (10):

$$\frac{dR^*}{dq} = - \frac{(1 + r_s)}{P^2} - \pi^* f(\pi^*) \frac{d\pi^*}{dq}.$$ (11)

Since, as noted above, $d\pi^* / dq$ must be positive, the entire expression in (11) is negative. This means that any increase (decrease) in regulatory costs will produce a fall (rise) in the interest rate paid by SEC bond issuers. In effect there is a supply shift away from INT financing toward SEC debt issues when q rises.   Q.E.D.

An increase in the reserve requirement leads to an expansion in the use of SEC financing, to growth in the market for high-risk bonds, and to a reduction in their interest rate. This is all accompanied by a reduction in the average risk of SEC bond issues, as reflected in a fall in P. The impact of changes in the distribution of borrowers on segmentation is considered in the appendix.

DEFAULT INCIDENCE AND MARKET SEGMENTATION

Let us now change the assumption that all corporate borrowers seek to borrow a fixed sum ($1). Instead, each borrower will now have a demand curve of the following form:

$$B_i = \rho - R_i.$$ (12)

Here, B_i is the amount of funds borrowed by the ith borrower, assumed to be a fraction of $1 million, and ρ is some parameter, constant across borrowers. R_i is the interest rate paid by borrower i. The total amount of funds borrowed would be

$$B = \int_0^1 B_i f(i) di = (1 + \rho) - \int_0^1 (1 + R_i) f(i) di.$$

As we have seen, the market will be segmented so that up to some partition value, π^*, all borrowers issue securities, while above π^* borrowing is from banks. The former borrowers pay the rate, $R_i = R^*$, that solves equation (5). The latter pay R_i, where R_i solves equation (1). Using equations (1) and (5), the total amount of funds borrowed by corporate borrowers is therefore

$$B = 1 + \rho - \int_0^{\pi^*} (1 + R^*) f(\pi) d\pi$$

$$- \int_{\pi^*}^1 \frac{1 + r_s}{(1 - q)\pi} f(\pi) d\pi. \tag{13}$$

It is noted that shifts in the segmentation partition (π^*) affect the total amount of funds borrowed, because some borrowers move along their loan demand curve when the interest rate changes.

Let us define D as the expected fraction of all funds borrowed by all corporate borrowers that are lost in default. For each category i, $(1 - \pi_i)$ is lost in default. Therefore, the aggregate proportion of all funds lent that are lost in default (for all corporate borrowers) is

$$D = \frac{(1+\rho)(1-\bar{\pi}) - \int_0^{\pi^*} (1+R^*)(1-\pi) f(\pi) d\pi - \int_{\pi^*}^1 \frac{(1+r_s)(1-\pi)}{(1-q)\pi} f(\pi) d\pi.}{B} \tag{14}$$

where $\bar{\pi}$ is the mean π for all borrowers and where B is defined in equation (13). The numerator of (14) is the expected number of dollars lost in default.

Proposition IV: Whenever the regulatory cost variable q increases (decreases), causing the "market share" of SEC financing to increase (decrease), the incidence of default risk (D) increases (decreases).

Proof: Consider the impact on D of a small change in q. The impact could be expressed as the following:

$$\frac{dD}{dq} = \frac{\partial D}{\partial q} + \frac{\partial D}{\partial \pi^*} \frac{d\pi^*}{dq} + \frac{\partial D}{\partial P} \frac{dP}{dq}, \tag{15}$$

where $d\pi^*/dq$ is given in equation (10). The second term on the right-hand side of equation (15) can be shown to vanish because $\partial D/\partial \pi^* = 0$. Therefore

$$\frac{dD}{dq} = \frac{\partial D}{\partial q} + \frac{\partial D}{\partial P}\frac{dP}{dq}, \tag{15'}$$

Now the first term on the right-hand side of (15') is proportional to

$$-\int_{\pi^*}^{1}\left[\frac{1}{\pi}[1-\pi-D]f(\pi)\right]d\pi. \tag{16}$$

Note that $(1 - \pi_i)$ is the default rate for category i borrowers. Since default rates for INT borrowers ($\pi^* \le \pi_i \le 1$) must be smaller than for the economy as a whole (D) due to the adverse selection of SEC customers, the term $[1 - \pi - D]$ in (16) must be negative and so (16) must be positive.

The last term in (15) has the same sign as dD/dP, and that is proportional to

$$\int_{0}^{\pi^*}(1-\pi-D)f(\pi)d\pi. \tag{17}$$

Over the range $0 \le \pi_i \le \pi^*$, the SEC borrower default risk $(1 - \pi_i)$ exceeds the aggregate default incidence D due to adverse selection for SEC financing, and so (17) is positive. Therefore (15) and (15') are positive.

Q.E.D.

Any change in the regulatory environment that increases the cost disadvantage of bank lending compared to SEC financing leads to an increase in the SEC "market share" and to an increase in the aggregate rate of default on corporate borrowing throughout the entire economy. In effect, capital funds are redirected away from the banking finance regime, and the reallocation leads to a growth in the incidence of corporate default.

Technological expansion or growth in the economy may be represented by a shift in the ρ parameter in the borrowers' demand function. When ρ rises, borrowing will rise in tandem for all customers at any given interest rate.

Proposition V: An upward shift in the demand for credit, as captured by an increase in ρ, must lead to an increase in the aggregate default incidence.

Proof: The impact of ρ on D is

$$\frac{\partial D}{\partial \rho} = \frac{1}{B} [(1 - \bar{\pi}) - D]. \tag{18}$$

π^* and P are not affected. The expression in brackets in (18) consists of the *unweighted* average default probability $(1 - \bar{\pi})$ minus the aggregate default incidence D. The latter is the average *weighted* default rate using borrowing amounts as weights. Now INT borrowers pay a lower interest rate than SEC borrowers and so borrow larger amounts. Therefore D is less than $(1 - \bar{\pi})$ and so (18) is positive.   Q.E.D.

CONCLUSION

The remarkable expansion in high-yield bond financing occurred at the same time that regulatory costs imposed on the commercial banking system in the United States were generally rising. These costs reduced the "comparative advantage" of the banks and created cost savings opportunities for borrowers financing through security issuing. It is notable that the growth in the high-yield market continued both during periods of high interest rates and low interest rates. While expanded securitization has occurred in many markets, for medium and long-term financing it has been most dramatic at the low end of the borrower-quality spectrum.

In this chapter, we have developed a model to explain the partitioning of the market for this corporate debt into two segments: bank lending and directly issued debt securities. We have shown that this segmentation leads to the emergence of the market for high-yield bonds. Due to asymmetric information the directly issued securities are restricted to the low-quality end of the risk spectrum. These bonds are shown to be both high-yield and high-risk compared to bank loans. The relative market shares of bank lending and high-yield securities are affected by regulation. As regulatory costs imposed on banks increase, the market for high-yield securities expands. At the same time, the average riskiness of high-yield bonds declines and the average promised yield falls. Finally, the overall incidence of default risk across the market increases when the high-yield bond market expands.

We now have a possible explanation for the growth in the market for high-risk debt securities in recent years. As some banking regulations have been tightened in recent years, as bank costs of funds have risen following phasing out of Reg Q and the introduction of capital requirements, there has been a shift in the segmentation of the market toward high-yield securitization. Our model predicts that the aggregate nationwide default incidence on corporate debt will increase whenever bank regulation is tightened or bank costs of funds rises. As the high-yield bond market expands, the bonds involved become somewhat less "junky", i.e., default rates fall somewhat, and the (promised) yield falls somewhat.

Our model might also explain differences in the use of high-yield bond financing across countries. The higher are reserve requirements and the tighter are other regulatory restrictions, the more high-yield bonds would be used as a source of financing. This might explain why the U.S. high-yield market is more developed than in some other Western countries.

APPENDIX TO CHAPTER 16

In this appendix, we will consider how changes in the distribution of corporate borrowers alter the market segmentation and pricing in the model.

1. *Changes in the Mean-Preserving Spread of* π.

Consider the variable π_i' defined as

$$\pi_i' = (1 + a)\pi_i - aE(\pi_i) ,$$

where a is some parameter and $E(\pi_i)$ is the mean value of π. Note that $E(\pi') = E(\pi_i)$ and that the variance $V(\pi_i') = (1 + a)^2 V(\pi_i)$.

We now assign π_i' to each borrower instead of his original π_i, assuming that the probability density function f remains the same as before. In effect we are transforming the distribution of repayment probabilities, keeping the mean constant but altering the variance.

For $a = 0$, equation (9) would of course still hold and the partition cutoff value would remain $\pi'* = \pi*$. Let us substitute π_i' for π_i and totally differentiate (9) with respect to $\pi*$ and a, evaluated at $a = 0$. We end up with $d\pi*/da$ being proportionate to $[\pi* - E(\pi)]$. The sign of this is positive (negative) whenever the partition cutoff value of π exceeds (is less than) the mean value.

Therefore, a mean-preserving increase in the spread of the π values, or an increase in borrower heterogeneity, will raise (lower) the partition whenever the partition value is more (less) than the mean repayment ratio. P would move in the same direction as π^* and the SEC interest rate would move in the opposite direction, reflecting changes in the riskiness of SEC borrowers.

2. Variance-Preserving Changes in the Mean of π

Now let us change the definition of π' to $\pi_i' = \pi_i + aE(\pi_i)$. Note that $V(\pi_i') = V(\pi_i)$, but that $E(\pi_i') = (1 + a)E(\pi_i)$.

Once again we substitute π' for each borrower's repayment probability. We differentiate (9) and evaluate for $a = 0$. The resulting $d\pi^* / da$ is proportionate to $-E(\pi_i)$, which is negative. Therefore, any increase (decrease) in the variance-preserving mean of π must decrease (increase) the partition value π^*. SEC borrowers would become more (less) risky as a group and the SEC interest rate would rise (fall).

Notes

1. A notable exception is Berlin and Loeys (1986).
2. Low-grade corporate bonds are generally defined as speculative bonds with a rating below BBB (Standard and Poor's) or Baa (Moody's), or unrated non-bank corporate debt. The low-rated bonds are grouped into several rating categories (e.g., BB, B, CCC, etc.). Different categories carry different yields on average. In our model, a simplified equilibrium will be described where all the high-yield bonds have the same yield. For an in-depth discussion of high-yield bonds ratings and yield distributions see Altman and Nammacher (1987).
3. For example, from 1986 to 1989, commercial credit extended through bank loans dropped from $69.5 billion to $39.3 billion. Over the same period, the volume of outstanding low-rated debt grew by about $60 billion.
4. While the same borrower may enter both markets, his riskiness and credit worthiness may be very different in each of the two due to differences in collateralization, restrictive covenants, debt seniority, etc. Hence, the dichotomy according to type of transaction rather than by the identity of borrowers is appropriate.
5. These costs reflect the broad spectrum of restriction, limitations, and regulations under which financial intermediaries operate. Within the model, it is easiest to think of q as a reserve requirement.
6. Note that in our model default risk is assumed to be independent of general market returns and risks on other assets. Therefore, co-variances of returns play no role in the model. While diversified portfolios of high-yield securities could be constructed to reduce investor exposure, our emphasis will be on default risks of individual instruments.

7. If default risk were to depend positively on loan size and interest, as in Stiglitz and Weiss (1981), our results below would still hold. In some cases, they would even be strengthened, as SEC financing would produce low-quality bonds with even higher default risks.
8. They are prohibited from hiring banks to collect information for them or from inferring information by observing bank lending.
9. If investors in SEC bonds had partial information about borrowers, then a heterogeneous securities market could emerge.

References

Altman, E. I., and Nammacher, S. A. (1987). *Investing in junk bonds: Inside the high-yield debt market.* New York: John Wiley & Sons.

Altman, E. I., and Nammacher, S. A. (1985a). *The default rate experience on high-yield corporate debt.* New York: Morgan Stanley & Co.

Altman, E. I., and Nammacher, S. A. (1985b). *Portfolio analysis of the high-yield debt market.* New York: Morgan Stanley & Co.

Baer, H. Z., and Pavel, C. A. (March/April 1988). Does regulation drive innovation? *Economic Perspectives.* Federal Reserve Bank of Chicago, 3–15.

Berlin, M., and Loeys, J. (1986). The choice between bonds and bank loans. Federal Reserve Bank of Philadelphia working paper No. 18.

Bernanke, B. S. (June 1983). Nonmonetary effects of the financial crisis in the propagation of the Great Depression. *American Economic Review,* 257–276.

Blume, M. E., and Keim, D. B. (July/August 1987). Lower-grade bonds: Their risks and returns. *Financial Analysts Journal,* 26–33.

Fama, E. (1985). What's different about banks? *Journal of Monetary Economics, 15,* 29–36.

Jensen, M. C. (July 1986). The takeover controversy: Analysis and evidence. Harvard Business School working paper.

Loeys, J. (November/December 1986). Low-grade bonds: A growing source of corporate funding. *Business Review.* Federal Reserve Bank of Philadelphia.

Stiglitz, J. E., and Weiss, A. (June 1981). Credit rationing in markets with imperfect information. *American Economic Review, 71,* 393–410.

Taggart, R. A., Jr. (September 1986). The growth of the 'junk' bond market and its role in financing takeovers. Boston University working paper.

Issuers, purchasers, and purposes of high-yield noninvestment grade bonds. (February 1988). Washington DC: Government Accounting Office Report GGD 88-SSFS.

CHAPTER 17

RECENT TRENDS IN CORPORATE LEVERAGE: CAUSES AND CONSEQUENCES

Ben S. Bernanke
John Y. Campbell[*]

Several financial innovations in the 1980s have encouraged American corporations to increase their use of debt. High-yield bonds, share repurchases, debt-financed takeovers, defenses against takeovers, and management buyouts have accompanied a steady increase in the interest burden of the corporate sector. These developments have aroused concern in the media, in Congress, and at the Federal Reserve Board.

We recently completed a study of trends in corporate leverage for the Brookings Institution.[1] Here we summarize our empirical findings (the first section following), discuss alternative explanations (second section), and briefly draw some lessons for the public policy debate (final section). Throughout, our focus is on the overall level of debt and not on the particular financial instruments or strategies used by corporations.

---

[*]Ben S. Bernanke and John Y. Campbell are both Professors of Economics and Public Affairs at Princeton University.

RECENT TRENDS

The Federal Reserve's Flow of Funds Accounts are the basic source of data on aggregate financial trends. The accounts show that corporate debt, measured at book value, has grown much faster than nominal GNP since the end of the 1981-82 recession. The cumulative growth rate of corporate debt over 1983-86 was about 45 percent, while nominal GNP grew by 29 percent. The growth rates in 1987 were 12 percent and 6 percent, respectively.

Although the growth of corporate debt has outpaced nominal GNP, it has not exceeded the growth of corporate equity values. The Flow of Funds Accounts show that the ratio of corporate debt to the sum of corporate debt and equity (the latter measured at market value) was 0.44 in 1982 and only 0.42 in 1986. In 1987, the ratio rose back to 0.44.

These aggregate data provide a snapshot of the state of corporate finance, but they are lacking in detail. Our Brookings study examined a sample of large, publicly traded corporations whose balance sheets are recorded on the COMPUSTAT data tape. The sample included about 700 firms in 1969, and grew to about 1,400 firms in 1986. For each firm, we constructed both "stock" measures of leverage (such as the debt-asset ratio, the ratio of the market value of debt to the market value of debt plus equity), and "flow" measures (such as the ratio of nominal interest expense to cash flow before interest, depreciation, and taxes).

As one would expect from the aggregate numbers discussed above, we found that debt-asset ratios have not risen much during the 1980s. But the ratio of interest expense to cash flow has increased to unprecedented levels. For the sample as a whole (that is, treating the interest and cash flow numbers as if they came from a single firm), the ratio was in the range 0.12 to 0.15 from 1969 to 1979. In 1982, during a severe recession, the ratio rose to 0.22; and in 1986, after several years of economic expansion, the ratio was still 0.20. The increase in the interest burden is even more pronounced among the more highly levered firms; the 90th percentile of the interest expense ratio never exceeded 0.53 in the 1970s, but it rose to 1.18 in 1982, and 1.65 in 1986.

How should one interpret these numbers, and in particular the contrast between relatively constant debt-asset ratios and sharply higher interest expense ratios? At a purely mechanical level, the discrepancy is due to the 1980s bull market in stocks, which has driven up price-earnings ratios. Corporate equity values have kept pace with the growth of debt, while both have outpaced earnings.

High stock prices embody market forecasts of robust growth in corporate earnings. If this growth is realized, then the interest expense ratio will return to more normal levels and the level of debt will not cause financial difficulties to corporations. On the other hand, there could be serious problems if a recession drives down earnings.

To get a better idea of the potential scope of these problems, we simulated the effects of a recession on our sample of firms. We asked what would happen if the changes in cash flow, stock prices, and interest rates that actually occurred in 1973-74 or 1981-82 were to occur again at the end of our sample in 1986. These two recessions had rather different effects in our simulations. In the 1973-74 scenario, the stock market declines sharply; we found that about 10 percent of firms would become at least technically insolvent because the market value of their assets would fall below the value of their debt. In the 1981-82 scenario, the stock market is fairly stable, but cash flow falls and interest rates rise; we found that about 10 percent of our firms would be unable to meet their interest obligations without further borrowing. The 1973-74 case would be a "solvency" crisis, while the 1981-82 case would be a potential "liquidity" crisis.

INTERPRETATION

What is responsible for the unusual increases in corporate debt that have occurred in the 1980s? An answer to this question is essential if we are to evaluate the costs and benefits to society of these developments.

The most straightforward view of corporate leverage is that it is determined by a balance between two opposing forces: the tax advantage to debt, on the one hand, and the cost of bankruptcy, on the other. According to this view, a shift toward increased use of debt must be due either to an increased tax advantage of debt, or reduced concern about bankruptcy, or both.

There is some debate about whether the tax advantages of debt have increased in the 1980s. The tax advantages of debt will be great when marginal corporate tax rates and the marginal tax rate paid by a stockholder on the dividends and capital gains she receives from the firm are high, relative to the rate paid by a bondholder on interest received. The Tax Reform Act of 1986 has lowered the marginal personal income tax rate and has increased the statutory rate of capital gains tax; on the other hand, it has reduced the statutory rate of corporate income tax from 46 percent to 34 percent. Overall, the effect on the incentive to issue debt depends on the tax rate of the marginal investor, and there is little agreement about what this tax rate is.

The tax advantages of debt are also increased by high inflation and nominal interest rates, since nominal interest payments are fully deductible even if in part they represent repayment of principal to compensate for inflation. The decline in inflation and nominal interest rates since the late 1970s is therefore a factor which works to reduce the tax advantages of corporate leverage.

However, there may be a more subtle way in which the tax advantages of debt have increased in the 1980s. Ten years ago many corporations believed that highly levered capital structures would provoke an Internal Revenue Service challenge to the deductibility of their interest payments, and that share repurchases would be treated by the IRS as equivalent to dividend payments. Over the last decade both these beliefs have been abandoned as the IRS has been "the dog that didn't bark."

The other side of the traditional coin is the constraint on leverage caused by expected bankruptcy costs which rise with the level of debt (because the probability of bankruptcy increases). It is sometimes argued that the expected bankruptcy costs of leverage have fallen in the 1980s because of the financial innovations associated with high-yield debt. For example, the practice of "strip financing," in which investors hold debt and equity in the outstanding proportions, blurs the distinction between debt and equity. In the event that the company experiences financial difficulties, there will be no costs caused by conflicts between equityholders and bondholders; these are the same people. Strip financing is a way to relabel "equity" as "debt," and to transform taxable "dividend" payments into tax-deductible "interest" payments. There are no extra bankruptcy costs associated with this type of leverage.

Even in the absence of strip financing, bankruptcy costs are reduced if the holders of corporate debt are a few large investors who can participate in a restructuring plan. In Germany and Japan, corporate debt-asset ratios are far higher than they are in the U.S., but bankruptcy costs are kept to a minimum because large banks play a leading role in the provision of finance and the management of the corporate sector. It is sometimes claimed that the development of the high-yield debt market has reduced bankruptcy costs in a similar way. The argument is not that the holders of high-yield debt could play the role of Japanese and German banks, since these investors are quite widely dispersed and include mutual funds, insurance companies, and other outsiders. Rather, it is argued that the investment banks who place the debt (or the LBO specialists who take companies private) would act to reduce bankruptcy costs in the event of financial difficulties.

So far we have not distinguished between the social costs of bankruptcy, and the costs to investors. But there have been two important changes in the 1980s which may have reduced the perceived costs of bankruptcy to investors, even if they have not reduced the true social costs of bankruptcy.

First, the constraints on lenders with fiduciary responsibilities have been relaxed in the 1980s. Pension funds, for example, have become more free to invest in low-grade corporate debt as the interpretation of the "prudent man" rule has become less strict.

Secondly, the deregulation of the financial system has worsened the well-known distortions caused by deposit insurance. Insured financial institutions have an incentive to make risky investments because their stockholders receive any unusual gains while the FDIC or FSLIC pays for any unusual losses. In a regulated environment, financial institutions are limited in their ability to respond to this incentive, and it is partially offset by monopoly profits which are created by regulatory barriers to entry. In the deregulated environment of the 1980s, banks and particularly savings and loans institutions find high-yield debt an attractive investment opportunity.

Tax and bankruptcy considerations are not the only factors which may influence the degree of corporate leverage. Recently Michael Jensen has emphasized the desirable incentive effects of debt. Corporate managers do not necessarily act in the interests of shareholders, and debt can be a powerful device which forces them to do so. In particular, in a mature industry with a large cash flow, such as the U.S. oil industry, the optimal policy for shareholders may be to pay out cash flow and let the corporation shrink. Debt contracts commit managers to pay out cash, rather than engaging in wasteful investments. Incentives are also an important advantage of management buyouts, which eliminate the distinction between managers and shareholders altogether.

This "back-to-the-wall" theory of corporate finance can explain the trends of the 1980s if manager-shareholder conflicts have become more serious in the last decade. But it is hard to know what direct evidence of this there might be.

LESSONS FOR PUBLIC POLICY

We have discussed a number of different reasons why the use of debt may have become increasingly attractive in the 1980s. Some of these are also considerations which should lead public policymakers to take a benign view of the increase in leverage. If the development of the high-yield debt market has reduced the costs associated with the failure of a corporation to meet its interest payments, or if the need for an effective set of managerial incentives has increased, then the use of debt benefits society as well as the parties involved.

In our view, however, the most important advantages which accrue to highly levered firms are private benefits but not social benefits. American corporations have learned that they can dramatically reduce their tax bills by borrowing, and American financial institutions have learned that the deposit insurance system rewards high-yield risky investment. Neither borrowers nor lenders are appropriately taking into account the social costs of leverage.

What are the social costs of increased leverage? It is important when discussing these not to fall into simple errors: For example, funds raised in financial markets to bankroll leveraged buyouts do not generally draw resources away from physical investment, since shareholders can be ex-pected to reinvest rather than consume most of what they get for their tendered shares. Similarly, the productive assets of bankrupt firms are not lost to society, even though ownership may change. And the legal and administrative costs of bankruptcy, although a drain on public resources such as the court system, are not sufficiently large to provoke concern.

The social costs of bankruptcy or financial distress lie not in these things, but in the potential disruption of firm operations or of the financial system. For example, it is possible that a few major bankruptcies could lead to a generalized "liquidity crisis," reminiscent of the Penn Central incident in 1970. Fundamentally solvent firms might in this case find themselves unable to undertake new borrowing or even to roll over maturing debt. The banking system, suddenly called upon to supply large amounts of liquidity under previously established lines of credit, might also find itself in trouble. This could have real effects on economic activity.

A second possibility is a "solvency crisis." Suppose that, for some set of reasons unrelated to financial structure, the economy were to enter a recession, leading to falling earnings and perhaps rising interest costs (as in

1973-74). Given high leverage inherited from the past, some firms could find it difficult to service debt on an ongoing basis. To make interest payments, they would likely have to cut back on investment commitments and possibly reduce employment, all of which would tend to exacerbate the .recession. Thus, with high initial leverage, any adverse shock to the economy might be "magnified." This increases the premium on avoiding recession in the first place; Ben Friedman has argued that this might have inflationary and other undesirable consequences.

It should also be kept in mind that, despite the emphasis of this paper on the debt of large corporations, and the recent attention in the media to takeovers and buyouts of very large firms, there are other sectors of the economy that are much more financially precarious than corporations. The savings and loan industry is the most obvious example. Possible interactions and contagion effects with other sectors—and the limited ability of policy-makers to deal with problems on several fronts simultaneously—increase the potential risks of corporate leverage.

For these reasons, it seems to us that there is an urgent need to reduce the distortions in our tax code and financial system which artificially encourage the use of debt contracts.

Notes

1. Ben S. Bernanke and John Y. Campbell (1988). "Is There a Corporate Debt Crisis?, *Brookings Papers on Economic Activity, 1*, 83–125.

CHAPTER 18

JUNK BONDS: IT'S TOO SOON TO TELL

*Seth A. Klarman**
Louis Lowenstein†

Warren Buffett has observed that you can get into more trouble with a good idea than a bad one, because the good idea may continue to be implemented well beyond its rational limitations. We believe this to be true of the tremendous growth in the market for newly issued high-yield bonds. The junk bond market has boomed for many reasons, among them the dissemination of potentially misleading information concerning the riskiness of junk bonds, the fact that these bonds have been issued only during economic good times accompanied by generally declining interest rates and rising values for corporate assets, and the great demand for these bonds by buyers using other people's money.

We believe the junk bond jury is still out. Only when junk bonds have been tested over a full economic cycle, or longer, we will be able to accurately evaluate the investment attractiveness of junk bonds. Until then we hope that accurate information concerning the risks of junk investing is widely disseminated and that we increase the accountability of those purchasing junk bonds with other people's money.

---

*Seth A. Klarman is Managing Director, The Baupost Group, Inc.
†Louis Lowenstein is Professor of Law at Columbia University.

The 1980s have witnessed an explosive growth of credit in many parts of society, including the government, consumer, and corporate sectors. The debate about corporate sector debt, which is our concern here, tends to focus heavily on takeovers and on public issue junk bonds. That tends to distort the analysis. For us, the issue is not takeovers as such or junk bonds as such, but the total amounts of debt incurred by particular companies from whatever source—banks or bonds—and for whatever purpose—takeovers, LBOs, or restructurings.

There are no black and white distinctions between junk loans by banks and junk bonds issued to mutual funds, thrifts, and insurance companies. The problem is not a junk bond problem, it's a junk credit problem. In most takeovers, over 50 percent of the debt is bank debt; the banks may be senior, but everyone is at risk. Having said that, nothing eharacterizes the easy availability of credit better than the junk bond market, where new issue volume has exploded from about $1 billion in 1981 to over $34 billion in 1986 and $31 billion last year. Investors are betting heavily that historical default rates on low-rated bonds accurately reflect the default risk of newly issued junk bonds.

RISKS OF JUNK BOND INVESTING

We believe that most newly issued junk bonds have significantly greater default risk and greater potential loss upon default than the pre-1980s junk bonds known as 'fallen angels.' Fallen angels are bonds of former investment grade credit which have declined in credit quality; they are usually moderate coupon bonds of a company trading well below par value. Frequently, fallen angels have substantial tangible assets behind them, assets which can be sold during economic hard times. Newly issued junk bonds usually have relatively few tangible assets behind them and far more goodwill. They also have a lot farther to fall, since they are issued at par. Fallen angels usually are not downgraded to below investment grade until the bonds have dropped well below par value. Another difference between the two is that the market usually has very low expectations for fallen angels and very high expectations for newly issued junk bonds. Financial market expectations are often inversely correlated with future returns. In any event, the return over past decades from fallen angels is not at all predictive of the risks or returns of today's different breed of newly issued junk bonds.

Many studies have demonstrated low historical default rates on low rated bonds, with corresponding high returns to investors. These studies have necessarily looked back at junk bonds during a period of explosive growth of new junk issuance and economic good times during which interest rates declined significantly. After six years of economic good times, when many companies would typically have built up cash reserves and tangible book value to withstand the inevitable business downturn, junk bond issuers are instead perched at the threshold of financial distress. Economic good times must continue for junk issuers to remain viable. Many issuers not only must continue to do well but, in fact, must do even better in order to meet their increasing debt burden which results from pay-in-kind and zero coupon obligations. This is a far cry from the fallen angel of yesteryear with low market expectations and more room for positive surprises.

If a personally euphoric outlook did not convince one to invest in junk bonds during these boom years, understatement of the the junk bond default rate may have done the trick. At best, default rates are a poor approximation of the risks of junk bond investment. We believe that because of the tremendous growth in junk bonds outstanding, calculations of the default rate are understated. Bonds do not default immediately; cash must be squandered, and business must worsen (or at least fail to improve), both of which take time. Thus the default numerator lags the rapidly growing total junk outstanding denominator in the default rate calculation. Furthermore, many recent junk issues are zero coupon, increasing rate, or pay-in-kind bonds, which are less likely than cash-pay bonds to default in the near-term. The possibility of default has been pushed back, but not reduced. Indeed, such securities may be more likely to default than cash-pay securities because the debt burden is growing and is not met from current cash flows. One should not take the absence of default during a period when default is being deferred as a sign of fiscal health. In other words, a junk bond issuer can be in real trouble long before it finally defaults.

Many troubled junk bond issues have in recent years undergone voluntary restructuring. Holders exchange their bonds for new securities, usually accepting less than par value in return. Although holders accept a loss to avoid a potentially greater decline from a default, voluntary restructurings are generally not included in default rate calculations. The default rate calculation thus understates losses and credit risk in the junk bond marketplace.

Because junk bond default rates may understate investors' losses, one calculation that might be of interest would be a calculation of the total return to investors from all the junk bonds issued in a given year. Such a calculation would incorporate bad news such as voluntary restructurings and market declines, as well as good news such as market price apprecia- tion, credit upgrades, and calls at a premium to par. The total return calculation, over a complete economic cycle of junk bond issuance and not just during the halcyon days, would provide a yardstick to investors of the yield necessary from junk paper to offset credit losses and market declines. Despite the tremendous amount of research involving junk bonds, it is unfortunate that a calculation of the total return from junk bond investing over the years has not been more publicly available.

OWNERSHIP OF JUNK BONDS

A high percentage of junk bonds outstanding are owned by thrift institu- tions, insurance companies, and mutual funds. Thrifts and insurance companies are attracted to junk bonds by the prospect of high current returns. Federal insurance of thrift deposits had tended to foster a "heads I win, tails you lose" attitude in thrift executives vis-à-vis the U.S. govern- ment. If they buy junk bonds, they currently earn fat spreads and fat salaries. If the bonds don't default, they earn high returns and become rich. If the junk bonds eventually default, the government bears virtually all of the losses. Remember that thrifts are in business and are able to attract relatively low-cost deposits only because of the FSLIC insurance. If depositors were obliged to evaluate the creditworthiness of a thrift institu- tion to determine the safety of their money, the mattress industry would have a banner year. Certainly the depositors would never accept the risk of junk bond assets without junk bond returns.

Many insurance companies invest policyholders' funds in junk bonds. Policyholders assume that insurers are investing their money prudently, and have virtually no knowledge of the insurer's assets underlying their policy. The lure of high current returns and a low historical default rate is hard for many insurance companies to resist.

Mutual funds are another major receptacle for junk bonds. Individual investors have believed the mutual fund sales pitch promising professional management, diversification, liquidity, and double digit yields. We don't think the risks have been adequately spelled out. For example, today's junk bond market is notoriously illiquid, because the distribution of the securities is not widespread. Compounding this problem is the fact that some of the open-end mutual funds are more than 90 percent invested, trying to maximize yield. Too little attention has been given to this lack of liquidity. Ben Graham pointed out over 50 years ago that low-grade bonds constitute a relatively unpopular form of investment. If there is an economic downturn, and if investors in high-yield mutual funds want to get out, we may have once again the picture of large elephants trying to squeeze through small doors that we saw in the stock market crash of 1987. Since few of the junk bond mutual funds have significant cash reserves, when investors want their money, *the funds will have to sell, regardless of price.*

Very simply, the junk bond mutual fund business is driven by the appearance of earnings rather than the substance. Mutual funds are one of the largest participants in the junk bond market, owning about 30 percent of the total junk bonds outstanding. What sells these so-called high-yield mutual funds is their advertised yield. The yield is about all that counts. And just as in the 1960s and 1920s, the accountants are letting operators hide behind old rules to conceal new tricks.

The trick here is quite simple. For a moment, assume you own all of Federated Department Stores, with no debt at all. You would be earning about $400 million before taxes. Not bad, but that's all you earn. Now watch what happens when we repackage Federated with junk bond financing. Because Federated has promised to pay interest at the rate of $600 million a year, some in cash, some not, institutional investors are telling the world that they are earning *from Federated* 50 percent more than Federated itself is earning. A dollar there is turned into a dollar and a half here. Not since the alchemists turned base metals into gold has there been anything like it. Even then it was not so richly rewarding.

If Federated has earnings of $400 million, and if the senior lenders have claims on the earnings that equal or exceed that amount, then what the junior bondholders as a group have bought is at best a common stock. As common stock, there would be little confusion about the lack of earnings. (Common stock would, in fact, be the superior security, because the investors would have voting control and would also own the entire claim to the earnings in excess of $400 million, not just a slice of it.) But when a clearly paupered common stock is dressed up to look like a princely bond, there is the opportunity for deception. You can put a 14 percent coupon on that bond. You can put a 17-3/4 percent coupon on it, as Federated did. But if there are no earnings for that junior bondholder, the more likely it is that investors will be misled by the form of the instrument.

ALLEGED MACROECONOMIC BENEFITS OF JUNK BOND ISSUANCE

Glen Yago has argued that companies which issued junk bonds from 1980-1986 grew faster than industry in general in several 'key' measures including employment, productivity, sales, and capital investment. Yago concludes that junk securities hold the key for America to recover its economic leadership in the world.

We take issue with Yago from two perspectives. First, Yago is asking the wrong question. He has focused on a handful of short-term measures to argue the macroeconomic benefits of junk bond issuance. Even if Yago is correct, which we doubt, a more important question needs to be answered first. This concerns whether junk bonds are an attractive investment opportunity for buyers and an attractive way for issuers to raise capital. If a few years from now, issuers won't issue or, as is more likely, buyers won't buy, then Yago's macroeconomic arguments are a moot point. Only if junk bonds are attractive to purchasers as well as issuers is there a reason to even consider Yago's arguments. And on this matter, we believe the junk bond jury is still out. We will not be able to accurately evaluate the investment attractiveness of junk bonds until they have been tested over a full economic cycle, or longer.

Even if junk bonds do pass the test of investment attractiveness over time, we take issue with Yago's arguments concerning the macroeconomic benefits of junk bond issuance. Yago points out that high-yield companies have increased employment faster than industry average. This is not surprising, as companies that raise capital, whether through debt or equity, are likely to use it to grow. Some junk bond issuers grow internally, others through acquisition. Yago does not distinguish between the two, even though growth through acquisition is of minimal (if any) macroeconomic value compared with internally generated increases.

We also question the relevance of employment data viewed alone. Not all new jobs contribute equal value to our economy. First Jersey Securities raised money for numerous small 'growth' companies, many of which were corporate shells, blind pools, and businesses of marginal reputation. Are these jobs as good as any? Are the jobs created by First Jersey themselves for boiler room securities salesmen valuable for our economy?

Yago's sales growth and growth in invested capital data for junk bond issuers are also not surprising as companies that raise money are obvious candidates to invest and grow. Yago points to the above-average productivity of junk bond issuers as measured by sales per employee. Sales per employee is but one of many possible productivity measures, and is a far from perfect test. Sales per employee would be high, for example, at companies that are skimping on research and development, or on customer service. Sales per employee would naturally be higher at faster growing small companies that are more likely issuers of junk bonds than at larger, more mature companies that are not typical junk bond issuers. When a junk bond issuer buys a business and hacks away at overhead, sales per employee may rise in the short term at uncertain long-term cost.

We would be far more interested in learning about the economic value of the growth that Yago describes. Was this growth profitable? Was economic value built? If so, junk bond issuers will continue to tap the capital markets for future growth. If not, the past growth is irrelevant as disappointed issuers will not use the junk financing mechanism in the future.

While Glenn Yago marvels about fast growing junk bond issuers such as Kinder Care and Charter Medical, he does not mention such junk bond dogs as Revco Drug Stores, the largest leveraged buyout to fail thus far. While the success of Kinder Care or Charter Medical is anything but certain, the failure of Revco is a sure thing. While Yago's companies have grown and invested, Revco has stagnated. Instead of investing in modern, well-located stores, point-of-sale terminals, pharmacy computers, inventory control and costing systems, or even remodeling, Revco has used virtually all available cash flow to service its debt. Less than two years after taking on over a billion dollars of debt and preferred stock, Revco defaulted, leaving behind a core business far less profitable than before its buyout and in worse business condition than any of its competitors. Clearly, junk bonds are not a panacea for everyone.

The surge in junk bond issuance during the 1980s has coincided with strong economic growth and generally declining interest rates. Prices paid for most businesses have increased during this decade, in large part due to the ready availability of debt financing. As a result of a strong economy and rising asset values, many early issuers of junk bonds have successfully managed to survive and in some cases prosper. Rising asset values, which relate more to psychological success than business success, have helped many junk bond issuers, as inadequate cash flows were bailed out by asset sale proceeds. Rising asset values have given confidence to borrowers and lenders alike, resulting in more easy credit bidding up asset prices further in a self-fulfilling way. Asset values do not rise to the sky, and the same influences that prolonged asset price inflation on the way up may well prolong asset price decreases on the way down.

After a complete cycle of economic growth and a slump of interest rate rises as well as declines and of asset value decreases as well as increases, we will be better able to assess the success of junk bonds. Will junk bond issuers prosper or go bankrupt? Will investors revel in excess returns or paper their walls with reminders of an era of credit market excess? Will Mike Milken be remembered as a financial genius and economic savior, as someone who carried a good idea too far, or as yet another Wall Street legend who built a financial empire on shaky foundations?

COMMENTS ON OTHER CONFERENCE PAPERS

The Bernanke and Campbell paper updates and summarizes their original Brookings paper.[1] It makes a significant contribution to thinking about debt. It is an excellent analysis of what they, with extraordinary restraint, have called the "reduced concern about bankruptcy" visible today. That loss of quality is captured especially well in their data showing sharply deteriorated coverage of interest charges in those companies that are, at any given time, at the bottom of the heap. And this deterioration is, of course, visible in the marketplace.

We agree that quality is best tested by liquidity rather than solvency. (Liquidity is the ratio of income before interest charges and income taxes to interest expense and other fixed charges. Solvency is a balance sheet concept, meaning the ratio of debt to equity, with equity measured either by book value or market value.) The liquidity test is more important, because it measures a company's ability to pay its interest charges as they accrue. Solvency ratios depend either on book values, which often are not meaningful, or on market values, which fluctuate widely.

We particularly concur with their analysis of the social costs of excessive leverage, the so-called contagion effects. Companies are like banks in the sense that weakness among some may be quickly transmitted to others. The problem is that companies which are in trouble will cut back on capital spending and other investments and inventories more deeply than those that are not. Our concern is that too many of us seem to ignore the cumulative impact of what is happening.

One addition we would make to what Bernanke and Campbell have said is that the moral hazards that explain the willingness of banks to take large risks may also explain what is happening at the insurance companies and mutual funds, which together own over 60 percent of the junk bonds, and which are under increasing pressure to maximize short-term performance. There is no FDIC for the high-yield mutual funds, but they seem quite ready to take remarkable risks. High-yield mutual funds are sold by yield, a fact which their advertising bears out.

With respect to the Melnick and Plaut paper, we think that they missed an essential point that Bernanke and Campbell—and Perry and Taggart— captured; namely, that banks are no more risk-averse than are public issue bondholders. Just look at the history of bank lending to LDCs, to real estate developers, and to oil companies; just look at the failing S&Ls. It is banks, not bondholders, that have been suffering heavy losses. Unfortunately, this misunderstanding of credit markets played a central part in the Melnick and Plaut paper.

CONCLUSION

It is too early to tell if junk bonds are good for both issuers and investors. Issuers will benefit if junk bonds represent capital available at a cost that permits an increase in the economic value of their businesses. Investors will benefit if junk bonds provide a total return, after credit losses, that is above market returns on a risk-adjusted basis. Our economy will benefit if junk bonds provide economic growth and a buildup of economic value without adversely impacting either issuers or investors.

Junk bonds remain untested through an economic cycle. Until they are, issuers and investors are gambling on economic good times and continuing asset value increases. Glenn Yago has been attracted, like a moth to a flame, to the early success of a financial market innovation. Until junk bonds have weathered the test of time, we should avoid blanket statements about their benefits and issuers and investors alike should choose to err on the side of caution.

Notes

1. B. Bernanke and J. Campbell (1988). "Is There a Corporate Debt Crisis?", *Brookings Papers on Economic Activity, 1*.

CHAPTER 19

WHAT EXPLAINS THE GROWTH IN HIGH-YIELD DEBT?

*Jan G. Loeys**

Chapters 15, 16, and 17 presented in this section, each from its own point of view, attempt to address the question "Why did high-yield bonds emerge out of nowhere to become such an important part of the total corporate bond market?" The various hypotheses discussed in this session can be reduced to two basic answers: (1) High-yield bonds replace equity, and (2) high-yield bonds replace other forms of debt, including bank loans—in each case presumably because high-yield bonds offer a more efficient form of financing.

Ben Bernanke and John Campbell investigate whether various forms of debt, among which high-yield bonds, have replaced equity and have thus raised corporate leverage. The evidence for this hypothesis, according to the authors, is mixed at best.

Corporate debt has grown faster than GNP this decade but remained stable when compared with the market value of equity. Bernanke and Campbell cannot find evidence that debt has become less expensive at the margin than equity—in terms of tax advantages or expected bankruptcy costs. And in the Brookings paper underlying their paper, they admit that

*Jan G. Loeys is Vice President of J. P. Morgan Co., Inc. The opinions expressed in this chapter are his own and do not necessarily represent the views that his employer, J.P. Morgan Co., Inc., may have on these issues.

only a small part of the increase in corporate debt can be traced to high-yield bonds.[1] So changes in desired leverage do not seem to offer the explanation we seek.

Arie Melnik and Steven Plaut follow the opposite approach, arguing that high-yield bonds replaced bank loans because a rise in the burden of bank regulation has reduced the competitiveness of bank loans. I would generally agree that high-yield bonds are substitutes for other types of debt contracts, but I do not think that bank regulation is the main culprit here.

First, the authors do not provide strong evidence of a rise in the burden of bank regulation. These regulatory 'taxes' would consist of deposit rate deregulation, minimum capital requirements, reserve requirements, and deposit insurance premia. On the first, it is not clear that the phase-out of the Federal Reserve's Regulation Q has increased bank costs. The elimination of deposit rate ceilings more likely merely moved banks from non-price to price competition and, if anything, improved the scope for bank intermediation. Even so, most of the disintermediation of banks has been on the wholesale side, where Regulation Q had been fully circumvented.

With respect to capital standards, banks have indeed been forced to raise capital-to-asset ratios from the lows they had reached five years ago, but these ratios are still way below the levels they had reached during the sixties and early seventies, before the start of the high-yield bond market. Reserve requirements have actually come down since the early seventies, in particular for large banks. Finally, FDIC premia have remained unchanged, except for the abolishment of the rebate, but this may be offset by the increased value of deposit insurance due to a rise in the number of bank failures. In sum, there is no overwhelming evidence of a big rise in the burden of bank regulation in the United States, nor in Europe for that matter.

A second problem with the Melnik and Plaut paper is that their results are counterfactual. In their model, banks specialize in information gathering and know each individual borrower's probability of default. Bondholders know only the average default probability for all firms in the economy. As a result, low-risk borrowers prefer bank loans as they can get a loan at the riskless rate plus a low individualized default premium. Higher risk firms must borrow in the bond market at a higher rate, equal to the riskless rate plus the average default rate for the economy. This result is clearly counterfactual: it has been the lowest-risk, highest-quality corporations that have moved to the securities markets.

Even so, there is not necessarily an equilibrium in this model. In this model, bondholders must know that the average default risk of firms that cannot obtain a bank loan and thus must issue bonds is higher than that for the whole economy. As bondholders then raise the default premium on bonds, the lowest-risk firms among those issuing bonds will find it more profitable to get a bank loan instead, thereby again raising the average default risk of firms left issuing bonds. Bondholders again must raise the default premium on bonds, and so on, until all firms get bank loans and no one issues bonds. The authors just assume that this unravelling will not take place, without explaining why one should accept this assumption.

If this model does not work, then how does one explain the growth of high-yield bonds? I think the best approach here is not to analyze this phenomenon purely as a change in the identity of the intermediaries—from banks to other financial intermediaries—but as a change in the nature of the debt contract, away from customized, renegotiable lending arrangements with a single lender and without a secondary market, such as bank loans or privately placed debt, towards more standardized, marketable forms of debt—that is, securities.

Why would such a shift have taken place? Two years ago, when I investigated this issue, I came up with the following hypotheses, some of which Kevin Perry and Robert Taggart also allude to in Chapter 15.[2]

A first explanation is that specialized financial intermediaries, such as banks, have lost part of their comparative advantage in information gathering and monitoring. Technological improvements in data manipulation and telecommunications have greatly reduced the costs of obtaining and processing information about the conditions that determine the value of a borrowing firm. Any analyst now has computerized access to a wealth of economic and financial information at a relatively low cost.

So, for many institutional investors, the costs of being informed about less-than-top-quality borrowers have dropped enough that they feel comfortable in owning securities issued by these firms without having to follow each and every move by these borrowers. As Mitchell Berlin and I showed in a theoretical model, such an extension of the securities market starts at the top, with the highest-quality borrowers gradually gaining access to the securities market as information costs fall, which is what I think we have seen in this market.[3]

A second factor, mentioned by Perry and Taggart and referred to by Fred Joseph in Chapter 8, is a shift in investor preferences toward marketable instruments away from debt contracts with extensive customized covenants that require regular renegotiation, and thus have no secondary market. Increasing interest rate volatility and unstable funding sources have induced some institutional investors such as insurance companies to switch from privately placed bonds—which are more a loan than a security—toward high-yield bonds, which have at least some form of a secondary market.

Third, discussions about the alleged rise in corporate leverage usually mention that investors might have become more willing to take on risk, partly because hedging and diversification techniques have become so much more abundant. This hypothesis has some merit. After all, the perception of increased risk is presumably what killed off the high-yield bond market during the thirties, and what induced investors then to let specialized intermediaries—such as banks—manage this type of risk for them. The finding during the seventies that default losses on high-yield bonds compared favorably with their promised yields, and continued relatively low loss rates since then—despite a major recession in 1982 and a stock market crash in 1987 reminiscent of 1929—all have widened the acceptability of this product among a growing number of investors.

Jack Guttentag and Dick Herring discussed this kind of risk preference shift a few years ago.[4] They argued that investors' perception of the chance of a financial crisis of the type that could bring down this market declines with the length of time that has elapsed since the last crisis occurred. They give the example of a driver who has just witnessed an accident and then drives very carefully for a while. But as time passes and the image of the accident recedes from his mind, the driver will get less and less careful. It is this behavior—the increased willingness to take on risk just because there hasn't been a crisis for such a long time—that, according to Gutentag and Herring, sets up the conditions conducive to another crisis, and that critics of high-yield bonds are trying to warn us about.

Finally, a caveat is in order here. Substituting securities for bank loans does not mean that we are eliminating financial intermediaries, only that we are changing the process of financial intermediation, from one where banks perform this function from beginning (deposits) to end (commercial loans), into one where the intermediation process is unbundled, with different firms specializing in underwriting, guaranteeing, and funding the debt.

Banks are allowed to function as guarantors through letters of credit or loan commitments, but until recently, were not allowed to contribute to the underwriting function, despite the fact that this 'subfunction' is subsumed in their traditional all-in-one, deposits-to-commercial-loan function. This explains why banks have tried for years to convince Congress and bank regulators to revise the Glass-Steagall Act, and why the Federal Reserve recently has seen fit to allow bank holding companies to engage in corporate debt activities through Section 20 companies.

Notes

1. B. Bernanke and J. Campbell (1988). "Is There a Corporate Debt Crisis?", *Brookings Papers on Economic Activity, 1*, pp. 83–125.
2. J. Loeys (November/December 1986). "Low-Grade Bonds: A New Source of Corporate Funding," *Business Review*, Federal Reserve Bank of Philadelphia, pp. 3–12.
3. M. Berlin and J. Loeys (June 1988). "Bond Covenants and Delegated Monitoring," *Journal of Finance*, pp. 397–412.
4. J. Guttentag and R. Herring (December 1984). "Credit Rationing and Financial Disorder," *Journal of Finance*, pp. 1359–1382.

PART 4

PUBLIC POLICY ISSUES OF HIGH-YIELD DEBT

CHAPTER 20

ECONOMIC IMPACTS OF HIGH-YIELD SECURITIES AND PUBLIC POLICY RESPONSE

*Glenn Yago** *

DEMYSTIFYING DEBT: INTRODUCTION

Struggles over the access, allocation, and cost of credit are common in the American political economy. In different decades, debt in the U.S. provided important access not merely to capital, but to land ownership, college, housing, and self-employment for a large share of the population.

There was a residual Tory influence after the American Revolution (that survives) that tried to apply restrictive measures to credit access for veterans, farmers, and industrial workers. Resistance to extending credit contributed to the rise of the Populist Party and progressive strains within both the Republican and Democratic parties at the turn of the century. During the twenties, Senator Henryk Shepsted and the "Sons of the Wild Jackasses" represented Democratic Party mavericks that identified with LaFollette Republicans from Wisconsin arguing for more expansive credit policies and access to capital markets. In the thirties, Franklin Roosevelt and Huey Long within the Democratic Party proposed creation of new debt

*Glenn Yago is Associate Professor of Management and Policy at the W. Averell Harriman School for Management and Policy, Economic Research Bureau, State University of New York at Stony Brook.

instruments for farmers, small businessmen, and homeowners during the Depression. Those measures became the centerpiece of new mortgage and credit instruments that financed the postwar recovery and were promoted by legislation during both the Truman and Eisenhower administrations. Political affinities on this issue have shifted within and between parties. Debt was viewed alternately as the balm and bane of economic growth. Resistance to debt was symbolic of either the preservation of privilege or financial prudence.

Today, the debt debate resonates earlier perspectives on economic vice and virtue. Consumer, foreign, government, and corporate debt are all painted with the same brush as "speculative" investment. Rarely, in this debate, is distinction made about the purpose of debt—consumption versus production—and its economic impacts. As in any political discourse during an era of rapid economic change, unfamiliar innovations become the focus of fear of what those changes portend. Embedded and confounded in this debt debate are high-yield securities, which today hold a prominent and vulnerable position.

Though the debt debate is usually held in economic terms, very little empirical, economic evidence is put forward. This is surprising since the facts are relatively simple and straight about the composition of debt and the social and economic effects of high-yield securities. The findings from my own study and those of other researchers is relatively consistent. My purpose today is to review these findings and then explore the political dimensions of the policy debate and proposals that have emerged.

THE ROLE OF DEBT IN CORPORATE CAPITAL STRUCTURE

Recent cumulative evidence about the performance of U.S. firms relative to their foreign competitors suggests that higher capital costs is a significant element in the weakening of U.S. competitiveness. Many companies find it difficult to adapt to competitive pressures and changing market trends because banks will not extend credit or the firm's size or market conditions make equity offerings undesirable. These problems of capital allocation and their impact on corporate capital structures are reflected in macroeconomic terms in our national accounts. The U.S. rate of capital investment has been traditionally lower than that of our major trading partners. Net nonresidential fixed investment, or additions to productive capacity, hovers between 1.5% - 2.9% of GNP. This figure is considerably lower than during the 1960s and most of the 1970s, and roughly half the level of investment by most EEC nations and Japan. Capital investment rates peaked in the mid-1980s and have since declined.

Even when capital is available, its costs may be prohibitive. The weighted average real costs of various investments was 10.7% in the United States according to the International Trade Commission (1983) and Hatso-poulos (1983), but only 4.1% in Japan. In long-term research and develop-ment, the Japanese cost of capital was 2.4%, compared to 10.1% in the United States. Overall, U.S. firms faced capital costs that were 7%-9% higher than their European and Japanese trading partners.

Both the amount and composition of debt have been strongly influ-enced by the relatively lower costs of debt capital. Corporate debt as a

FIGURE 20–1
Credit market debt[a] as a percentage of total sources of funds[b]

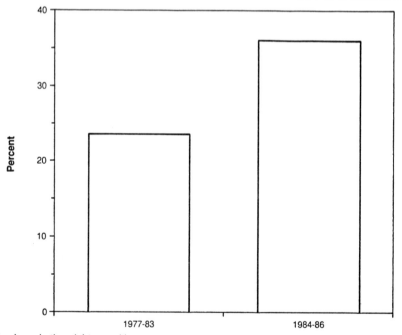

[a]Bonds and other debt securities
[b]Bank loans, private placements, and credit market debt

Source: Federal Reserve Flow of Funds Accounts

FIGURE 20–2
Composition of credit market debt

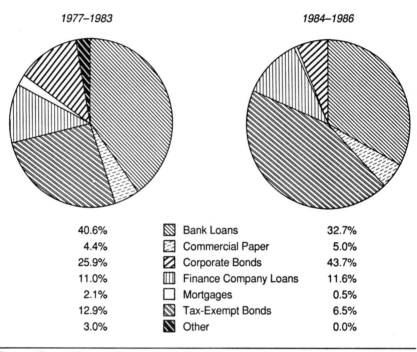

		1977–1983		1984–1986
40.6%	▨	Bank Loans		32.7%
4.4%	▧	Commercial Paper		5.0%
25.9%	▨	Corporate Bonds		43.7%
11.0%	▥	Finance Company Loans		11.6%
2.1%	☐	Mortgages		0.5%
12.9%	▨	Tax-Exempt Bonds		6.5%
3.0%	◼	Other		0.0%

Source: Federal Reserve Flow of Funds Accounts

proportion of GNP rose from 34% in 1983 to 42% in 1987. As Figures 20–1 and 20–2 show, Federal Reserve data shows that as the absolute levels of corporate debt increased, the composition of debt shifted away from bank loans and towards the capital markets. As a percent of total, bank loans fell 8%, while the combined credit market share of corporate debt increased 13%.

Is this debt excessive? Again the question needs to be more precisely stated as excessive to whom for what purpose? Relative to the underlying market value of the equity grown through debt, corporations do not appear overly leveraged (Bernanke and Campbell, 1988). Debt-equity ratios fell from 84% to 74% from 1983 to the present. By this measure, Meltzer and Richard (1987) have shown that corporate debt peaked in the mid-seventies and has declined since then. Debt increases have resulted in equity growth and increased share prices. According to U.S. Department of Commerce figures on corporate profits, the capacity to service debt has remained relatively stable even though absolute levels of debt have risen. Interest coverage (income/interest payments) has hovered between 6.2 - 6.4 between 1974 and 1986.

Relative to foreign corporations, U.S. companies also appear to be underborrowed. In the manufacturing sector, German and Japanese corporations averaged 66% and 64% of debt in their respective capital structures compared to 30% for similar U.S. firms. Foreign manufacturers showed a lower after-tax cost of capital, increased volume, and profitability growth rates, and reduced short-term pressures for share/price performance. As a percent of GNP, corporate debt is 100% in Japan, 70% in Germany, 65% in Canada, and only 42% in the United States.

Examining evidence from the oil and tobacco industry, Jensen (1986) showed that when cash flow was used to service debt, other value increasing transactions ensued through changes in corporate strategy, acquisitions, product introductions, and development of new markets. In those industries, the weight of debt acted as an anchor, forcing management to maximize efficiency and productivity to meet interest payments.

STRUCTURAL CHANGES IN THE CAPITAL MARKETS AND THE RISE OF HIGH-YIELD SECURITIES

As Perry and Taggert (1987) have detailed, a variety of factors including financial deregulation, pension fund deregulation, interest and inflation rate volatility, and the globalization of capital markets created conditions conducive to the rise of high yield bonds.

As we noted in Figure 20–2, comparing the composition of credit market debt in 1977-1983 with that in 1984-1986, we find that tax-exempt bonds decreased as a source of capital from 12.9% to 6.5%. Commercial banks became less responsive to businesses as a source of capital as indicated by bank loan declines. Mortgages decreased slightly from 2.1% to 0.5%. Finance company loans increased slightly from 11.0% to 11.6%. Commercial paper also increased somewhat, from 4.4% to 5.0%.

The junk bond revolution began when investors realized that on a risk-adjusted return basis, junk bonds could be excellent investments, outperforming investment-grade bonds over time. Once distribution channels for these high-yield bonds were established and the market was supported by investors, companies began issuing bonds that were below investment grade from their inception. In 1983, the amount of high-yield securities began to rise sharply (Figure 20–3). Due to the growth of new non-investment-grade issues, by 1987 junk securities represented approximately 24% of all outstanding corporate debt (Figure 20–4). However, as high-yield debt grew, it followed rather than led trends in increased corporate indebtedness. While high-yield debt ratcheted up sharply from 1977-1987, the increase is nothing like the ninefold increase in corporate debt outstanding in the U.S. during the same period. During that same period, U.S. corporations assumed $1.8 trillion in new debt. Of that new

FIGURE 20–3
High-yield securities' share of total corporate debt, 1977–1987

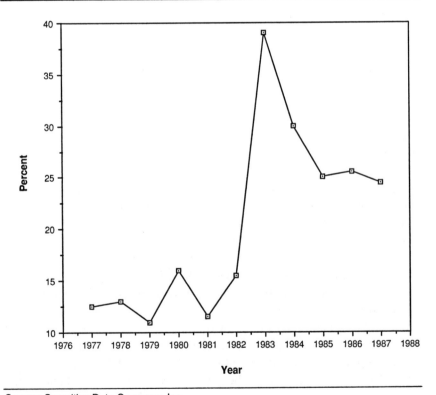

Source: Securities Data Company, Inc.

debt, $622 billion or 34.7% was raised through investment-grade bonds and $164.5 billion or 9.1% was raised through high-yield issues.

As junk bonds outperformed their investment grade counterparts, confidence in the rating system as a determinant of bond value declined. The structure of corporate and personal taxes, increased capital needs for restructuring, and shifts in the relationship between outstanding debt and default risk attracted both issuers and investors to the junk bond market (Fridson and Wahl, 1987; Altman and Nammacher, 1985; Pozdena, 1987; Schrager and Sherman, 1987).

The opening of the high-yield bond market gave issuers affordable access to fixed-rate funding, without the covenants and restrictions associ-

FIGURE 20–4
High-yield and total corporate debt issued, 1977–1987

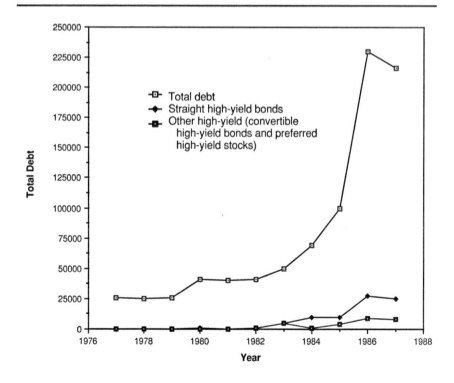

Source: Securities Data Company, Inc.

ated with bank loans and private placements. By issuing high-yield bonds, corporations could also avoid costly and dilutive common stock offerings, reducing their dependence on an erratic and unpredictable stock market. The contract between issuer and investor made explicit a long-term endorsement of a company's growth plan in exchange for guaranteed high-yield returns. With greater flexibility and lower capital costs, issuers could more effectively respond to changing market trends and deploy their assets more swiftly towards new objectives.

RISK ASSESSMENT AND THE FINANCIAL IMPACT OF HIGH-YIELD SECURITIES

The requirements of financial risk assessment can be at odds with the competitive risks of corporations seeking to enter new markets. Rating agencies such as Moody's and Standard & Poor's have developed their own criteria for determining whether or not a company will receive an investment grade rating. New companies may lack the size, capital structure, or history needed to qualify as investment grade. Companies that are entering new markets, introducing new products, or facing structural or strategic changes may be unable to document past performance and give an adequate indication of future performance. As a result, such companies are typically denied investment grade ratings.

Many of the assumptions of the financial risk inherent in investment grade ratings are not upheld by financial experience in the marketplace:
- in examining variations between investment grade bonds and their relative default risk, Broske (1987) found that bond rating assignments were poor predictors of default probability.
- while default rates of junk bonds were relatively higher than for investment grade issues, the default rate has been skewed by significant bankruptcies (e.g., LTV, REVCO). When adjustments are made for the duration of the issue and the firm's underlying asset base, high-yield bonds showed lower total risk (Altman and Nammacher 1986).
- Blume and Keim (1987) found an annualized compound monthly rate of return of 11.04% for junk bonds compared to 9.6% for long-term Treasury bonds.
- Altman (1988) indicates that over time, yields for junk bonds have expanded while risks have remained unchanged.

- Pound (1987) showed that firms raising new capital through debt issues were rewarded by the market with higher stock prices.
- WEFA (1988) found that except for consumer credit cards, the risk adjusted return on high-yield bonds has been consistently greater than on other types of assets generally held by thrift institutions. Similarly, a study by a regional bank showed that high-yield corporate bonds outperformed commercial loans in a number of dimensions relevant to portfolio management—liquidity, asset/ liability management, financial information, diversification, yield spreads, and credit quality.

Debt issues must do more than reconfigure a company's financial structure to prove economic benefit.   Corporate performance can be measured in the variety of ways the firm pursues and accomplishes higher value operations and strategies. To test whether high-yield securities as a financial instrument achieved this objective, I would like to review the evidence that emerged—from my own and other studies of available data on the use of funds from high-yield issues and the impact of those funds in financing employment, productivity, sales, capital investment, and capital spending—and other studies in this field.

USE OF FUNDS

In our study of high-yield issues from 1980-1986, we found that 74.7% of the proceeds were earmarked for corporate growth, and 21.9% were used for acquisition financing (Tables 20–1 and 20–2). Only 3.25% were used in unsolicited takeovers—disproving the popular myth that high-yield securities are primarily used to fund hostile acquisitions in the public market.

Lehn, et al. (1986) found that junk bonds represented a relatively small portion of tender-offer financing. For 1985, the year of the study, junk bonds represented one-sixth of all tender offer financing, less than one-quarter of financing against large targets; and less than one-third of financing in hostile deals.

In the General Accounting Office's recent study of high-yield bonds, an examination of corporate takeover financing from 1985-86 revealed that junk bonds represented only 12% of the total amount financed. In short, while the use of junk bonds for takeovers varies by the time interval of study and number of cases included, there appears to be nowhere near the level of use suggested by the popular press and political perception.

TABLE 20-1
Use of proceeds by industry—Firms issuing high-yield securities in 1980-1986[a]

Industry (SIC)	Issue Amount	General Corporate Purpose	Refinancing			Acquisition Financing						N
			Bank Debts	Other Debts	Recap	Friendly Acquisition	Possible Future Acquisition	LBO	Refinancing Acquisition Debts	Takeover Refinancing Debts	Selling Security Holders	
Agricultural Products (01, 02)	177.0	31.4 (17.74)	97.6 (55.14)	48.0 (27.12)								4
Mining (10-14)	5146.1	1501.0 (29.17)	3091.3 (60.07)	87.4 (1.70)		21.0 (0.41)	3.0 (0.06)		351.4 (6.83)		91.0 (1.77)	51
Construction (15-17)	225.2	98.4 (43.69)	117.6 (52.22)	6.7 (2.98)		2.5 (1.11)						7
Manufacturing Durable (24, 25, 32-39)	10825.9	4524.0 (41.79)	3550.1 (32.79)	627.7 (5.80)	529.4 (4.89)	31.0 (0.29)	422.2 (3.90)		750.8 (6.94)	386.1 (3.57)	3.9 (0.04)	214
Manufacturing Nondurable	6354.7	2353.7 (37.04)	1539.2 (24.22)	732.1 (11.52)		358.3 (5.64)	25.5 (0.40)	41.2 (0.65)	1234.5 (19.43)		70.3 (1.11)	84
Transportation (40-47)	4461.8	3381.1 (77.78)	619.2 (13.88)	169.5 (3.80)		77.8 (1.74)	111.6 (2.50)		1.5 (0.03)		101.0 (2.26)	58
Communications (48)	4130.1	2583.6 (62.56)	493.7 (11.95)	292.6 (7.08)		340.7 (8.25)	347.6 (8.42)		71.9 (1.74)			25
Public Utilities (49)	7798.3	2386.6 (30.60)	2428.0 (31.13)	1977.7 (25.36)					926.5 (11.88)		79.4 (1.02)	68
Wholesale (50, 51)	1775.9	564.8 (31.80)	875.5 (49.30)	184.7 (10.40)		7.4 (0.42)			143.6 (8.09)			44
Retail (52-59)	5748.6	2973.1 (51.72)	1280.7 (22.28)	515.5 (8.97)	21.0 (0.27)	253.7 (4.41)	238.3 (4.15)		487.6 (8.48)			92
Finance (60-62, 67)	7364.6	5687.2 (77.22)	703.5 (9.55)	354.5 (4.81)		145.7 (1.84)	285.9 (3.62)	40.2 (0.51)	162.8 (2.06)		506.9 (6.41)	130
Insurance (63, 64)	1854.8	502.7 (27.10)	25.0 (1.35)	371.7 (20.04)		709.4 (38.25)	47.6 (2.57)		198.4 (10.70)			20
Real Estate (65)	2994.9	1047.1 (34.01)	1124.9 (37.56)	635.0 (21.20)		144.4 (4.82)	10.3 (0.34)		33.4 (1.12)			42
Business & Professional (73, 89)	1813.6	664.7 (36.65)	634.2 (34.97)	158.9 (8.76)		100.00 (5.51)	212.3 (11.71)		43.7 (2.41)			44

TABLE 20–1—continued

Industry (SIC)	Issue Amount	Refinancing				Acquisition Financing						N
		General Corporate Purpose	Bank Debts	Other Debts	Recap	Friendly Acqui-sition	Possible Future Acquisition	LBO	Refinancing Acquisition Debts	Takeiver Refinancing Debts	Selling Security Holders	
Leisure & Repair (70, 72, 75-79)	3122.7	1652.4 (52.92)	664.9 (21.29)	245.8 (7.87)	17.4 (0.56)	144.9 (4.64)	38.7 (1.24)		356.1 (11.40)		2.2 (0.07)	38
Health & Educational (80, 82)	3016.8	1444.7 (47.89)	440.9 (14.61)	222.7 (7.38)		470.1 (15.58)	77.8 (2.58)		360.8 (11.96)			61
Total	67351.6	31396.5 (46.62)	17686.3 (26.26)	6630.5 (9.84)	567.8 (0.84)	2799.5 (4.16)	1828.2 (2.71)	81.4 (0.12)	5123.0 (7.61)	386.1 (0.57)	854.7 (1.27)	982

[a]Only 755 firms with readily available performance data are included. All dollar figures are in millions. Number in parentheses are percentages (over issue amount).

Source: Drexel Burnham Lambert

TABLE 20-2
Use of proceeds by industry—Manufacturing firms issuing high-yield securities in 1980-1986[a]

Industry (SIC)	Issue Amount	Refinancing				Acquisition Financing						N
		General Corporate Purpose	Bank Debts	Other Debts	Recap	Friendly Acqui- sition	Possible Future Acquisition	LBO	Refinancing Acquisition Debts	Takeiver Refinancing Debts	Selling Security Holders	
Food & Kindred Products (20)	1461.6	789.8 (54.04)	172.8 (11.82)	206.5 (14.13)		201.9 (13.81)		41.2 (2.82)	49.2 (3.37)			18
Textile Mill Products (22)	376.4	117.9 (31.32)	162.5 (43.17)	20.0 (5.31)					36.1 (9.59)		40.0 (10.63)	8
Apparel (23)	195.7	46.5 (23.76)	117.3 (59.94)	22.7 (11.60)					9.2 (4.70)			7
Lumber & Wood Products (24)	52.8	15.3 (28.98)	28.7 (54.36)	4.9 (9.28)							3.9 (7.39)	2
Furniture & Fixtures (25)	96.1	49.4 (51.40)	42.9 (44.64)	3.8 (3.95)								3
Paper & Allied Products (26)	1442.1	159.7 (11.07)	578.1 (40.09)	186.7 (12.95)					487.3 (33.79)		30.3 (2.10)	11
Printing & Publishing (27)	981.1	131.2 (13.37)	123.6 (12.60)	64.7 (6.59)		96.5 (9.84)	11.3 (1.15)		553.8 (56.45)			11
Chemicals & Allied Products (28)	44.6	250.4 (56.32)	71.7 (16.13)			33.0 (7.42)	2.0 (0.45)		87.5 (19.68)			12
Petroleum & Coal Products (29)	692.5	524.6 (75.75)	167.9 (24.25)									6
Rubber & Plastic Products (30)	760.7	333.6 (43.84)	145.3 (19.10)	231.5 (30.42)		26.9 (3.54)	12.2 (1.60)		11.4 (1.50)			11
Stone, Clay & Glass (32)	470.4	150.3 (31.95)	110.7 (23.53)	101.3 (21.53)					108.1 (22.98)			11
Primary Metal Industries (33)	1040.0	302.7 (29.11)	506.5 (48.70)	226.5 (21.78)					4.3 (0.41)			15
Fabricated Metal Products (34)	1178.6	505.6 (42.90)	213.0 (18.07)	80.3 (6.81)			177.3 (15.04)			202.3 (17.16)		17
Machinery (except Electrical) (35)	799.8	408.4 (51.06)	251.7 (31.47)	10.3 (1.29)			35.5 (4.44)		93.7 (11.72)			25

TABLE 20–2—continued

Industry (SIC)	Issue Amount	Refinancing				Acquisition Financing						N
		General Corporate Purpose	Bank Debts	Other Debts	Recap	Friendly Acqui- sition	Possible Future Acquisition	LBO	Refinancing Acquisition Debts	Takeover Refinancing Debts	Selling Security Holders	
Electric & Electronic Equipment (36)	3185.4	1585.4 (49.77)	1209.6 (37.97)	45.0 (1.41)		76.8 (2.41)			84.5 (2.65)	183.8 (5.77)		72
Transportation Equipment (37)	2479.8	678.6 (27.37)	779.3 (31.43)	91.4 (3.69)	529.4 (21.35)	22.0 (0.89)	48.2 (1.94)		330.7 (13.34)			31
Instruments (38)	874.7	433.3 (49.54)	229.8 (26.27)	14.7 (1.68)		9.0 (1.03)	84.4 (9.65)		103.5 (11.83)			26
Miscellaneous Manufacturing (39)	648.3	395.0 (60.93)	177.9 (27.44)	49.5 (7.64)					26.0 (4.01)			12
Total Manufacturing	17180.6	6877.7 (40.21)	5089.3 (29.62)	1359.8 (7.91)	529.4 (3.08)	389.3 (2.27)	447.7 (2.61)	41.2 (0.24)	1985.3 (11.56)	386.1 (2.25)	74.2 (0.43)	298

[a]Only 256 manufacturing firms with readily available performance data are included. All dollar figures are in millions. Numbers in parentheses are percentages (over issue amount).

Source: Drexel Burnham Lambert.

JOB CREATION AND RETENTION: THE EMPLOYMENT EFFECTS OF HIGH-YIELD SECURITIES

The claim that junk bonds are used largely for "bust up shutdown takeovers" that destroy jobs abounds in the popular press and academic articles (Lowenstein, 1985; Herman and Lowenstein, 1986). Yet there appears to be no consistent empirical evidence to support these claims. In fact, the evidence that emerges indicates that the impacts of restructuring and reinvestment financed through high-yield securities has the opposite generally accepted effect.

Paulus and Gay (1986) indicate that intensive restructuring activity is associated with greater productivity gains and can be used as a defensive response to import penetration. Lichtenberg and Siegel (1987) examined 19,000 manufacturing plants in 1972-1981, and found that companies tend to sell plants that lack a comparative advantage. Low levels of efficiency increased the likelihood of ownership change. They also found that companies that changed ownership through mergers, acquisitions, or divestitures showed increases in total factor productivity. In short, new owners of firms operated plants more efficiently.

The generally cited counter-evidence comes from Ravenscraft and Scherer (1987, pp. 68-70) who found that the pretakeover accounting profits of target firms of 95 tender offers during 1957-1975 were not statistically, significantly different from the corresponding profits of other firms in the same industries. Moreover, they found no evidence that the postmerger profitability of acquired assets in a larger sample of firms from 1950-76 increased significantly in relation to their premerger levels (Ravenscraft and Scherer, 1987, pp. 101-103). In fact, firms not sold off had profitability decline among conglomerate acquisitions and smaller companies, while equal-sized companies had some profitability increases. Critics use these studies as evidence against acquisitions and the debt financing used to accomplish them.

A closer reading of the evidence suggests an alternative and more likely interpretation more consistent with recent studies. The evidence stops in Ravenscraft and Scherer's study for the most part in 1977 (prior to the advent of the contemporary high-yield market). An exception is some data on sell-offs that goes until 1981 and consists primarily of divestitures from the conglomerate acquisition wave of the 1960s and 1970s. The present merger and acquisition wave that began in 1982, financed in part by high-yield securities, can be best characterized as deconglomerization; the undoing of earlier mergers that had poor strategic and economic justification (Mitchell and Lehn, 1988).

Brown and Medoff's study (1987) of Michigan companies confirms that, over time, mergers and acquisitions result in efficiency and employment gains. My own studies of plant closings in New York and New Jersey (1986) indicated that shutdowns could be attributed to restructurings in less than 2% of the cases. Bhide (1988) examined a sample of twelve hostile takeovers completed in 1985 and found no evidence of takeover-caused production loss. Rather, the data showed that companies lost 4,000-5,000 jobs prior to the takeover between 1981-85, 7% per year, due to uncompetitiveness. Posttakeover job loss was primarily due to corporate staff reductions which averaged 200-300 jobs per company.

Basically, the research on employment to date can be summarized as follows:

- large firms shrink faster than smaller firms (Ghemawat and Nalebuff, 1987);
- firms that reduce costs, introduce new products and production processes that revitalize and reverse maturing product cycles (Abernathy and Hayes, 1985);
- small- and medium-size firms provide the major sources of new jobs and are best at retaining existing ones.

If leverage helps firms maximize efficiency and grow, high-yield firms should have higher than average levels of employment gain and retention. To test this hypothesis, we analyzed employment changes among those high-yield issuers for which employment data were available, and compared them to changes in total industry employment.

To correct for the addition of new issuing firms, we studied high-yield firms using cohort analysis, i.e., analyzing the change in employment from the year the firm first issued a high-yield security to 1986, the final year for which industry totals were available. In each cohort from 1980 to 1985, high-yield firms far and away outstripped industry rates of employment growth. The average annual increase in employment among high-yield firms was 6.68%, compared to only 1.38% for industry as a whole (Table 20–3).

From 1980 through 1983, industry as a whole experienced net job losses, while high-yield firms showed relatively steady employment gains. In subsequent years, total industry employment improved, but not enough to match the rate of job creation among high-yield firms. Disaggregating

TABLE 20–3
Changes in employment, high-yield firms vs. industry totals

	Average Annual Change, 1980–1986				
	High-Yield Firms			*Industry Total*	
Industry	*N*	*Absolute*[a]	*Percent*	*Absolute*[a]	*Percent*
A. Breakdown by Industry Group					
Agricultural Products (01, 02)	3	–0.518	–1.344	0.342	72.555
Mining (10–14)	28	1.556	2.887	–25.107	–7.215
Construction (15–17)	4	0.249	1.386	–6.205	–3.560
Manufacturing Durable (24, 25, 32–39)	148	–8.058	–0.892	–152.512	–2.199
Manufacturing Nondurable	69	–1.894	–0.411	–38.963	–1.001
Transportation (40–47)	28	23.527	6.992	113.922	11.369
Communications (48)	13	1.670	8.316	–1.455	–2.025
Public Utilities (49)	30	3.654	4.039	3.923	0.871
Wholesale (50, 51)	38	–4.823	–4.211	25.339	10.242
Retail (52–59)	62	60.001	13.848	187.586	6.303
Finance (60–62, 67)	45	7.308	10.263	16.320	7.944
Real Estate (65)	23	2.093	8.203	1.737	5.319
Business & Professional (73, 89)	33	5.917	7.823	22.567	12.121
Leisure & Repair (70, 72, 75–79)	25	11.257	124.125	27.970	8.271
Health & Educational (80, 82)	34	41.037	17.787	49.135	16.975
Total	**583**	**142.976**	**6.679**	**224.599**	**1.379**
B. Further Breakdown by two-digit SIC for Manufacturing Industries					
Food & Kindred Products (20)	12	–0.418	–0.347	47.049	5.532
Textile Mill Products (22)	6	–3.516	–6.543	6.146	10.579
Lumber & Wood Products (24)	2	0.267	16.834	0.246	1.683
Furniture & Fixtures (25)	1	0.583	9.712	6.042	8.129
Paper & Allied Products (26)	8	5.138	6.773	6.296	1.609
Printing & Publishing (27)	7	0.379	1.430	13.402	4.433
Chemicals & Allied Products (28)	9	0.026	0.509	–29.873	–4.064
Petroleum & Coal Products (29)	5	–0.301	–1.533	–57.918	–5.079
Rubber & Plastic Products (30)	7	–5.294	–6.529	–24.066	–7.375
Stone, Clay & Glass (32)	9	0.456	1.368	–2.176	0.988
Primary Metal Industries (33)	9	–4.492	–2.760	–14.727	–2.251
Fabricated Metal Products (34)	11	3.459	10.008	–8.925	–1.922
Machinery (except Electrical) (35)	15	–1.161	–0.160	–25.947	03.680
Electric & Electronic Equipment (36)	63	–0.658	–0.073	–20.866	–1.742
Transportation Equipment (37)	17	–5.850	–2.453	–99.544	–3.280
Instruments (38)	21	–0.663	–1.836	5.911	1.119
Miscellaneous Manufacturing (39)	10	1.853	7.860	7.474	12.318
Total Manufacturing	**217**	**–10.192**	**–0.742**	**–191.476**	**–1.774**

[a]Absolute changes are in thousands of jobs.

Source: COMPUSTAT Data, S&P, 1980–86.

total employment effects, we found some interesting patterns among industries. Other than agriculture, where there were too few cases, high-yield companies were relatively consistent in outperforming their industries. This was particularly evident in high-yield firms:

- where employment grew in high-yield companies but fell at the industry level (e.g., communications);
- where employment grew faster among high-yield firms, e.g., retail and finance;
- where employment shrank among high-yield firms, but less than overall industry declines, e.g., manufacturing.

PRODUCTIVITY EFFECTS OF HIGH-YIELD SECURITIES ON FIRM PERFORMANCE

A popular charge against industrial restructuring in general, and junk bonds in particular, is that they are simply financial reshuffling or "paper entrepreneurism" and fail to create genuine value within the U.S. economy. Our study, however, suggests the reverse. Often restructuring involves transfers of ownership, new management and work practices, strategic acquisition of market share, or development of new production or distribution processes that improve cost efficiencies and redeploy assets toward higher rates of return.

As Table 20–4 indicates, the distribution of high-yield financing parallels the distribution of mergers, acquisitions, and divestitures throughout the 1980s. High-yield financing has been concentrated in sectors that have faced deregulation or intense competition from abroad. Paulus and Gay (1987) have shown that productivity increases have been concentrated in those areas of the economy where restructuring has occurred. Their work led us to examine the relationship between high-yield financing, restructuring, and productivity in various sectors of the economy. Using the Bureau of Labor Statistics' productivity index, we found that in most industries where high-yield financing and restructuring were intensive, productivity increases were considerable (Table 20–5). Mining, manufacturing, finance, and public utilities achieved substantial productivity increases. Transportation and communications had high levels of high-yield financing, but their restructuring intensity was lower and they experienced productivity declines. Despite low levels of high-yield financing and restructuring, retail trade firms achieved substantial productivity gains.

TABLE 20–4
Comparative distribution of corporate restructuring and
high–yield financing: Summary table, 1980–87

	Share of...		
	Mergers, Acquisitions, or Divestitures	Firms Issuing High-Yield Bonds	Output
Mining and Natural Resource Extraction	17.4	4.9	3.4
Manufacturing	40.5	33.71	22.2
Deregulated Industries			
Transportation and Communications	10.4	6.96	6.4
Finance, Insurance, and Real Estate	18.2	19.6	4.4
Subtotal	**86.5**	**65.17**	**36.2**
Balance of U.S. Economy	13.5	34.83	63.8

Source: Paulus and Gay, 1987; Economic Research Bureau, 1988; Industrial Productivity: BLS Productivity Index.

Among manufacturing industries, high yield financing, restructuring, and productivity increases were again closely associated. This pattern was particularly evident in primary metals, fabricated metals, transportation equipment, food and kindred products, and paper and allied products. With the exception of rubber and plastic products, wherever high-yield securities were intensively used, productivity increases occurred.

Another measure considered in the study was market productivity as measured by sales per employee as opposed to physical output per employee hour. This measure allowed us to investigate a broader range of industries. Overall, sales per employee grew faster in high-yield firms than for industry totals (3.13% versus 2.41%) (see Table 20–6). Within manufacturing, sales per employee also grew faster in high-yield companies than for the industry totals (4.71% versus 2.85%). There was considerable diversity in market productivity performance between industries. In the Class of 1983 analysis, high-yield firms showed higher rates of growth in sales per employee than industry totals in the post-1983 period. High-yield manufacturing showed a dramatic increase in sales per employee between the before and after periods—market productivity jumped 7.38% for high-yield firms while the rate of increase dropped by more than half for manufacturing firms as a whole.

TABLE 20–5
Junk bond intensity, productivity change, and restructuring intensity

Industry (SIC)	Junk Bond Intensity Index[a]	Change of Productivity Index[b]	Restructuring Intensity Measure (RIM)[c]
A. Breakdown by Industry Group			
Agricultural Products (01, 02)	0.125		
Mining (10–14)	1.690	33.95	5.8
Construction (15–17)	0.053		
Manufacturing Durable (24, 25, 32–39)	0.902	8.55	1.5
Manufacturing Nondurable	1.209	4.26	1.8
Transportation (40–47)	1.712	−0.62	0.8
Communications (48)	1.636	−34.78	0.9
Public Utilities (49)	3.332	22.82	0.9
Wholesale (50, 51)	0.307		0.1
Retail (52–59)	0.812	4.29	0.4
Finance (60–62, 67)	3.970	13.34	4.4[d]
Insurance (63, 64)	1.746		2.5
Real Estate (65)	0.406		0.1
Business & Professional (73, 89)	0.480		0.7
Leisure & Repair (70, 72, 75–79)	1.260	0.85	0.8[d]
Health & Educational (80, 82)	0.712		0.3
B. Further Breakdown by two-digit SIC for Manufacturing Industries			
Lumber & Wood Products (24)	0.136	3.25	2.2
Furniture & Fixtures (25)	0.442	3.00	0.4
Stone, Clay & Glass (32)	0.944	7.33	0.9
Primary Metal Industries (33)	1.978	11.06	1.5
Fabricated Metal Products (34)	1.691	3.62	1.4
Machinery (except Electrical) (35)	0.604	6.80	1.0
Electric & Electronic Equipment (36)	0.947	8.43	1.6
Transportation Equipment (37)	1.427	19.37	1.6
Instruments (38)	0.317	8.27	2.8
Miscellaneous Manufacturing (39)	1.114		1.5
Food & Kindred Products (20)	5.404	6.04	3.8
Textile Mill Products (22)	0.284	6.31	1.2
Apparel (23)	0.391		0.9
Paper & Allied Products (26)	3.677	3.88	1.3
Printing & Publishing (27)	1.628		0.9
Chemicals & Allied Products (28)	0.552	−0.13	2.2
Petroleum & Coal Products (29)	0.490	25.33	0.4
Rubber & Plastic Products (30)	1.361	−13.08	0.8
Total Manufacturing	**1.005**	**6.25**	**1.6**

[a]The Junk Bond Intensity Index is the ratio of the share of Junk Bond (dollar amount) issuance for each industry relative to that same industry's share of GNP during 1983–86.

[b]The Change of Productivity Index is the difference of the industry's productivity (output per employee–hour, 1977 = 100) between 1983 and 1985.

[c]RIM is the ratio of the share of Merger & Acquisition activities accounted for by each industry relative to that same industry's share of U.S. output during 1980–85.

[d]Average of Industries' RIMs in this Industry Group.

Source: Drexel Burnham Lambert; COMPUSTAT, S&P; Survey of Current Business, DOC; Worldwide Economic Outlook, Morgan Stanley; Productivity Measures, DOL.

TABLE 20–6
Changes in sales per employee—high-yield firms vs. industry totals[a]

| | | Average Annual Change, 1980–1986 | | | |
| | | High-Yield Firms | | Industry Total | |
Industry	N	Absolute	Percent	Absolute	Percent
A. Breakdown by Industry Group					
Agricultural Products (01, 02)	3	−0.847	2.171	2.035	15.519
Mining (10–14)	28	−2.081	0.231	10.615	7.875
Construction (15–17)	4	5.727	8.424	−0.937	−0.219
Manufacturing Durable (24, 25, 32–39)	157	3.978	5.209	7.100	7.940
Manufacturing Nondurable	60	3.894	4.025	−2.088	−0.970
Transportation (40–47)	28	2.727	3.291	−0.470	−0.428
Communications (48)	13	19.537	18.282	19.311	16.334
Public Utilities (49)	30	8.227	3.297	9.007	4.151
Wholesale (50, 51)	38	14.287	8.523	12.548	6.103
Retail (52–59)	62	3.539	6.159	2.690	3.354
Finance (60–62, 67)	45	16.306	9.977	4.785	3.799
Real Estate (65)	23	−1.707	−0.122	14.252	9.269
Business & Professional (73, 89)	33	−0.521	−0.341	7.012	11.005
Leisure & Repair (70, 72, 75–79)	25	−1.576	−1.393	2.821	8.575
Health & Educational (80, 82)	34	2.208	7.638	0.854	2.431
Total	**583**	**2.798**	**3.127**	**2.705**	**2.405**
B. Further Breakdown by two-digit SIC for Manufacturing Industries					
Food & Kindred Products (20)	12	3.350	5.275	−0.168	−0.133
Textile Mill Products (22)	6	−4.855	8.602	2.849	6.727
Apparel (23)	5	1.088	3.690		
Lumber & Wood Products (24)	2	9.353	11.533	4.566	5.425
Furniture & Fixtures (25)	1	3.844	7.212	2.330	4.324
Paper & Allied Products (26)	8	7.000	7.129	6.411	5.734
Printing & Publishing (27)	7	3.376	5.967	5.853	7.411
Chemicals & Allied Products (28)	10	0.407	0.651	5.045	5.218
Petroleum & Coal Products (29)	5	−34.887	−6.975	0.198	0.683
Rubber & Plastic Products (30)	7	9.692	10.015	4.509	6.621
Stone, Clay & Glass (32)	9	1.967	1.946	5.071	5.926
Primary Metal Industries (33)	9	3.184	2.822	2.205	2.606
Fabricated Metal Products (34)	11	4.122	5.405	4.777	6.241
Machinery (except Electrical) (35)	15	2.984	5.144	4.465	5.229
Electric & Electronic Equipment (36)	62	4.835	8.611	7.886	8.743
Transportation Equipment (37)	17	4.221	5.334	9.425	10.274
Instruments (38)	21	4.481	7.604	4.928	6.060
Miscellaneous Manufacturing (39)	10	6.246	9.656	6.261	10.571
Total Manufacturing	**217**	**3.938**	**4.713**	**3.450**	**2.852**

[a]Only 583 high-yield firms with readily available employment and sales data are included. Sales per employee are in thousands of dollars.

Source: COMPUSTAT Data, S&P, 1980–86.

SALES IMPACT OF HIGH-YIELD SECURITIES

Sales growth is a key indicator of a company's market position and competitive strength. In our analysis of sales performance, high-yield firms showed an annual growth rate of 9.38%, compared to 6.42% in general (Table 20–7).

In mining and nondurable manufacturing, industry sales decreased moderately (–1.43% and –1.00%), while high-yield firms increased sales 1.46% and 3.56%, respectively. In four other industries, high-yield firms increased their sales twice as fast as their industries—retail trade, finance, insurance, and leisure and repair services. In agriculture, durable manufacturing, real estate, and business and professional services, the rate of sales growth was lower relatively for high-yield firms.

Analyzing manufacturing separately, we found that high-yield firms showed a 5.57% increase in sales, outperforming total manufacturing, which grew only 3.78%. High-yield firms in lumber and wood products, fabricated metals, primary metals, and rubber and plastics grew twice as fast as their respective industries. In both rubber and plastics and primary metals, high-yield firms showed greater sales gains than their industries, showing that investment grade companies in these sectors had net sales losses. Growth in the remaining industries was relatively lower.

The more detailed analysis of the Class of 1983 showed that among firms that issued high-yield securities, average annual sales growth after issuing was almost twice the rate before issuing: 10.02%versus 5.10%. Sales growth among industry in general was a more modest 2% increase. Within manufacturing, high-yield firms reversed a declining sales trend, turning it into a rapid positive growth (from -4.32% to 7.42%). Meanwhile, overall manufacturing sales growth was much less dramatic (from 3.05% to 4.41%).

HIGH-YIELD SECURITIES AND CAPITAL EXPENDITURES

While both the debt and equity portions of capitalization increased for high-yield firms, it is most important from the business and public policy perspective to examine the data on the actual amount spent on construction or acquisition of property, plant, and equipment. Net nonresidential fixed

TABLE 20–7
Changes in sales—high-yield firms vs. industry totals[a]

Industry	N	Average Annual Change, 1980–1986			
		High-Yield Firms		Industry Total[c]	
		Absolute[b]	Percent	Absolute	Percent
A. Breakdown by Industry Group					
Agricultural Products (01, 02)	3	7.682	1.270	1.240	23.113
Mining (10–14)	29	174.129	1.462	–8.140	–1.434
Construction (15–17)	5	196.598	9.618	10.579	5.327
Manufacturing Durable (24, 25, 32–39)	158	3957.541	7.006	658.251	8.705
Manufacturing Nondurable	61	1347.391	3.562	–96.557	–1.002
Transportation (40–47)	28	3301.440	10.162	100.844	10.908
Communications (48)	15	681.987	28.531	192.147	17.288
Public Utilities (49)	30	1778.682	7.317	113.374	6.010
Wholesale (50, 51)	38	820.910	5.282	76.571	11.841
Retail (52–59)	63	5736.610	21.751	261.189	10.061
Finance (60–62, 67)	48	2763.907	20.576	259.751	8.786
Insurance (63, 64)	6	463.641	35.496	141.378	15.296
Real Estate (65)	24	331.061	10.107	8.182	14.973
Business & Professional (73, 89)	33	318.600	8.727	34.109	20.394
Leisure & Repair (70, 72, 75–79)	27	905.237	15.506	4.296	1.923
Health & Educational (80, 82)	36	2006.086	26.493	20.987	19.574
Total	**604**	**24791.502**	**9.384**	**1778.202**	**6.417**
B. Further Breakdown by two-digit SIC for Manufacturing Industries					
Food & Kindred Products (20)	13	329.584	5.771	37.159	5.467
Textile Mill Products (22)	6	75.366	2.865	7.680	7.004
Apparel (23)	5	30.577	3.920	9.144	10.214
Lumber & Wood Products (24)	2	50.633	30.804	7.118	5.634
Furniture & Fixtures (25)	1	54.250	14.703	5.268	12.740
Paper & Allied Products (26)	8	1172.430	13.392	35.502	7.407
Printing & Publishing (27)	7	184.774	9.989	29.827	12.104
Chemicals & Allied Products (28)	10	29.962	1.871	22.683	2.939
Petroleum & Coal Products (29)	5	–692.934	–8.477	–241.491	–4.390
Rubber & Plastic Products (30)	7	217.632	2.878	2.112	1.162
Stone, Clay & Glass (32)	9	167.730	5.451	7.897	4.998
Primary Metal Industries (33)	9	163.063	3.316	0.062	0.753
Fabricated Metal Products (34)	11	653.306	20.758	11.331	4.435
Machinery (except Electrical) (35)	15	242.339	5.977	136.303	8.310
Electric & Electronic Equipment (36)	63	1368.088	9.129	227.728	12.300
Transportation Equipment (37)	17	692.639	4.468	224.460	9.362
Instruments (38)	21	139.518	8.273	31.605	8.085
Miscellaneous Manufacturing (39)	10	425.974	25.081	6.480	13.345
Total Manufacturing	**219**	**5304.932**	**5.573**	**561.694**	**3.778**

[a]Only 604 high-yield firms with readily available sales data are included.
[b]Absolute changes for high-yield firms are in millions of dollars.
[c]Industry totals are in 100 millions of dollars

Source: COMPUSTAT Data, S&P, 1980–86.

investment has remained comparatively low in the U.S. relative to foreign competitors, and the capacity to add and mobilize productive capacity through investment is key to a successful transition of the economy. Capital expenditures are a key indicator of a firm's growth and response to changing market trends.

Overall, high-yield firms showed an annual growth rate in capital expenditures that was more than twice that of total U.S. industry (10.61% versus 3.83%) (see Table 20–8). High-yield firms outstripped the growth rates of their respective industries in durable and nondurable manufacturing, transportation, communications, retail trade, real estate, business and professional services, leisure and repair services, and health and educational services. Lower or declining levels of expenditures were present in remaining industries.

High-yield issues were primarily concentrated in the manufacturing sector. Manufacturing firms have faced a critical demand for retooling and modernization in the face of foreign competition. During our study period, 220 high-yield manufacturing firms accounted for 39.38% of the increases in capital spending for all publicly traded manufacturing firms. The annual growth rate of capital spending among high yield manufacturers was more than four times that of total manufacturing (9.59% versus 2.09%). In comparing the Class of 1983 to all firms that year, the rate of capital spending from 1983-1986 was over three times higher than for industry in general (13.66% versus 3.67%). Within manufacturing, high-yield firms far outperformed industry levels of capital spending after 1983 (17.97% versus 0.59%). In fact, high-yield firms managed to reverse declining levels of capital spending from the pre-issue period, moving from –4.89% to 17.97%, while manufacturing investment overall remained essentially flat.

ECONOMIC IMPACTS: SUMMARY

Though diversity exists by firms within industries—and variation in high-yield effects persist between industries depending on a variety of economic, social, and management factors—the overall economic impact of high-yield securities on firm and industrial performance appear consistently positive.

Aggregate numbers are convincing, but industry and firm stories are even more telling. In our study, we examined a variety of high-yield firms

TABLE 20–8
Changes in capital expenditures—high-yield firms vs. industry totals[a]

Industry	N	Average Annual Change, 1980–1986 High-Yield Firms Absolute[b]	Percent	Industry Total[c] Absolute	Percent
A. Breakdown by Industry Group					
Agricultural Products (01, 02)	3	7.682	1.270	1.240	23.113
Agricultural Products (01, 02)	3	1.241	3.603	0.182	12.386
Mining (10–14)	29	−245.674	−7.344	−10.775	−7.310
Construction (15–17)	5	−0.184	1.442	−0.012	5.279
Manufacturing Durable (24, 25, 32–39)	159	249.249	6.276	26.614	6.015
Manufacturing Nondurable	61	417.184	15.532	−9.691	−0.529
Transportation (40–47)	28	1274.891	26.178	10.033	8.973
Communications (48)	15	153.117	29.284	24.509	9.539
Public Utilities (49)	30	49.622	1.897	10.683	2.980
Wholesale (50, 51)	37	−53.503	−1.535	0.270	3.112
Retail (52–59)	63	323.654	26.979	14.884	13.443
Finance (60–62, 67)	34	46.247	19.750	3.173	29.918
Real Estate (65)	22	56.086	27.144	0.589	21.961
Business & Professional (73, 89)	33	174.166	29.554	2.633	23.174
Leisure & Repair (70, 72, 75–79)	26	357.953	22.443	6.982	17.708
Health & Educational (80, 82)	36	376.300	32.827	2.415	9.712
Total	**581**	**3180.349**	**10.605**	**82.489**	**3.830**
B. Further Breakdown by two-digit SIC for Manufacturing Industries					
Food & Kindred Products (20)	13	39.792	17.049	2.025	6.432
Textile Mill Products (22)	6	5.158	10.363	0.580	15.532
Apparel (23)	5	6.211	37.897	0.097	6.311
Lumber & Wood Products (24)	2	1.382	82.472	0.305	9.003
Furniture & Fixtures (25)	1	3.739	37.501	0.162	20.973
Paper & Allied Products (26)	8	370.124	33.375	2.365	4.157
Printing & Publishing (27)	7	65.167	37.780	2.028	14.979
Chemicals & Allied Products (28)	10	12.403	17.389	2.681	2.600
Petroleum & Coal Products (29)	5	−87.918	−20.344	−21.927	−3.415
Rubber & Plastic Products (30)	7	6.245	10.890	2.460	16.428
Stone, Clay & Glass (32)	9	−26.021	−2.991	−0.542	−2.304
Primary Metal Industries (33)	9	−29.453	−4.066	−1.515	2.816
Fabricated Metal Products (34)	11	127.022	102.077	0.441	6.925
Machinery (except Electrical) (35)	15	1.220	4.042	−0.762	−0.834
Electric & Electronic Equipment (36)	64	85.284	6.967	13.114	8.030
Transportation Equipment (37)	17	67.764	8.102	13.125	8.233
Instruments (38)	21	−0.813	1.511	1.957	5.651
Miscellaneous Manufacturing (39)	10	19.127	31.623	0.328	14.530
Total Manufacturing	**220**	**666.433**	**9.694**	**16.923**	**2.086**

[a]Only 581 firms with readily available data are included.
[b]Absolute changes for high-yield firms are in millions of dollars.
[c]Industry totals are in 100 millions of dollars

Source: COMPUSTAT Data, S&P, 1980–86.

and industry restructurings to investigate the management strategies that facilitated recovery and growth. After years of decline, the textile industry began to turn around last year, benefiting from the modernization of plant and equipment estimated to be between $16-20 billion. Plants are running at near capacity (12.5 billion pounds of output out of 13 billion pounds of capacity). At both Stevens and Burlington, restructuring brought companies into better focus, and divested divisions are operating more efficiently.

In the copper industry, management invested in modernization and new technology and eliminated marginal operations. Variable costs of production were reduced 20%-30%. In the paper industry, capacity utilization is up to 93.2%. Paper companies got out of real estate, chemicals, and textile investment and focused on manufacturing paper. Productivity increased 6% last year, and plant and equipment investment has been rising annually since 1984. Companies like Stone Container, Great Northern Nekoosa, and others have targeted market segments and consolidated towards higher margin, higher market share positions within their industries.

The internal growth of high-yield firms and their growth through industry restructuring has been a response to, not a cause of, fundamental economic changes. The growth of the high-yield market was a response to the need of firms to finance changes requisite for growth and competition. Debt generally, and high-yield debt specifically, can be mismanaged and abused like any financial instrument. But, so far, the evidentiary record suggests that while debt is no guarantee of economic success, it limits the excuses managers can make about pursuing negative present value projects in industries as diverse as oil, paper, steel, financial, or health services. For the most part, high-yield debt has impelled managers towards reinvestment strategies focused on core business segments and the basic requirements for global competition.

PUBLIC POLICY AGAINST HIGH-YIELD SECURITIES: REGULATING THE ECONOMY OUT OF AN INVESTMENT-LED RECOVERY

Regardless of the economic impact of high-yield securities, the public policy response has been an overwhelming reaction to regulate the market's success. Let us review the dimensions of public policy responses at the federal and state level to the rapid expansion of the market for high-yield securities. Both federal and state legislation have been proposed or enacted in a number of public policy areas (see Table 20–9).

Federal Policies Regulating High-Yield Securities
Securities Regulations

As numerous measures were introduced to further police cheating in the securities markets, high-yield securities became a target of concern over fair market practices. As part of tender offer proposed regulations, revisions were proposed in the Securities Exchange Act to restrict the issuing of securities that would cause a reduction in the national bond rating of an existing security. Additionally, a moratorium was also proposed on hostile takeovers financed by junk securities (leaving hostile takeovers financed conventionally by cash laden large corporations and foreign investors unhindered) along with the prohibition of junk security holdings by federally insured institutions. As of this writing, the high-yield market has been subjected to considerable legislative distortion. On July 27, 1989, the House and Senate adopted a provision that would bar savings and loans from owning high-yield bonds. Thrifts must divest currently held bonds over a five-year period. The evidentiary record of this study and other academic research were discounted by Congress. Further reports by the General Accounting Office and Data Resources, Inc. (on the impact of a recession on high-yield bonds) and Wharton Econometric Forecasting (on high-yield bonds compared to other savings and loan investments in the past) were also neglected in deliberations. Other measures on interest deductibility and merger and acquisition regulation are still under deliberation.

Federal Reserve Policy

During the hostile takeover battle between Mesa Petroleum and Unocal, Unocal petitioned the Federal Reserve Board in May 1985 requesting that margin requirements in Regulation G be applied to debt securities issued by a shell corporation involved in a tender offer. The Fed did apply Regulation G to certain types of transactions and a Senate Bill was later introduced to further amend margin requirements used in acquisitions.

TABLE 20-9
Existing and proposed regulations of high-yield securities

Federal		Federal and State		State	
Securities	Federal Reserve	Banking	Tax	Savings & Loans/ Commercial Banks	Insurance
S.634—Bill to amend Securities Exchange Act and restrict new securities that would cause a reduction in bond rating. HR.687—Moratorium on hostile takeovers financed by junk securities and prohibition of junk security holdings by federally insured institutions.	Regulation G margin requirements application to debt securities issued by a shell corporation in takeovers. S.1847—Bill to amend margin requirements for financial instruments used in acquisitions.	S.1653—Junk Bond Limitation Act of 1987. Limit junk securities held by federally insured institutions (current cap is 11%).	Interest—Deductibility of debt. Reclassification of high-yield securities regarding qualification for interest exclusion.	Restrictions on investments in high-yield securities by state-chartered banks and savings and loans—California, Texas, Florida.	Restrictions on investments in high-yield securities—Maryland, Texas, New York.

Banking Policy

The Senate and House Banking Committees and the Comptroller of the Currency authorize national banks to invest in corporate debt securities according to a risk-based capital reserve requirement that is currently defined as not exceeding 10% of the bank's capital and surplus in any one issue. As a general rule, securities considered speculative (like non-investment grade securities) may not be held by national banks as investment securities. Somewhat contradictory is the fact that unrated issues are not necessarily regarded as speculative. Those securities may not exceed 5% of the bank's capital and surplus and are subject to the prudent banking judgment rule—that the issuer be able to meet its obligations and that the security be able to be sold with reasonable promptness at a price corresponding to fair market value.

Federal savings and loans and savings banks (thrifts) are chartered and regulated by the Federal Home Loan Bank Board. While allowed to invest in corporate debt, the securities must be investment grade and marketable. They can consider high-yield securities as commercial loans and invest up to 10% of their assets in those instruments.

Tax Legislation

Last year, the Senate Finance and House Ways and Means Committee considered punitive measures against debt securities that would limit the tax deductibility of acquisition-related debt. A recent study by the Securities and Exchange Commission (Lehn and Mitchell, 1988) documents the impact of the announcement of this provision upon the slide in share values that became the October Crash of 1987. Nevertheless, resistance to tax increases and requirements of federal deficit reduction may make interest deductibility a convenient target with serious implications for businesses and the capital markets they depend upon. A proposal has been adopted to reduce the intercorporate dividends-received deduction from 70% to 50%. Also, provisions to limit interest deduction on acquisition debt and the taxing of the market discount on bonds will probably be introduced in the next Congress.

Additionally, Congress recently mandated that the Treasury Department revise Subchapter C of the federal tax code. The forthcoming revision may recommend that certain high-yield securities are reclassified from debt to equity and thereby eliminated from the interest exclusion associated with debt.

State Regulations Affecting High-Yield Securities Banks and Thrifts

State law authorizes investments by state-chartered banks according to rules of "prudence" and permits investment in corporate debt obligations subject to the same limits imposed on national banks. Insofar as state banks become members of the Federal Reserve System and obtain FDIC insurance, they are subject to federal rules and the practices of FDIC examiners.

Savings and loans chartered and supervised by various states operate under the regulations set by the state legislatures. California, Texas, and Florida will allow investment in high-yield securities up to 40%, while other states have adopted the Federal cap (11%). Other states are considering measures to limit high-yield securities investments further.

Insurance Companies

Life insurance companies currently account for over 30% of the high-yield bond market. Broad limits have been proposed in New York, Texas, Florida, and Maryland to restrict the percent of assets held in high-yield securities. While Maryland withdrew its proposal, the New York State Insurance Commission adopted a regulatory limit of 20% on publicly traded high-yield bond investments by life insurance companies headquartered in New York.

PUBLIC POLICY AND PRIVATE POWER: FINANCIAL COMPETITION AND REGULATION IN THE CAPITAL MARKETS

Until recently, the stability of the high-yield securities market remained unshaken in spite of judicial scrutiny, legislative pressure, the stock market crash, and continued long-term economic problems. Nevertheless, regulatory impulses persist without regard for empirical evidence of economic impacts. Frequent initiatives to regulate a seemingly effective and expanding market are worthy of considerable reflection. While the text of the policy discourse is primarily economic, what drives it is political.

The resounding success of the high-yield market as a source of capital for internal growth and industrial restructuring has been accompanied with increasing political controversy and legislative scrutiny. No other financial security instrument (debt or equity) has undergone as much investigation. The market grew faster than regulators could write new rules. When the legal history of the case against high-yield securities is finally written, it would be worthy of further scholarly investigation to explore how double standards were applied for noninvestment grade versus investment grade securities and why selective prosecution and investigation was undertaken.

THE POLICY DISCOURSE

As we have seen, the gap between political perception and the economic reality about high-yield securities is considerable. High-yield securities have been confounded with an assortment of factors to which they are often only tangentially related, if at all.

- High-yield bonds are ascribed with causing takeovers.
- "Junk" securities are blamed for bad loan portfolios of failing thrifts, banks, and pension funds.
- High-yield debt is the most visible and vulnerable of all debt, given the fact that it is new and different.

The problems of failed banks and thrifts resulted from bad real estate, energy, and agricultural loans and not from high-yield debt. The policy discourse has remained unconfused by the facts that have begun to emerge from academic research and government investigation about the positive economic and financial consequences of high-yield securities. Beyond a textual analysis of the discourse in the popular press and legislative debates, the next obvious question is: Why does the misunderstanding persist? I believe there are political and conceptual limits to the current policy debate about high-yield securities.

POLITICAL LIMITS: INTEREST GROUP POLITICS
AND CAPITAL MARKETS

The most obvious question about the heat surrounding high-yield securities is: Whose ox was gored? As the evidence suggests, it was not the investors who enjoyed rates of return in high-yield markets hundreds of basis points higher than other financial instruments; it was not businesses hungry for capital to finance their growth that were previously "unbankable" or subject to onerous banking restrictions; not employees, customers, and vendors that enjoyed the heightened levels of economic activity financed by high-yield securities; and not shareholders whose equity values grew with debt financed growth.

Returning to the earlier review of changes in credit markets, we saw that high-yield securities grew at the expense of bank debt and that high-yield companies grew at the expense of the hegemony of many established firms. As William Carney has succinctly noted:

> There are two reasons why junk bonds have come under attack—other explanations are mostly window dressing. First, junk bonds have made it easier for new challengers to enter the market for corporate control. Second, they are a valuable financing innovation for midsize companies that were traditionally ignored by large underwriters and had to pay higher interest rates at commercial banks. To the extent that junk bonds compete with existing lenders, these institutions predictably have responded by seeking to regulate competitors who exploit this new tool.

When the General Accounting Office investigated problem thrifts and insurance company insolvencies, they could find no evidence of high-yield defaults affecting the investment portfolios of those companies. Problem banks and thrifts were the consequence of agriculture, energy, and real estate commercial loans. However, in legislative hearings, it has become clear that commercial banks and insurance companies have been most interested in utilizing regulations to restrict competition for loans and access to capital markets. In New York, for example, only two insurance companies exceeded the 20% limit on high-yield investments, First Executive Life and Presidential Life—two insurance companies that were challenging more established names in the insurance industry.

The use of political regulation to restrict economic competition between established enterprises and their challengers has a long history in railroads, communications, energy, and other industries. It is ironic that during an era of financial deregulation that facilitated the expansion of the high-yield market, counter pressures from vested interests seek to re-establish protective regulation that could introduce dangerous rigidities in capital markets that require flexibility to adapt to change.

CONCEPTUAL LIMITS TO HIGH-YIELD REGULATION

The expressed purpose of financial regulatory policy, and not the hidden political agenda of interest group politics discussed above, is to base transactions on legal and accounting standards derived from historical principles of safety, soundness, and financial prudence. These principles hopefully counterbalance the risks inherent in a market economy and the need to keep the markets fair and equitable.

Regulations emerge that confirm, as Michael Milken has suggested, the victory of form over content in public financial policy. A high-yield security that is traded in public markets with considerable liquidity and rigorous due diligence has limited risk as an investment instrument. Commercial loans that accomplish the same purpose and have fewer self-regulatory provisions to ensure safety and soundness as the high-yield market are much more risky. While the content of these financial instruments is fundamentally the same, the form results in more onerous regulation for high-yield securities.

This is, in part, the result of interest group influences on legislative deliberations and the inherent tension between regulatory rulemaking and risk analysis and the markets that are subject to them. Our tools of risk analysis in public policy are antiquated and static, based on the balance sheet which is a snapshot of a firm's financial condition.

While our current analysis of risk for measures of soundness and safety are static, the markets they seek to regulate are dynamic, given the technological changes in capital and product markets. The growth of the high-yield market took advantage of new advances in credit analysis that could capture the dynamic of rapidly changing markets, while regulatory policy continues to rely upon static financial models. If public policy is to keep economic growth alive in the U.S., its tools need to catch up with the rapidity of changing needs for businesses seeking access to the capital markets.

References

Altman, E. I. (1988). *Measuring corporate bond mortality and performance*. New York University.

Altman, E. I., and Nammacher, S. A. (1987). *Investing in junk bonds: Inside the high-yield debt market*. New York: John Wiley & Sons.

Bernanke, B., and Campbell, J. (1988). Is there a corporate debt crisis? *Brookings Papers on Economic Activity, 1*.

Blume, M., and Keim, D. (December 1984). Risk and return characteristics of lower-grade bonds. University of Pennsylvania, The Wharton School, Rodney L. White Center for Financial Research.

Broske, M. S. (September 1987). Do investment grade bonds differ from one another in default risk? Oklahoma State University, College of Business Administration working paper 87–18.

Brown, C., and Medoff, J. (May 1987). The impact of firm acquisitions on labor. Washington DC: National Bureau of Economic Research.

Fridson, M., and Wahl, F. (July 1987). Fallen angels versus original issue of high-yield bonds. *High performance: The magazine on high-yield bonds*. Morgan Stanley.

General Accounting Office (February 1988). *Financial markets: Issuers, purchases and purposes of high-yield, noninvestment grade bonds*.

Ghemwat, P, and Nalebuff, B. (January 1987). The devolution of declining industries. *Discussion papers in economics*. Princeton University, Woodrow Wilson School of Public and International Affairs, No. 120.

Hatsopoulos, G. (1983). *High costs of capital: Handicap of American industry*. Waltham, MA: Thermo Electron Corporation.

Herman, E., and Lowenstein, L. (April 1986). The efficiency effects of hostile takeovers. Columbia Law School, Center for Law and Economic Studies working paper.

Jensen, M. (1986). Agency costs of free cash flow, corporate finance, and takeovers. *American Economics Association Papers and Proceedings, 76*.

Lehn, K., et al. (1986). Noninvestment grade debt as a source of tender offer financing. (Study commissioned by) Securities Exchange Commission, Office of the Chief Economist.

Lichtenberg, F., and Siegel, D. (1987). Productivity and changes in ownership in manufacturing plants. Columbia University Graduate School of Business (prepared for Brookings Institution microeconomic conference).

Lowenstein, L. (1985). Management buyouts. *Columbia Law Review, 85*.

Meltzer, A., and Richard, S. (1987). Mortgaging America's corporations. Carnegie Mellon University.

Paulus, J., and Gay, R. (1987). Is America helping herself: Corporate restructuring and global competitiveness. *World Economic Outlook.*

Perry, K., and Taggert, R., Jr. (September 1987). The growing role of junk bonds in corporate finance. Boston University, Department of Finance.

Pound, J. (March 1987). Why corporations restructure. Yale University, Department of Finance.

Pozdena, R. (April 1987). Junk bonds: Why now? *Federal Reserve Bank of San Francisco Weekly Letter.*

Ravenscraft, D., and Scherer, F. (1987). *Mergers, selloffs, and economic efficiency.* Washington DC: Brookings Institution.

Schrager, R., and Sherman, H. (January 1987). Junk bonds and tender offer financing. Investor Responsibility Research Center.

Yago, G. (1986). Plant closings in New York: Causes, consequences, and policy implications. Economic Research Bureau, W. Averell Harriman School for Management and Policy working paper HAR-86-001.

Wharton Econometric Forecasting Associates (WEFA). (September 1988). The risk-adjusted returns for major investments available to thrift institutions.

CHAPTER 21

EFFECTS OF LBOs ON TAX REVENUES OF THE U.S. TREASURY*

Michael C. Jensen
Steven Kaplan
Laura E. Stiglin†

We examine the tax effects of leveraged buyouts (LBOs) in which a group of investors (including managers) take a company private, a topic that is receiving increasing attention from legislators, the business community, and the press. In examining the tax implications of these transactions, many observers have focused on the interest deductibility of the debt used to finance them. It has been noted that LBO firms' increased debt payments generate sufficient tax deductions to ensure that many of them do not pay income taxes in the period immediately following the LBO. Some argue these transactions are being subsidized by the federal taxpayer in the sense that they cause net losses of tax revenues to the U.S. Treasury.[1] Our analysis, based on 1988 tax law and data from buyouts in the period 1979-

*A version of this chapter appeared in *Tax Analysts Tax Notes*, vol. 42, no. 6 (February 6, 1989). The authors are indebted to Alan Auerbach, Gregg Balantine, and Mark Wolfson for helpful suggestions.

†Michael C. Jensen is Edsel Bryant Ford Professor of Business Administration at the Harvard Business School. Steven Kaplan is Assistant Professor of Finance, University of Chicago. Laura Stiglin is a principal with The Analysis Group, Belmont, Massachusetts.

1985, indicates these arguments are incorrect. Under our assumptions, net Treasury revenues from LBO firms increase on average by about 61 percent over the prebuyout payments. Our estimates indicate that at a total dollar volume of LBO transactions of $75 billion per year, the Treasury would gain about $9 billion in the first year and about $16.5 billion per year in present value of future net tax receipts.

What has often been overlooked is the fact that there are five ways in which LBOs can generate incremental revenues to the U.S. Treasury. First, because they create substantial realized capital gains for shareholders, LBOs give rise to increased capital gains taxes. Second, LBO firms realize significant increases in operating income, which are also taxable. Third, many of the creditors who finance LBOs are taxed on the interest income from LBO debt payments. Fourth, LBO firms contribute to tax revenues by using capital more efficiently. Finally, many LBO firms sell off assets triggering additional corporate taxes on the capital gains. Offsetting these incremental revenue gains are increased interest deductions on the large debt commonly incurred, and lower tax revenues on dividends because LBOs generally do not pay dividends on common equity.

THE AVERAGE LBO

Developing correct assumptions for quantifying the tax implications of LBOs is difficult, and requires detailed knowledge of the effects of LBOs on income and expenses for all parties to the transaction. Complete data are probably unavailable anywhere. The assumptions employed here are based, wherever possible, on data collected and analyzed by Kaplan (1989b) in the most complete study of LBOs to date. His study investigates the sources of value increases following an LBO, and the division of value between pre- and postbuyout investors. Kaplan's sample includes data on 48 of the 76 buyouts greater than $50 million that were announced between January 1, 1979 and December 31, 1985.

We estimate the tax revenue effects of LBOs using an example characterizing the average buyout transaction. As Table 21–1 shows, Kaplan finds the average prebuyout value of equity is $360 million and the average gain to prebuyout shareholders is 40 percent. Thus, the buyout purchase price for the common equity is approximately $500 million. Equity in the average LBO equals approximately 14 percent of the total capitalization of the buyout firm, and the average transaction generates $400 million in incremental debt. We assume the average tax basis for prebuyout shareholders equals 80 percent of the prebuyout value, approximately $290 million, implying taxable capital gains to the prebuyout shareholders of $210 million. Finally, Kaplan finds a postbuyout sale value of $750 million,[2] implying another $250 million, or 50 percent, gain in value between the buyout and the time when the firm is sold or taken public.

We estimate the tax effects of the average LBO based on reasonable representations of actual investor and firm behavior and use tax rates effective under the 1986 Tax Reform Act. Details of the calculation of the tax effects of these transactions on the U.S. Treasury are explained below. In summary, Table 21–1 shows that, on average, LBOs generate tax increases that are 194 percent of the tax losses they cause. The average LBO purchase of $500 million generates $227 million in present value (at 10 percent) of tax revenue increases versus $117 million in present value of tax losses for the Treasury. The $110 million net increase in present value of tax revenues converts at a 10 percent interest rate to an annualized net increase in taxes of $11 million or 61 percent more than the $18 million annual federal taxes the average LBO firm would have paid if nothing had changed.[3] In the year after the buyout, we estimate the Treasury gains $77 million in taxes against a loss of $17 million for a net gain of $59 million. This constitutes a 228 percent gain over the tax receipts attributable to these firms in the previous year. At a total volume of $75 billion per year, these transactions are thus generating about $16.5 billion in present value of tax revenues for the Treasury, and on a current account basis, they are generating approximately $9 billion per year. The derivation of these estimates is discussed below.

Because it is difficult to precisely estimate the tax effects for any particular deal without having direct access to IRS data, we also estimate the tax effects under conservative assumptions that tend to understate the Treasury's gains from LBOs and to overstate its probable losses. Under these assumptions, the estimates indicate the Treasury does a little better than just break even on the transaction. We find that the assumptions necessary to generate a break-even scenario are sufficiently conservative that it is unlikely the Treasury will lose revenues on the average transaction. Thus, reasonable assumptions and the best empirical evidence to date on the effects of LBOs suggests that, rather than losing tax revenues, the U.S. Treasury is a likely beneficiary from leveraged buyouts.

TABLE 21–1
Tax revenue implications of an average LBO

Based on sample average assumptions from Kaplan's(1988) study of all LBOs greater than $50 million announced in the period 1979 through 1985 (in $ millions)

1. Critical values for the average LBO

Prebuyout market value of equity	$360
Buyout purchase price	500
Incremental debt	400
Tax basis for prebuyout shareholders (.8 × 360)	290
Postbuyout value of equity	750
Taxable capital gain to prebuyout shareholders	210
Capital gain to buyout investors	250

INCREMENTAL TAX GAINS TO THE TREASURY

Capital Gains. The first way in which LBOs contribute to tax revenues is through the capital gains tax. The capital gain for shareholders of the average LBO is approximately $210 million. This represents the difference between the buyout purchase price of $500 million and the original $290 million tax basis for prebuyout shareholders. Since stock prices have increased dramatically in the last five years, it is likely that our assumed tax base of 80 percent of the prebuyout equity value is conservatively high. A substantial portion of the shareholdings will be held in tax-exempt form, such as pension funds. We assume that only 70 percent of the capital gains at this stage are received by taxable investors, and that they are taxed at a 28 percent rate. In Kaplan's sample, 30 percent of prebuyout equity is held by institutions such as pension funds, banks, mutual funds, endowments, and investment advisors. We conservatively assume all these institutions are tax exempt. To the extent that some of these gains are received by corporations, the higher 34 percent corporate rate is appropriate and so too for individuals in the 33 percent bracket. We use the 28 percent rate recognizing that some investors in the 28 percent bracket may realize capital losses to offset a portion of these capital gains. Therefore, immedi-

TABLE 21–1—Continued

2. *Net incremental tax revenues to U.S. Treasury*

	Present Value at 10%	Year after Buyout[a]
Incremental tax revenues		
Capital gains taxes	$54.2	$41.2
($210 × .7 × .28) + [($250 × .3 × .28) × .62]		
Taxes on increased operating income	85	8.5
($100 × .25 × .34) × 10		
Taxes on LBO creditors' income	40.8	6.8
($400 × .6 × .5 × .34)		
Taxes from increased capital efficiency	29.9	3.0
($44 × .2 × .1 × .34) × 10 × 10		
Taxes on sale of assets ($500 × .2 × .5 × .34)	17	17
Total incremental revenues	$226.9	$76.5
Incremental tax losses		
Tax deductibility of interest payment on debt	−81.6	−13.6
($400 × .6 × .34)		
Taxes on forgone dividend payments	−35.3	−3.5
(.05 × $360 × .7 × .28)		
Total incremental losses	−$116.9	−$17.1
Net incremental tax revenues to U.S. Treasury	$110.0	$59.4
Ratio of gains to losses	1.9	4.5

[a]See *Net Incremental Tax Revenues* section (p. 289) of text for discussion of assumptions for the year after buyout calculation.

Assumptions:

LBO marginal corporate tax rate	34%
Capital gains and dividend tax rates on individual and corporate investors	28%
Discount rate	10%
Percent of debt that is permanent	60%
Percent of interest that is received by taxable investors	50%
Percent of stock owned by taxable shareholders at buyout	70%
Percent of stock owned by taxable shareholders at postbuyout sale	30%
Percent increase in LBO operating income	25%
Percent decrease in LBO capital expenditures	20%
Dividend yield as a percent of prebuyout equity value	5%

ately upon the firm being taken private, capital gains tax revenues increase by $41.2 million:

$$\$210 \text{ million} \times 0.70 \times 0.28 = \$41.2 \text{ million}. \qquad (1)$$

In the absence of a buyout, investors will realize a stream of capital gains over time through normal trading. If half of all such gains were recognized, they would amount to $360 \times (1-.8) / 2 = \$35$ million. If they were recognized uniformly over a five-year period the tax gain would be reduced by $7 \times .7 \times .28 = \$1.37$ million per year, and this has a present value of $5.2 million. Rational planning implies that taxes from such "voluntary" realizations of capital gains are likely to be small since investors can plan them to coincide with offsetting deductions. Many such gains are never taxed when they go through well-planned estates at death. We therefore ignore additional explicit adjustment for these gains.[4]

Within three to seven years, the firm's new managers are likely to sell their interests, repurchase stock, or undertake an initial public offering, generating a second round of capital gains tax revenues. Our estimate is that these transactions occur on average about five years after the buyout. Kaplan's findings suggest that the second-round capital gains equal $250 million for the average transaction depicted in Table 21–1 ($750 million minus $500 million). However, by the time the second sale occurs, the majority of stock is typically held by nontaxable institutional investors. Assuming that 30 percent of the gain is taxable at a 28 percent tax rate, tax revenues equal $21 million:

$$\$250 \text{ million} \times 0.30 \times 0.28 = \$21 \text{ million} \qquad (2)$$

and, discounted back five years to the time of the buyout at 10 percent, this totals $21 \times .62 = \$13$ million. Thus, including both phases of capital gains, the average LBO generates $41.2 + \$13 = \$54.2$ million in incremental tax revenues.[5]

Increased Operating Income. LBO firms exhibit substantial increases in operating income, and such additional income is another source of tax revenues to the Treasury. Operating income among the firms in Kaplan's sample increased on average by 42 percent over the $100 million prebuyout level by the third year after the buyout. Part of this income growth is explained by general business conditions and industry trends, some of which may be due to the reaction of competitors to the increased efficiency of the LBO firm itself. But even after controlling for these industry and business cycle effects, LBO operating income is approximately 25 percent higher than it would have been otherwise, yielding an average industry-adjusted increase of $25 million per year.[6] Assuming these incremental earnings are taxed at a corporate marginal rate of 34 percent, the firm's annual tax revenues will increase by $8.5 million.

$$\$100 \times 25 \times 0.34 \; = \; \$8.5 \text{ million.} \tag{3}$$

Using a 10 percent discount rate to capitalize this tax stream yields a tax increase of $85 million in present value. To the extent that any of the increase in operating income results from reductions in wages, this is an overestimate of the tax benefits to the Treasury. Kaplan shows that employment increases after buyout. The increase is less than the industry average by a statistically insignificant amount. There is no good data available on what happens to wage rates after buyouts, but if they change in either direction, the effects should be incorporated in the above estimate.

Taxes on LBO Creditors' Income. The third way LBOs augment tax revenues is through taxes paid by LBO creditors on incremental interest income. However, some portion of LBO debt is often retired quickly. We assume that 60 percent of the average LBO's $400 million incremental debt is permanent and that this is a net increase in total aggregate debt. In any LBO, some combination of taxable and nontaxable institutions holds the debt, with banks holding a major part. A substantial portion of the debt can be held by tax-exempt entities. We assume the average tax rate paid by debt holders is about half the 34 percent corporate rate, which is equivalent to assuming 50 percent of the debt is held by tax-free institutions, with the remaining paying the 34 percent rate. We also conservatively assume that total assets held by tax-exempt institutions rise by their holdings of this new debt. This yields increased revenues of 40.8 million:

$$\$400 \text{ million} \times 0.6 \times 0.5 \times 0.34 = \$40.8 \text{ million.} \tag{4}$$

Increased Capital Efficiency. The fact that LBO firms use their capital more efficiently also generates tax revenues. Given their enhanced incentives to maximize shareholder value, LBOs eliminate wasteful capital projects that would have been undertaken in the absence of a buyout. These funds are returned to shareholders, who can invest them to earn a taxable return.

Capital expenditures of prebuyout firms average $44 million per year, or 7.7 percent of total capital. After an LBO, these capital expenditures are cut by roughly 20 percent. Assuming these expenditures would have earned only enough to offset tax depreciation, the annual increase in tax revenues derived from investing the resources elsewhere in the economy to return a cost of capital of 10 percent is:

$$\$44 \text{ million} \times 0.2 \times 0.1 \times 0.34 \times 10 = \$2.99 \text{ million.} \qquad (5)$$

This is the *annual* increase in present value of taxes received by the Treasury that result from increased efficiency of capital utilization. Capitalizing this annual tax stream at a 10 percent rate, the present value of tax revenue increases from improved capital efficiency equals $29.9 million. Given the losses experienced in past diversification mergers and acquisitions, there is reason to believe the gains in efficiency of capital utilization are even larger because the free cash flow that is trapped in such organizations does not just earn a low return, it tends to be wasted. See Jensen (1986, 1988).

Taxes on Sale of Assets. The final source of increased tax revenues associated with the typical LBO derives from asset sales following the buyout, and these generate further capital gains taxes. We have assumed that, on average, firms sell 20 percent of their assets ($100 million) at prices consistent with the buyout price, these assets have a tax basis of 70 percent of the prebuyout equity value (.7 × .2 × $360 = $50 million), these sales all occur in the first year, and are taxable at the 34 percent corporate rate. These sales, on average, yield $17 million in additional tax revenues to the Treasury:

$$\$500 \text{ million} \times .20 \times .5 \times .34 = \$17 \text{ million.} \qquad (6)$$

For most plant and equipment, a 70 percent tax basis represents depreciation for 3 years or less. We believe this is a conservative assumption. To the extent that the sale prices of these assets are reflected in the tax basis of the purchasers, future tax revenues will be lower, and to the extent these sales put the assets in more productive hands, future operating revenues and taxes thereon will rise.

INCREMENTAL TAX LOSSES TO THE TREASURY

Interest Deductions. The largest potential tax loss associated with LBOs comes from the additional interest deductions generated by their increased debt. Assuming, again, that 60 percent of the average $400 million of incremental debt is permanent, and that interest deductions are worth 34 cents on the dollar, the Treasury's tax loss from increased interest deductions equals $81.6 million:

$$\$400 \text{ million} \times 0.6 \times 0.34 = \$81.6 \text{ million}. \tag{7}$$

We ignore the increase in federal taxes that is due to lower state taxes. We also have assumed in this calculation that all of this debt is a net addition that would not have occurred in the absence of the buyout. This leads to an overestimate of the tax losses to the Treasury.

In addition, it can be argued that the only part of the interest payments that represent a tax loss to the Treasury is that portion representing the riskless rate, because the risk premium for defaults will on average not be paid and will show up as income from forgiven debt.

Forgone Dividend Payments. The Treasury also loses tax revenues on an LBO's forgone dividend payments. Assuming that, on average, firms pay annual dividends equal to the Kaplan sample average of 5 percent of their market value, the average LBO firm would pay .05 × $360 = $18 million in annual dividends prior to the buyout. If 70 percent of these dividends had been taxable at a 28 percent rate, the elimination of dividends following the LBO would reduce annual tax revenues by $3.5 million:

$$\$360 \text{ million} \times 0.05 \times 0.7 \times 0.28 = \$3.5 \text{ million} \tag{8}$$

Capitalizing this tax stream at 10 percent, the present value of the tax loss equals $35 million.

NET INCREMENTAL TAX REVENUES TO THE U.S. TREASURY

In summary, the $226.9 million in present value of gains in tax revenues to the U.S. Treasury from the average LBO transaction exceed the $116.9 million in present value of losses by $110 million dollars. As mentioned in the introduction, at a 10 percent interest rate, this converts to an equivalent annualized perpetual gain of $11 million which is an increase of 61 percent over the average $18 million tax payment by the Kaplan sample in the year prior to the buyout. Because of the highly nonuniform nature of the changes in tax revenues to the Treasury, this $11 million is the best estimate of the annual equivalent change.

The last column of Panel 2 of Table 21–1 calculates the change in federal tax payments that occur on average in the year after the buyout for those who are interested in those estimates. On this current account basis the Treasury is a winner, gaining $76.5 million in taxes while losing $17.1 million for a net gain of $59.4 million—a 230 percent gain over what they would have received if tax payments had remained at the $18 million pre-buyout level. This is a temporary increase because much of the gains, i.e., the capital gains taxes, are front end loaded.

In the calculation of the tax changes in the year after the buyout, the $41.2 million in additional capital gains taxes to shareholders are the same as in the present value analysis. We ignore tax payments on the postbuyout gains on sale of the company because they occur roughly five years in the future. The $8.5 million taxes on increased operating income and the $3 million on increased capital efficiency in the first year are included under the assumption that at the margin, after carryback allowances, this income is taxable to the corporation. Kaplan finds that in about half the cases LBOs pay no federal taxes in the first year, and this implies these increased taxes will be lower to the extent the firms have unused tax deductions. In the third year after the buyout, the typical LBO firm has no unused tax deductions. The $6.8 million taxes on the LBOs' creditors income assume that no debt is retired in the first year. To the extent this is an overestimate, it is more than compensated for by our use of an interest rate of 10 percent on the debt. Since the actual interest rate is closer to 12 percent, the debt could be as low as 83 percent of the beginning amount and still be consistent with these creditor tax payments. Similarly, on estimating the lost revenues to the Treasury, we assume the entire debt is outstanding for the year and that all deductions are actually used. As noted above, to the extent these deductions are not used, the estimated tax losses of $13.6 million to the Treasury are too high.

To test the sensitivity of the assumptions in the average LBO example described in Table 21–1, a set of conservative assumptions that tend to understate the Treasury's gains and overstate its losses are applied to the same average LBO transaction. As shown in Table 21–2, this analysis

TABLE 21–2
Tax revenue implications of an LBO based on conservative
assumptions

Scaled to the size of the average LBO in Kaplan's (1988) sample
(in $ millions)

1. *Critical values for the average LBO*

Prebuyout market value of equity	$360
Buyout purchase price	500
Incremental debt	400
Tax basis for pre-buyout shareholders (.8 × 360)	290
Postbuyout value of equity	750
Taxable capital gain to prebuyout shareholders	210
Capital gain to buyout investors	250

2. *Net incremental tax revenues to U.S. Treasury*

	Present Value at 10%	Year after Buyout
Incremental tax revenues		
Capital gains taxes ($210 × .7 × .28)	$41.2	$41.2
Taxes on increased operating income	51	5.1
($100 × .15 × .34) × 10		
Taxes on LBO creditors' income ($400 × .8 × .35 × .34)	38.1	4.8
Taxes from increased capital efficiency	15.0	1.5
($44 × .1 × .1 × .34) × 10 × 10		
Taxes on sale of assets ($5004 × .24 × .54 × .34)	17	17
Total incremental revenues	$162.3	$69.6
Incremental tax losses		
Tax deductibility of interest payment on debt	−108.8	−13.6
($1004 × .84 × .34)		
Taxes on forgone dividend payments	−35.3	−3.5
($3604 × .054 × .74 × .28)		
Total incremental losses	−$144.1	−$17.1
Net incremental tax revenues to U.S. Treasury	$18.2	$52.5
Ratio of gains to losses	1.1	4.1

Changes in assumptions from Table 21–1	*Average*	*Conservative*
Percent of debt that is permanent	60%	80%
Percent of interest that is received by taxable investors	50%	35%
Percent increase in LBO operating income	25%	15%
Percent decrease in LBO capital expenditures	20%	10%

TABLE 21–3
Tax revenue implications of the RJR-Nabisco LBO

**Based on sample average assumptions from Kaplan's (1988)
study of all LBOs greater than $50 million announced in the
period 1979 through 1985 (in $ billions)**

1. Critical values for the RJR-Nabisco LBO

	Per Share Value	Total Value (billions)
Prebuyout market value of equity (227 million shares)	$55	$12.48
Buyout purchase price (at assumed cash value of $100)	100	22.70
Incremental debt (assuming convertible debt is converted to equity)	81	18.39
Tax basis for prebuyout shareholder (75% of prebuyout price)	41.25	9.36
Postbuyout value of equity (assuming total gain equals 109%)	115	26.11
Taxable capital gain to prebuyout shareholders	58.75	13.33
Capital gain to buyout investors	15	3.38

indicates tax gains and losses that approximately offset each other, with present value of tax gains of $162.3 million and tax losses of $144.1 for a net gain of $18.2 million, just slightly more than break even. In this calculation, we assumed that 80 percent of the debt is permanent rather than 60 percent, that only 35 percent of the interest is taxable to creditors rather than 50 percent, that the increase in operating income is 15 percent rather than 25 percent, and that the decrease in capital expenditures is 10 percent rather than 20 percent. We also assumed there are no tax gains on the final sale of the firm, perhaps because the firm is not sold or that other tax sheltering is available for these gains. All of these changes reduce the tax gains and increase the losses to the Treasury in present value terms. Interestingly, under these very conservative assumptions, the net gains to the Treasury in the year after the buyout fall only slightly from $59.4 to $52.5 million. Thus, based on the best empirical data available, LBOs appear to have, at worst, tax-neutral effects in present value terms and, more likely, tax-enhancing effects on the U.S. Treasury. In virtually all cases, the Treasury gains substantial revenues in the short run.

TABLE 21–3—Continued

2. *Net incremental tax revenues to U.S. Treasury*

	Present Value at 10%	Year after Buyout
Incremental tax revenues		
Capital gains taxes ($13.33 \times .6 \times .28$)	$2.24	$2.24
Taxes on increased operating income ($3 \times .25 \times .34$)10	2.55	.25
Taxes on LBO creditors' income ($18.39 \times .6 \times .35 \times .34$)	1.31	.22
Taxes from increased capital efficiency ($1.6 \times .2 \times .34$)10	1.09	.11
Taxes on sale of assets ($22.5 \times .25 \times (1-.4) \times .34$)	1.16	1.16
Total incremental revenues	8.35	3.98
Incremental tax losses		
Tax deductibility of interest payment on debt ($18.39 \times .6 \times .34$)	-3.75	-.62
Taxes on forgone dividend payments ($2.20 \times .227 \times .6 \times .28$)10	-.84	-.08
Total incremental losses	-$4.59	-$.70
Net incremental tax revenues to U.S. Treasury	$3.76	$3.28
Ratio of gains to losses	1.8	5.7

Assumptions:

Capital gains and dividend tax rates	28%
Corporate tax rate	34%
Discount rate	10%
Percent of debt that is permanent	60%
Percent of interest that is received by taxable investors	35%
Percent of stock owned by taxable shareholders at buyout	60%
Percent of stock owned by taxable shareholders at postbuyout sale	30%
Percent increase in LBO operating income	25%
Percent decrease in LBO capital expenditures	20%
Percent of dividends received by taxable investors	60%
Percent of assets sold in the first year	25%

We have ignored for simplicity the $100 million purchase of 1.3 million preferred shares. Total fees are about $710 million, and we have assumed these are taxable to recipients and tax deductible to RJR-Nabisco.

THE RJR-NABISCO LEVERAGED BUYOUT

Because the RJR-Nabisco LBO by Kohlberg, Kravis, and Roberts is so large, and involved such heated bidding, it has attracted much attention and controversy. Along with this have come accusations that the gains to shareholders are at the expense of the Treasury.[7] Table 21–3 contains our estimates of the implications of the transaction for the U.S. Treasury which indicate the Treasury is highly likely to gain rather than lose tax revenues. In present value terms, the increased revenue for the Treasury is $3.76 billion, $3.28 billion of which it will likely gain in the year following the buyout. These payments are more than eight times higher than the approximately $370 million in Federal taxes paid by RJR-Nabisco in 1987.[8] Indeed, at a rate of $370 million per year, the total present value of RJR-Nabisco's tax payments into perpetuity is only $3.7 billion, just slightly higher than the first year's tax revenues induced by the buyout.

To obtain these estimates of the RJR tax revenues after the buyout, we assume that 60 percent of the increased debt is permanent but none is retired in the first year, that 35 percent of the interest is received by taxable investors, that 60 percent of the prebuyout stock is owned by taxable investors, that 30 percent of the stock at the postbuyout sale is owned by taxable investors, that operating income rises by 25 percent, that capital expenditures decrease by 20 percent, and that 25 percent of the assets are sold in the first year with a tax basis of 73 percent of the prebuyout market value of equity. The 82 percent premium to the prebuyout shareholders in this case (assuming the cash value of the offer is $100, not the stated $109) was exceptionally high, perhaps because of the intense bidding. We have conservatively assumed that the total value increase in the LBO will be equal to the sample average of 109 percent in the period 1979 through 1985, implying a $15 per share gain for the buyout investors.

SUMMARY AND CONCLUSIONS

The typical LBO is more beneficial to the U.S. Treasury than many observers realize. Increased interest deductions and forgone dividend payments clearly have the potential to reduce tax revenues. However, the large capital gains that result from LBOs, increases in their operating income and capital efficiency, enhanced creditor income, and taxes on asset sales have the potential to increase tax revenues. The net effect of these tax changes varies across transactions; some LBOs may result in tax revenue reductions, while others may generate net new tax revenues. As the examples in our tables show, however, the preponderance of evidence indicates that in the aggregate these transactions generate revenue gains for the Treasury.

Based on the data from transactions over $50 million in the period 1979 through 1985, an average LBO transaction in 1989 increases tax revenues to the U. S. Treasury by $110 million on a present value basis, and by $59.4 million in the year after the buyout. The present value of gains translates to a permanent equivalent annual increase of approximately $11 million on average, or a 61 percent increase in taxes per buyout firm. Our conservative assumptions in Table 21–2, which we believe understate Treasury revenues, indicate that even in those circumstances the Treasury is likely to break even. Our application of the analysis to the RJR-Nabisco transaction indicates, contrary to popular views, that the transaction will enrich the Treasury by over $3 billion whether viewed from a short- or long-term perspective.

Policies that restrict these transactions will likely reduce future tax revenues received by the Treasury. At a total volume of $75 billion per year, LBO transactions are generating about $16.5 billion in present value of tax revenues for the Treasury per year, and on a current account basis, they generate approximately $9 billion per year. It appears that from a narrow tax policy perspective, great care should be taken in adopting policies that discourage LBO transactions.

Notes

1. See, for example, Saunders (1988).
2. These values come from several forms of transactions, including sale of the firm, an initial public offering of stock, or the repurchase of stock for the 21 firms for which complete data on final postbuyout sale prices or value is available.
3. A strictly comparable comparison would add the taxes paid by creditors and the capital gains taxes paid by stockholders to the $18 million benchmark. These numbers are extremely hard to obtain, but we believe they are generally insignificant in any event because the total prebuyout debt is very small and the unsheltered realized capital gains are also likely to be small.

4. To the extent investors are expecting a decrease in capital gains tax rates in the future, they have incentives to postpone realization of these imbedded gains, and to the extent those rates are lower than 28 percent, future taxes will be lower.

5. The desire of buyout firms to recognize the gains from the winners in their portfolio of firms early, to establish an attractive track record, tends to cause the more profitable deals to be sold first. Kaplan (1988) provides some evidence of this in his study, but the effect does not appear to be large. This may result from offsetting pressures by managers to sell earlier than would otherwise occur because they prefer to realize the payoffs from their equity investment earlier.

6. The change in operating earnings in the first year after the buyout is 15.6 percent. To the extent that any of these operating improvements are reflected in decreases in the economy-wide price level, they would not be taxed.

7. *Time* magazine, for example, in its cover story of December 5, 1988, "A Game of Greed," claims the U. S. taxpayers will lose between $2 and $5 billion in the long run, p. 69.

9. Total taxes paid by RJR-Nabisco in 1987 were $682, but $313 million of this were "foreign and other" taxes.

References

Jensen, Michael C. (Winter 1988). Takeovers: Their causes and consequences. *Journal of Economic Perspectives*, pp. 21–48

Jensen, Michael C. (Summer 1986). The takeover controversy: Analysis and evidence. *Midland Corporate Finance Journal*, pp. 1–27.

Kaplan, Steven. (July 1989a). Management buyouts: Evidence on taxes as a source of value. *Journal of Finance*, pp. 611–632.

Kaplan, Steven. (1989b). The effects of management buyouts on operations and value. *Journal of Financial Economics*, forthcoming.

Saunders, Laura. (November 1988). How the government subsidizes leveraged takeovers. *Forbes*, pp 192–196.

CHAPTER 22

DISCUSSION OF PUBLIC POLICY ISSUES OF HIGH-YIELD DEBT

F. M. Scherer[*]

When a paper reads as if it were written by Harry Truman's esteemed one-armed economist, as does Professor Yago's, I instinctively inquire what the other hand might be holding back. In particular, there is an intriguing tension in the evidence. On one hand, Yago's survey using Drexel Burnham data (Tables 20–5 and 20–6) reveals that only 22 percent of the high-yield debt issued between 1980 and 1986 was used to finance acquisitions. On the other hand, Professor Yago reports from research using COMPUSTAT data that the industry distribution of high-yield financing "parallels the distribution of mergers, acquisitions and divestitures throughout the 1980s." Is it possible that there was time-lagged slippage between the Drexel Burnham "acquisitions" and the much larger "general corporate purpose" categories? Professor Yago also finds that *firms* issuing high-yield debt had unusually high sales and capital expenditures growth rates, but no attempt is made to determine whether that growth was solely internal, or whether some of it may have been associated with mergers. Without such controls for intervening mergers, no solid inference can be drawn.

[*]F. M. Scherer is The Ford Motor Company Professor of Business and Government at the John F. Kennedy School of Government, Harvard University, and was formerly at Swathmore College.

The other paper assigned me, Professor Kaplan's, summarizes a most original and impressive empirical study. Among other things, both of the economists' arms are in full view—e.g., on whether there is selection bias in the availability of postbuyout financial information (there seems to be), on whether two-year postbuyout performance can be sustained, and on whether the decline in postbuyout capital outlays comes from avoiding bad investments or having to forgo good ones. Although I join in Kaplan's caveats, I am both surprised and tentatively persuaded by his finding that operating margins increased on average following buyout, and that the increases reflect heightened managerial incentives to run the tightest possible ship.

Through our statistical research and case studies, Ravenscraft and I observed similar tendencies. To quote our case study findings on leveraged buyouts:[1]

> The behavioral effects of moving from conglomerate ownership to this high-risk, high-potential-gain environment were striking. Cost-cutting opportunities that had previously gone unexploited were seized. Austere offices were substituted for lavish ones. Staffs were cut back sharply. New and more cost-effective field sales organizations were adopted. Inexpensive computer services were found to substitute for expensive in-house operations. Make versus buy decisions were reevaluated, and lower-cost alternatives were embraced. Efforts were made to improve labor-management relations by removing bureaucratic constraints that had been imposed by the previous conglomerate's headquarters. Tight inventory controls were implemented, cutting holding costs by as much as half. Low-volume items were pruned from product lines to trim inventories and reduce production set-up costs.[2] Tighter control was exercised over accounts receivable. . . .

What surprises me about the Kaplan results is that they are for whole, generally successful companies going private, whereas our study was confined to partial sell-offs of divisions that, for the most part, had been performing poorly prior to their divestiture. On average, we found for a large sample, the operating income of divested lines was *negative* in the year before sell-off commenced. It must be harder to improve the performance of a whole company already doing well than for a division that may have been mismanaged by its conglomerate parent. Because our study focused only on divisional sell-offs, we were unable to disentangle the effect of stronger managerial motivation in a highly leveraged structure from what happens when a simple organization replaces a complex one. With

Kaplan's sample, there were presumably no substantial changes in organizational complexity, so the managerial motivation variable stands out. And it seems to matter.

This is good news, but it is also bad news. The bad news is that it suggests a serious failure in the corporate governance mechanism of American capitalism. If high leverage and raising the median equity stake of the top two managers from 3.90 percent to 7.54 percent lead to more strenuous cost control, why were the managers resting on their oars before buyout? And if they were, why didn't the nonmanagement directors, who owned a surprisingly high 13.4 percent of prebuyout equity, crack the whip and rouse management to more strenuous efforts without buyout? Since most U.S. publicly listed corporations have lower outside director ownership shares than those in Kaplan's sample, are we to infer that similar efficiency gain opportunities go unexploited in the bulk of American industry?

If the answer to these questions is pessimistic, there are two main avenues of change. One is to reform corporate governance, finding ways to install outside directors who *will* take a serious interest in their charges and spur management to do its job to the best of its ability or, if that ability is insufficient to meet the challenges, find management that can and will do what it is paid well to do. The alternative is to continue the trend toward corporate structures with much higher leverage and larger inside management equity shares.

I see serious risks in the second approach. High leverage means higher risk, not only to the individuals and institutions who buy heavily leveraged companies' securities, but also to the economy as a whole. It is not a sufficient defense to say that high-yield bondholders have fared well thus far, because, as the recent Presidential campaign reminded us, we have experienced continuous and generally rising prosperity during the past six years—the heyday of high-yield debt financing. The real test will come when the inevitable recession arrives. Most of the Jeremiahs who have prophesied about that dreaded day have missed an important part of the point. Recessions are usually triggered by some shock, such as rising interest rates, that induces a cutback in real capital investment. In the next recession, the shock could come from deliberate Federal Reserve Board action, or a sudden rush on the vulnerable dollar and a withdrawal of foreign investors from U.S. financial markets. If the rise in interest rates (ratcheting short-term financing costs upward) and the decline in economic activity with the onset of recession cause cash flow problems for numerous highly leveraged companies, those firms' managers will have to take stern measures to avoid default. It is almost certain that they will react by cutting back real plant and equipment investment more than they would had they been less heavily burdened with debt. That *incremental* reduction in real investment will in its own right deepen the recession. And as additional workers in the capital goods industries lose their jobs, their spending on consumption will fall incrementally, with the negative multiplier effect reverberating through the economy. In short, an interest and investment-induced recession in a heavily leveraged economy is almost certain to be more severe than one in an economy populated by corporations whose financial structures have more shock absorption capability.

Although other factors played a more important role, this sort of debt-induced reaction is said by Professor Galbraith to have contributed to the severity of the depression beginning in 1929.[3] Curious about what changes have occurred since then, I sought comparative data on the financial structure of the U.S. corporate sector in 1929 and the end of 1988's first quarter.[4] The variable on which I focus is debt (short-term plus long-term) as a percentage of the book value of debt plus stockholders' equity. The comparisons are as follows:

	1929	1988
Manufacturing	15%	39%
Mining	15%	49%
Retailing	23%	50%
All three combined	17%	40%
Public utilities	42%	n.a.

The degree of leverage built into the manufacturing, mining, and retailing sectors eight months ago was much higher than it was in 1929. It approximates the leveraging of 1929's public utilities sector, which was the paramount locus of subsequent financial failure. And since the first quarter of 1988, leveraging has continued at a brisk pace. I estimate that the RJR-Nabisco buyout and Philip Morris' acquisition of Kraft alone will raise the manufacturing sector leverage ratio from 39 to 41 percent.

To the argument that we are approaching a peril point, two counter-arguments can be raised. For one, the economy is more stable intrinsically now than it was in 1929. We know more about how to combat recession, and we have more automatic stabilizers such as the income tax and unemployment compensation. This is true, but cautionary notes must be added. Although we know more macroeconomics now than decision-makers did in 1929, our flexibility to act upon that knowledge is declining. If a recession hits, the federal deficit is likely to balloon quickly into the $200 billion-plus range. Will we be able to take aggressive counter-cyclical measures under those conditions? Our newly won position as a net debtor nation in the world economy also limits our flexibility. Thus, if the Federal Reserve were to react by massively creating reserves, any sharp anti-cyclical decline in real interest rates would drive the dollar lower, and fears of inflation (pushing nominal interest rates higher) could trigger a run against the dollar.

It is also argued that extensive leveraging of U.S. industry is accept-able because other nations, such as Japan and Germany, have long been much more highly leveraged than we, and they have survived macroecon-omic shocks nicely. It is true that they have sustained more debt-rich capital structures, and it is equally true that their leverage, combined with tax laws similar to ours, gives their corporations an appreciable capital cost advan-tage over American companies relying more heavily on equity finance. But there is an important difference. In Japan, when financial crisis looms, government, the powerful banks, and industry work together to ensure that a serious shock does not escalate into a financial rout. Affiliated companies bail each other out, recession cartels are authorized, import restraints are imposed—a whole panoply of instruments is available to combat crisis. In West Germany since the restructuring following World War II, the Big Three of banking have wielded sufficient power to prevent ordinary shocks from becoming aggravated, and cooperation among government, the banks, and industry, though less close than in Japan, can be expected to facilitate concerted action against larger shocks. We in the United States have a different, more decentralized, more adversarial, system. Unless we are willing to make significant changes in that system, it is unlikely that we would be able to deal with the interacting problems of recession and high leverage nearly as quickly and effectively as Japan and Germany.

Thus, I see serious risks in a continued movement toward the leverag-ing-up of American industry. At the same time, I believe Professor Kaplan's paper has identified a weakness in the still predominant system of corporate governance. The safer route toward correcting that weakness seems, in my opinion, to be improving the governance system, rather than building ever more debt into corporate financial structures. I would propose among other things new rules limiting severely the number of boards upon which fully employed directors may sit, encouraging the nomination of outside directors by stockholding financial intermediaries, and requiring that a substantial fraction of outside directors' compensation be deferred and linked to the long-term (i.e., at least five-year) performance of company stock.

Notes

1. David J. Ravenscraft and F. M. Scherer (1987), *Mergers, Sell-offs, and Economic Efficiency.* Brookings Institution, p. 154.
2. This might help explain Kaplan's finding that postbuyout sales declined relative to industry trends.
3. John Kenneth Galbraith (1955), *The Great Crash,* New York: Houghton-Mifflin, p. 183.
4. My source for 1929 is *Historical Statistics of the United States: Colonial Times to 1957* (1960), Washington DC: U.S. Bureau of the Census, pp. 582–583 (based upon Internal Revenue Service data); and for 1988, *Quarterly Financial Report for Manufacturing, Mining and Trade Corporations* (First Quarter 1988), Washington DC: U.S. Bureau of the Census. For the 1929 data, I assumed that half of "notes and accounts payable" were interest-bearing debt to be added to "bonds and mortgages."